Dublin

DIRECTIONS

WRITTEN AND RESEARCHED BY

Paul Gray and Geoff Wallis

NEW YORK • LONDON • DELHI

www.roughguides.com

Contents

Introduction to

Dublin

Although a compact city, more than a quarter of the Republic of Ireland's population of almost four million lives within Dublin's boundaries, a figure swelled by more than a million tourist arrivals each year. While it was for centuries the fulcrum of Ireland's fight for independence from Britain, today celebrated in the numerous memorials that pay homage to the revolutionary struggle, the city has developed into a thriving modern metropolis, which embraced the European ideal far more readily than anyone ever expected.

Much of Dublin's centre has been redeveloped over the last few decades, leaving a wag to comment that "the city's only sights are building sites" as it – literally – builds upon Ireland's economic boom.

▲ Sunlight Chambers

So, alongside the city's historic buildings and monuments, you'll discover grand new hotels and clubs, stunning new street architecture and a recently inaugurated, state-of-the-art tramway system. It's this meeting of the old and the new, and the constant sense of anticipation, that gives the city its edge.

Bisected by the River Liffey, a waterway forming the city's geographical and spiritual core, Dublin's rich architectural

When to visit

Unless you're planning your trip to coincide with a major festival (see p.208), Dublin is definitely at its best in the spring and early autumn when the temperature remains generally mild and rainfall is often lower. Though the hottest months, July and August are also often the wettest, the tourist crowds are at their peak at this time and the city can seem oppressive.

▲ Liffey at night

history is vividly represented by cathedrals and churches, castles and bridges, grand Georgian squares and townhouses. The city's origins date back to ninth-century Viking times when the Norsemen saw the strategic potential of the sweeping Dublin Bay. They adopted the location's Irish name, Dubh Linn ("dark pool"), for their new home, soon amalgamating it with the nearby Celtic settlement called Baile Átha Cliath ("place of the hurdle ford") which remains the Irish name for Dublin. Later, the twelfth century saw Dublin conquered by the Anglo-Normans and it remained the locus of English (and, subsequently, British) control over Ireland for more than seven hundred years. Though just a few buildings survive from earlier times, much of the centre's form and character was created during the eighteenth and nineteenth centuries, reflected in its street layout and grand edifices such as the Four Courts and the Custom House. Many of these buildings played a pivotal role in Ireland's struggle for independence, whether during the rebellions of 1798 or 1803, or the Easter Rising of 1916; others featured prominently in the civil war that followed independence in 1921.

While the past continues to provide a redolent backdrop, Dublin is changing in other subtle ways as its population becomes less homogenous. The arrival and settlement of migrants, particularly from Africa and Eastern Europe, together with the city's longer-standing

▼ Book of Kells

and thriving Chinese community, has seen Dublin gradually inch towards multiculturalism. The effects of these changes are most visible in the city's restaurants, shops and street markets, broadening native tastes and expanding imaginations, while the newcomers have also added fresh impetus to Dublin's music and arts scenes.

Dublin has also become an increasingly style-conscious city. Where once it looked inwards for inspiration, today it is ever glancing both east and west, to Europe and America, catching new trends and invariably bringing a decidedly Irish slant to bear upon them. Much of that trendsetting reveals itself in the flourishing shops, bars, clubs, cafés, restaurants and galleries of the fashionable Southside, centring especially on and around Grafton Street and the redeveloped arts quarter Temple Bar. Rising against its erstwhile image as dowdy, occasionally seedy and somewhat down-at-heel, the Northside is also smartening up, and you'll find a plethora of new chic bars, cafés and restaurants, in particular around the quays of the Liffey. East of the centre, on both sides of the river, the former docklands are forming the nexus for the latest stage of regeneration.

Dublin is particularly renowned for its literary heritage, producing celebrated writers such as

▲ Grattan Bridge

▲ Dublin Castle

George Bernard Shaw, Oscar Wilde, Samuel Beckett, Brendan Behan and, of course, James Joyce, the author whose novels and short stories most incisively and intensely capture the life and spirit of the city. There is a long theatrical tradition, too, once focused mainly on the Abbey and the Gate theatres, but nowadays encompassing all manner of experimental shows and events.

The city's most famous musical export is the band U2, though other major figures include Sinéad O'Connor, Bob Geldof, the late Phil Lynott of Thin Lizzy fame, and, of course, those boisterous balladeers The

Dubliners themselves. Such talent continues to be nurtured by numerous cutting-edge venues covering all manner of musical genres. Traditional-music lovers are particularly well catered for by a wealth of pubs hosting regular, often excellent sessions. Dublin boasts a vibrant nightlife scene, too, with enough clubs to keep the hardiest party animal spoilt for choice.

However, there's no escaping the reality that Dublin has become one of Europe's most expensive cities, both for locals and visitors. While you probably won't spend too much cash using the city's reasonably priced and extensive transport network, the cost of eating and drinking has risen sharply in recent years. Despite this seeming exorbitance, whether you're just visiting for the weekend or staying a while longer it's still relatively easy to experience this invigorating city to the full without incurring the wrath of your bank manager. Accommodation, at least, is one area where you can save, by booking in advance and keeping abreast of midweek bargains,

▲ Gresham Hotel

and the city also offers a large number of free attractions.

For a taste of Ireland at large, it's very easy to slip out of Dublin to a host of varied nearby attractions, from fascinating Neolithic and monastic sites to opulent mansions once occupied by Ireland's ruling elite. Alternatively, cliff-top walks and exhilarating mountain vistas will bring the fresh air rushing into your lungs.

Dublin
AT A GLANCE

Kildare Street and Merrion Square

Lying on Kildare Street, the elegant but forbidding Leinster House, seat of the Irish Parliament, is neatly bordered at its four corners by the country's main cultural and touristic institutions: the National Museum, the National Library, the National Gallery and the Natural History Museum. To the east, the lawns of Merrion Square are a pleasant, quiet spot, surrounded by well-preserved Georgian terraces.

▲ Temple Bar

boisterous nightlife and for art. With bars and clubs, cosmopolitan restaurants, stylish shopping, galleries and arts centres, it's likely that you'll end up here at some stage.

Kilmainham

Just west of the city, the suburb of Kilmainham offers a taste of Ireland both old and new in the form of the Irish Museum of Modern Art, housed in the imposing Royal Hospital, and through the austere penal conditions on view at Kilmainham Gaol, a building with an iconic status in Ireland's struggle for freedom.

► National Gallery

Temple Bar

Hemmed in by the river and the former dam that is Dame Street, Temple Bar somehow manages to remain the city's hub both for

◄ Museum of Modern Art, Kilmainham

Phoenix Park

Whether you just fancy a stroll, watching sports such as hurling, polo, or, perhaps surprisingly, cricket, or taking a trip to the zoo, this sprawling parkland offers plenty of scope for relaxation and entertainment. The adjacent Farmleigh mansion, sumptuous former home of the Guinness family, should be included in everyone's agenda.

▲ Farmleigh gardens

The Inner Northside

Alongside some of Dublin's most renowned traditional-music pubs, this much regenerated area offers swish new clubs, bars and cafés, chain stores and bustling streets, historic monuments and edifices, a thriving street market and famous theatres, museums and galleries – something for everyone, in fact.

▼ Traditional music, *Hughes's* pub

▲ Trinity College

Grafton Street

In the centre of the city, Trinity College happily opens its doors to casual visitors to enjoy its grand architecture, wonderful collection of illuminated manuscripts and restful parkland. The main gate stands at the bottom (or, some say, the top) of Grafton Street, a pedestrianized arena for purposeful shoppers by day, rambling carousers by night.

◀ Christ Church Cathedral

The old city

The relics of British rule – Dublin Castle, City Hall, Christ Church and St Patrick's cathedrals – can be found in the former Anglo-Norman city centre, with the area's highlight the global treasure-house of the Chester Beatty Library. The old city's fringes, particularly South Great George's Street, are home to cafés and restaurants, hip shops and some great pubs, old and new.

Ideas

The big six

Wandering the streets of Dublin without a fixed plan, taking in street performances, Georgian squares and traditional pubs as the mood takes you, is one of this compact city's great pleasures. But there are a number of things you really shouldn't leave town without seeing, ranging from stark reminders of Ireland's colonial past at Kilmainham Gaol to the unexpected Oriental beauties of the Chester Beatty Library.

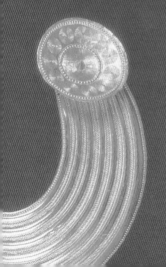

▲ **Chester Beatty Library**

An elegant, world-renowned display of manuscripts, prints and *objets d'art* from Europe, the Middle East and Far East.

P.112 ▸ THE OLD CITY AND SOUTH GREAT GEORGE'S STREET

▲ **Trinity College**

The gorgeously illustrated *Book of Kells* and the magnificent Long Room in the Old Library justly take pride of place amongst the treasures of Dublin's famous college.

P.70 ▸ TRINITY COLLEGE, GRAFTON STREET AND AROUND

▼ The Liffey

Bisecting the city, the river lies at the very heart of Dublin and has inspired many a writer and artist. A stroll along the Quays is an essential part of any trip to the city.

P.129 ▸ AROUND O'CONNELL STREET

▼ The National Gallery

A graceful showcase of European art since the fifteenth century – don't miss the vibrant Jack B. Yeats collection.

P.85 ▸ KILDARE STREET AND MERRION SQUARE

▲ Kilmainham Gaol

The notorious Gaol was where Ireland's revolutionaries were often incarcerated and, in some cases, executed. Tours provide a chilling evocation of nineteenth-century penal conditions.

P.126 ▸ THE LIBERTIES AND KILMAINHAM

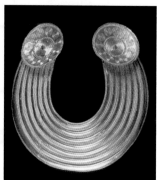

▲ The National Museum

Dazzling hordes of prehistoric gold and beautifully wrought Christian treasures to make your jaw drop.

P.83 ▸ KILDARE STREET AND MERRION SQUARE

Literary Dublin

Ireland has a rich and vivid literary heritage, much of it centred upon the capital. Many of the nation's greatest works were written by authors in sometimes self-imposed exile, including Samuel Beckett and James Joyce (see p.142). Contemporary writers like Roddy Doyle and Joseph O'Connor (brother of singer Sinéad) have continued to explore the city's vibrant life, often to great comic effect.

▲ **George Bernard Shaw**
The playwright spent most of his life in England but lived in Synge Street during his early years.
P.160 ▸ ALONG THE GRAND CANAL

▲ **Jonathan Swift**
The author of the great satirical novel *Gulliver's Travels* was once Dean of St Patrick's Cathedral, and is buried there.
P.116 ▸ THE OLD CITY AND SOUTH GREAT GEORGE'S STREET

▶ Oscar Wilde

Wilde lived in Merrion Square and this statue can be found in the park there. His social standing was ruined by a notorious court case, though whilst incarcerated he produced one of his greatest works, *The Ballad of Reading Gaol*.

P.86 ▸ KILDARE STREET AND MERRION SQUARE

▼ Brendan Behan

Northside-born Behan was an acclaimed novelist and dramatist but also very much a legend in his own lunchtime. *McDaid's* was one of his favourite pubs.

P.80 ▸ TRINITY COLLEGE, GRAFTON STREET AND AROUND

▼ Patrick Kavanagh

The poet and novelist from County Monaghan was a major figure in mid-twentieth-century Dublin literary life.

P.160 ▸ ALONG THE GRAND CANAL

▼ Dublin Writers Museum

The best place to begin your literary explorations of the capital and its authors.

P.142 ▸ NORTH FROM PARNELL SQUARE

DUBLIN WRITERS MUSEUM

James Joyce

Perhaps no other writer has encapsulated the life of a city more evocatively or more incisively than Joyce. His mammoth work *Ulysses* captures one eventful day in Dublin, setting the city as a vivid backdrop for the endeavours and excursions of the novel's rich tapestry of characters. *Portrait of the Artist as a Young Man* draws vividly upon Joyce's development, from child to struggling author, while his collection of short stories, *Dubliners*, is, too, rich in character and redolent of the city in description. Joyce spent most of his adult life living in Europe and the publication of *Ulysses* in Ireland was actually banned on the grounds of obscenity until the 1960s.

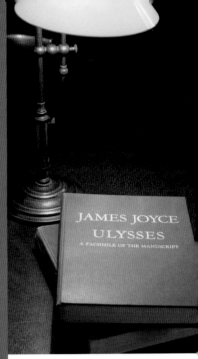

▲ The James Joyce Centre

Devoted to all things Joycean, the Centre celebrates both the author's life and his literary achievements.

P.142 ▸ NORTH FROM PARNELL SQUARE

▲ Bloomsday

Fans of Joyce annually celebrate the day on which *Ulysses* is set, many following in the footsteps of the central characters and some even dressing for the part.

P.208 ▸ ESSENTIALS

▲ Davy Byrne's pub

One of the protagonists of *Ulysses*, Leopold Bloom consumed a gorgonzola sandwich and a glass of Burgundy here.

P.79 ▸ TRINITY COLLEGE, GRAFTON STREET
AND AROUND

▶ St Stephen's Green

A warts-and-all bust of Joyce is just one of several fine historic monuments here.

P.91 ▸ ST STEPHEN'S GREEN TO THE GRAND
CANAL

▼ James Joyce Tower, Sandycove

A quirky collection of Joycean artefacts in the imposing Martello tower that was home to *Ulysses'* Buck Mulligan.

P.165 ▸ THE SOUTHERN OUTSKIRTS

Dublin tastes

Dublin's culinary reputation is fast improving, though prices can sometimes be off-putting. The pleasures of modern Irish cuisine (as well as the finer points of Guinness) are dealt with elsewhere, but there are plenty of traditional tastes that won't break the budget and will leave you with an evocative memory of the city.

▼ Leo Burdock's

The crisply battered fish and perfectly fried potatoes from Dublin's best-loved chipper are hard to beat.

P.118 ▶ THE OLD CITY AND SOUTH GREAT GEORGE'S STREET

▼ Sheridan's

Savour the tastes and aromas of Dublin's finest display of Irish cheeses.

P.76 ▶ TRINITY COLLEGE, GRAFTON STREET AND AROUND

▲ The Old Jameson Distillery

Learn the secrets of whiskey-making and sample a drop of the hard stuff.

P.148 ▸ FROM CAPEL STREET TO COLLINS BARRACKS

▲ King Sitric's Fish Restaurant, Howth

Local oysters, mussels, lobsters and fish – a great way to round off the Howth Cliff Walk.

P.174 ▸ THE NORTHERN OUTSKIRTS

▼ The Porterhouse

Sample an award-winning range of home-brewed stouts, lagers and bitters.

P.105 ▸ TEMPLE BAR

▼ Hot port

Drop into a traditional pub off Grafton Street, or indeed any Dublin bar worth its salt, for this fine winter warmer, spiked with lemon and cloves.

P.79 ▸ TRINITY COLLEGE, GRAFTON STREET AND AROUND

Musical Dublin

Whatever your musical tastes you're bound to find something to suit in Dublin. There are plenty of pubs hosting traditional music sessions, often of astonishingly high quality, while many others, from the tiny to the mega-bar, offer jazz, blues and up-and-coming rock bands. There's also a plethora of places for gigging and ligging, from small events to major concerts, and several classical music venues.

▲ Temple Bar Music Centre

A purpose-built venue with a justifiably lauded reputation for hosting left-field bands and singers.

P.106 ▶ TEMPLE BAR

▲ National Concert Hall

Home to the city's major classical music concerts and often other important musical events.

P.206 ▶ ESSENTIALS

▶ J.J. Smyth's

The Aungier Street bar is the focus for
Dublin's blues and jazz-fusion scene.

P.122 ▶ THE OLD CITY AND SOUTH
GREAT GEORGE'S STREET

▼ The Cobblestone

One of the best places to catch a traditional
session in the city, and also to sample locally
produced brews.

P.152 ▶ FROM CAPEL STREET TO
COLLINS BARRACKS

▼ U2

Unquestionably Ireland's most successful
musical export and singer Bono has become
one of the country's most powerful political
ambassadors. In its early days the band
played many small venues in the city, most
now defunct, but including the Project Arts
Centre.

P.101 ▶ TEMPLE BAR

Georgian Dublin

During a period of great prosperity in the eighteenth century, Dublin enjoyed its architectural heyday: from 1757 the Wide Streets Commissioners oversaw the building of tree-lined squares and boulevards that were worthy of a modern European capital. Famous architects and craftsmen were brought in to design both public set-pieces and intimate residences. Hard times, however, followed the complete transfer of political power to London in 1801, though this economic stagnation helped to ensure the survival of extensive areas of Georgian architecture to this day.

▲ Lower Fitzwilliam Street

An absorbing tour of a re-created Georgian townhouse on the corner of Merrion Square.

P.88 ▸ KILDARE STREET AND MERRION SQUARE

▲ Newman House

Fabulous stucco-work adorns what became Ireland's first Catholic university.

P.91 ▸ ST STEPHEN'S GREEN TO THE GRAND CANAL

▲ The Casino at Marino

Probably Ireland's finest Neoclassical building, executed with beautiful craftsmanship and witty sleight of hand.

P.172 ▸ THE NORTHERN OUTSKIRTS

◀ Fitzwilliam Square

This late-Georgian square, built on a more intimate scale than other examples in the city, was home to W.B. Yeats, among other notables.

P.93 ▸ ST STEPHEN'S GREEN TO THE GRAND CANAL

▶ The Custom House

Dominating the waterfront, the design of Gandon's magnificent edifice features numerous intricate exterior details and a grand dome.

P.133 ▸ AROUND O'CONNELL STREET

Guinness pubs

Few visitors leave Dublin without trying the hometown drink, the stout Guinness, even if it's just a "glass" (a half-pint). It really does taste better here, and locals argue about exactly which pub pours the best drop (is the travel-shy liquid better at *Ryan's*, just across the river from the brewery, than downstream at *Mulligan's*?). It's always granted the requisite two minutes' settling time halfway through pouring, and no matter how thirsty you are, you should let it settle again once it's fully poured.

▲ Mulligan's

Characterful, rambling haunt of *Irish Times* hacks, and who's to doubt their view that it purveys the best pint in the city?

P.81 ▸ TRINITY COLLEGE, GRAFTON STREET AND AROUND

▼ The Long Hall

Hopefully this long-time favourite, currently in the middle of a building site, won't change its atmospheric decor or its careful handling of the black stuff.

P.121 ▶ THE OLD CITY AND SOUTH GREAT GEORGE'S STREET

▲ The Palace Bar

Sip some of the finest Guinness in Dublin at the sociable bar or in the easy-going, glass-roofed back room.

P.81 ▶ TRINITY COLLEGE, GRAFTON STREET AND AROUND

▼ Ryan's

A long-time challenger to the claim that *Mulligan's* serves the best pint of the black stuff, this Parkgate Street bar is also a handy watering hole en route to Phoenix Park.

P.157 ▶ PHOENIX PARK

▲ The Gravity Bar

Perched on the seventh storey of the Guinness Storehouse, *The Gravity Bar* offers the literal chance to get high. The stout here is probably Dublin's best.

P.125 ▶ THE LIBERTIES AND KILMAINHAM

Dead Dublin

In few capital cities in the world are you made so vividly aware of local, and therefore national, history as in Dublin. Events and their colourful protagonists are each firmly rooted and commemorated in their location, evoking the diverse strands – Catholic, Anglo-Irish and even French Protestant – of the city's past.

▲ Irish Famine Memorial

Rowan Gillespie's stark bronze figures were commissioned to commemorate the 150th anniversary of the worst year of the Great Famine. More than a million people died between 1845 and 1849 and many others were forced to emigrate.

P.134 ▶ AROUND O'CONNELL STREET

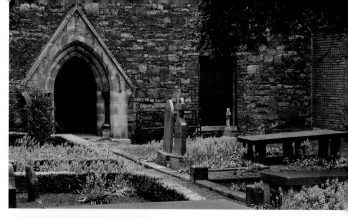

▲ Huguenot Cemetery

A small, well-tended tribute to these industrious seventeenth-century immigrants.

P.90 ▶ ST STEPHEN'S GREEN TO THE GRAND CANAL

◀ Glasnevin Cemetery

Tour Ireland's poignant national cemetery, followed by the traditional drink round the corner at *Kavanagh's*, also known as *The Gravediggers*.

P.170 & P.175 ▶ THE NORTHERN OUTSKIRTS

▼ St Michan's Church

Take a tour of the spooky crypt and its mummified remains.

P.147 ▶ FROM CAPEL STREET TO COLLINS BARRACKS

▼ The monuments in St Patrick's Cathedral

Eclectic reminders of the city's Protestant history, from a cast of Jonathan Swift's skull to a grandiose memorial to the mother of physicist Robert Boyle.

P.115 ▶ THE OLD CITY AND SOUTH GREAT GEORGE'S STREET

Bars and clubs

Dublin has a multitude of stylish, modern bars, some featuring startlingly idiosyncratic decor, with the Quays and surrounding streets one of the best areas to head for. The club scene too is thriving, though reflecting popular tastes some of the mega-clubs have closed in recent years, and smaller, more chic venues have sprung up in their stead. The streets west of Grafton Street, and Harcourt Street, south of St Stephen's Green, are the centres of the action.

▲ Anséo

This unpretentious watering hole on Camden Street is Dublin's DJ bar of the moment.

P.95 ▸ ST STEPHEN'S GREEN TO THE GRAND CANAL

▲ Rí Rá

A vibrant and long-standing venue – Monday's Strictly Handbag is the night to hit.

P.122 ▸ THE OLD CITY AND SOUTH GREAT GEORGE'S STREET

▲ Gaiety Theatre

A weekend makeover sees this renowned theatre transformed into one of the city's largest clubs with plenty of DJs and a very late licence.

P.81 ▸ TRINITY COLLEGE, GRAFTON STREET AND AROUND

▲ Sin É

The bar's name means "that's it" in Irish – enough said. If you're looking for a dark and conducive atmosphere, this is the place to go.

P.151 ▸ FROM CAPEL STREET TO COLLINS BARRACKS

◄ Dice Bar

Don't be deterred by the dark and brooding interior – there's plenty of life here and some great sounds.

P.151 ▸ FROM CAPEL STREET TO COLLINS BARRACKS

Dublin churches

Dublin city is not in truth a magnet for connoisseurs of religious architecture. Though Christianity has had a strong presence here since the fifth century, when St Patrick baptized converts in a well near his present-day cathedral, the area's finest early Christian remnants are well to the south of the city at Glendalough. However, the compelling interest of Dublin's churches lies in the stories that the stones and artefacts tell, from the wildly oscillating fortunes of St Audoen's to the miraculous survival of Our Lady of Dublin.

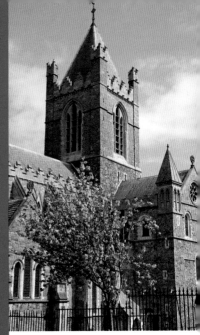

▲ Christ Church Cathedral

Originally built in the twelfth century but substantially reconstructed in the nineteenth, with an interesting display of treasures in the huge crypt.

P.112 ▸ THE OLD CITY AND SOUTH GREAT GEORGE'S STREET

▲ Glendalough

St Kevin's Church is just one of several important remains on view at this monastic site, gloriously set against the backdrop of the Wicklow Mountains.

P.182 ▸ DAY TRIPS

▼ Whitefriar Street Carmelite Church

This Catholic church enshrines Our Lady of Dublin, one of the few pre-Reformation wooden statues to survive in Ireland, and the remains of St Valentine.

P.117 ▸ THE OLD CITY AND SOUTH GREAT GEORGE'S STREET

▲ St Patrick's Cathedral

A quirky array of memorials adorn the national Anglican cathedral.

P.115 ▸ THE OLD CITY AND SOUTH GREAT GEORGE'S STREET

▼ St Mary's Pro-Cathedral

The renowned Palestrina Choir celebrates Latin Mass here every Sunday morning.

P.133 ▸ AROUND O'CONNELL STREET

▼ St Audoen's

Dublin's longest-functioning parish church bears witness to the troubled history of the city and the Church of Ireland.

P.114 ▸ THE OLD CITY AND SOUTH GREAT GEORGE'S STREET

Pub snugs

Blissfully resisting the pressures of modernization and conformity, many Dublin pubs have kept their snugs. Partitioned off by carved wood and cut-glass screens, these havens often have a private hatch to the bar and are perfect for making and breaking confidences. The pubs described here are all congenial places to drink, even if you can't take up residence in their coveted snugs.

▲ The Octagon Bar

The stylish bar at *The Clarence* bathes in artificial daylight, from which you can hide, if you wish, in the secretive, pew-like, modern snug.

P.105 ▸ TEMPLE BAR

▲ Doheny and Nesbitt

Atmospheric pub with a small, packed front bar, roomier back bar and three large snugs to choose from.

P.95 ▸ ST STEPHEN'S GREEN TO THE GRAND CANAL

▲ Kehoes

This former grocery-pub has a fine mahogany bar and plenty of cosy nooks and crannies.

P.80 ▶ TRINITY COLLEGE, GRAFTON STREET AND AROUND

▲ Toners

Efficient service and one glass-partitioned booth by the bar at this Spartan, sociable pub.

P.96 ▶ ST STEPHEN'S GREEN TO THE GRAND CANAL

▶ The Stag's Head

Ornate, stag-themed decor and good Guinness, but you'll have to come early to get a table in the large, dark snug.

P.122 ▶ THE OLD CITY AND SOUTH GREAT GEORGE'S STREET

Rebellious Dublin

Wherever you tread in Dublin you're bound to encounter some connection with Ireland's 700-year struggle for independence. Monuments recalling the past abound in the city: in statues, notably those of Daniel O'Connell and Charles Parnell on O'Connell Street; in buildings inextricably linked to key moments in the country's history, such as Dublin Castle and the General Post Office; and in memorials to those who fell during the process in Parnell Square and at the Croppy's Acre.

▲ Daniel O'Connell

A key figure in the struggle for Catholic Emancipation, O'Connell is celebrated in several notable Dublin monuments, including this one at City Hall.

P.107 ▸ THE OLD CITY AND SOUTH GREAT GEORGE'S STREET

◄ Kilmainham Gaol

The leaders of the Easter Rebellion were executed here – an event that, alongside many other incidents in Ireland's political history, is recounted in the Gaol museum's galleries.

P.126 ▸ THE LIBERTIES AND KILMAINHAM

▼ General Post Office

The locus of the 1916 Easter Rebellion, the GPO's portico still bears bullet marks.

P.131 ▸ AROUND O'CONNELL STREET

▼ Robert Emmet

Romantic nationalist hero, hanged after the failed rebellion of 1803, who is remembered for his powerful speech from the dock.

P.84 ▸ KILDARE STREET AND MERRION SQUARE

► Wolfe Tone

Leader of the unsuccessful French-supported Rebellion of 1798, who killed himself in prison and became the martyr figure for later revolutionary nationalism.

P.91 ▸ ST STEPHEN'S GREEN TO THE GRAND CANAL

Indulgent Dublin

It's easy to get through a lot of money during a stay in Dublin, recently ranked Europe's second-most expensive city. Some of the treats described here, however, won't break the bank – though you'll probably want to be on rock-star royalties to stay in *The Clarence's* penthouse. A growing number of the city's hotels open their spas to non-residents, with treatments and massages an optional extra.

▲ Black velvet

This champagne cocktail is a waste of good Guinness, some say. Enjoy it at *The Morrison* overlooking the river or in any of the major hotel bars.

P.137 ▸ AROUND O'CONNELL STREET

▲ Restaurant Patrick Guilbaud

A top-class French restaurant, using the best of seasonal Irish produce, with a good-value lunchtime menu.

P.89 ▶ KILDARE STREET AND MERRION SQUARE

▶ The penthouse suite at The Clarence

The heights of indulgence . . . your own piano, outdoor hot tub and peerless views of the Liffey.

P.193 ▶ ACCOMMODATION

▲ Tethra Spa at the Merrion Hotel

A luxurious escape offering wide-ranging treatments, a gym, a swimming pool decorated with murals of Neoclassical landscapes, and a marble steam room.

P.192 ▶ ACCOMMODATION

▲ Horse and carriage ride

See the sights in style.

P.90 ▶ ST STEPHEN'S GREEN TO THE GRAND CANAL

Outdoor Dublin

With attractive public gardens, elegantly designed squares and the sprawling expanse of Phoenix Park, Dublin provides a wealth of green space, with plenty of opportunities for a stroll or an alfresco picnic. Outside the city, the shores of Dublin Bay offer bracing walks, while hardier souls might fancy a dip in the sea.

▲ The Forty Foot Pool

A popular bathing place, summer and winter – brace yourself.

P.166 ▸ THE SOUTHERN OUTSKIRTS

▲ St Stephen's Green

Bang in the centre, the Green is great for people-watching and gives an outdoor history lesson through its fascinating monuments.

P.90 ▸ ST STEPHEN'S GREEN TO THE GRAND CANAL

◀ A picnic in Merrion Square

A great, generally quiet, setting on a sunny day: elegant lawns and flower-beds, with glimpses of the square's Georgian terraces above the treetops.

▶ Open-top bus tours

Taking a bus tour is one of the best ways to appreciate the city's daily life, as well as its attractions. The drivers and guides are ever informative and might even break into song at appropriate moments.

▼ Phoenix Park

Europe's largest walled park offers vast scope for investigation – visit the People's Garden, enjoy the zoo or take a tour of the magnificent Farmleigh mansion.

▶ The Botanical Gardens

Exotic gardens, rockeries and arboreta to explore – and you can duck into the Victorian glasshouses if it rains.

Sporting Dublin

Sport is an integral part of Irish life and no more so than in the capital. Gaelic football, hurling, soccer and rugby matches feature on pub TV screens and as a prominent part of daily conversation, and newspaper coverage seems boundless. Then there's also that well-known Irish fondness for a flutter, be it on the horses or the dogs.

▲ Dublin Marathon

The event is Ireland's largest road-race and takes place every October.

P.209 ▸ ESSENTIALS

▲ Croke Park

The national stadium for Gaelic games hosts several matches during the summer and the All-Ireland finals in September.

P.143 ▸ NORTH FROM PARNELL SQUARE

▶ Shelbourne Park

See the dogs in action and catch the trackside banter.

P.207 ▶ ESSENTIALS

▲ Leopardstown races

Home of the Irish Gold Cup in February, the closest racetrack to the city is a great place to experience local passion for the horses.

P.207 ▶ ESSENTIALS

▼ Lansdowne Road

Ireland's international rugby and soccer teams both play their home matches here, usually with at least three home games each per season.

P.207 ▶ ESSENTIALS

Gay and lesbian Dublin

Though attitudes to homosexuality have become more tolerant in recent years, Dublin's gay and lesbian scene remains relatively small, reflecting centuries of Catholic teaching and hardened attitudes. Apart from a few Southside bars, it's very much focussed on the Capel Street area. *Outhouse* and *GCN* (see p.210) are the best sources of information.

▲ GUBU

"Grotesque, unprecedented, bizarre and unbelievable" – don't miss the classic Busty Lycra night on Wednesdays.

P.151 ▶ FROM CAPEL STREET TO COLLINS BARRACKS

▲ The Front Lounge

Sophisticated and long-standing café-bar
that attracts an easy-going, mixed crowd.

P.104 ▸ TEMPLE BAR

▶ The George

Ireland's oldest and most popular gay bar
offers plenty of entertainment, as well as a
relaxed area for a quiet pint.

P.121 ▸ THE OLD CITY AND SOUTH
GREAT GEORGE'S STREET

▼ Yello

Up-and-coming bar/venue offering a range
of entertainment, including a wickedly funny
Friday karaoke session.

P.151 ▸ FROM CAPEL STREET TO
COLLINS BARRACKS

Modern art and architecture

Though small, Dublin's modern-art scene is thriving, thanks to a range of exhibition spaces, both public and commercial. Major shows tend to focus upon international artists, though native Irish art is gaining increasing coverage. In architecture, recent trends have seen a shift away from a merely functional modernism and there's a graceful eloquence present in many new constructions, as well as a striking range of "street sculpture", the most impressive example being the Dublin Spire, also known as The Spike.

▼ The Spike

The Northside's premier landmark, Ian Ritchie's 400-foot needle catches the sunlight during the day and broods ominously at night.

P.130 ▶ AROUND O'CONNELL STREET

▲ The Douglas Hyde Gallery

An attractive and prestigious venue for contemporary art in Trinity College.

P.71 ▶ TRINITY COLLEGE, GRAFTON STREET AND AROUND

▼ Irish Museum of Modern Art

IMMA displays a regularly changing selection of temporary exhibitions as well as those drawn from its own extensive collection of modern art from Ireland and beyond.

P.125 ▶ THE LIBERTIES AND KILMAINHAM

▲ The Gallery of Photography

It's always worth checking out the exhibits of Irish and international photo-works here.

P.100 ▶ TEMPLE BAR

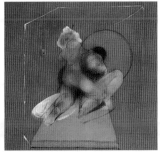

▲ The Francis Bacon studio

Though London-based, the painter Francis Bacon was Irish-born. Part of the Hugh Lane Gallery recreates his studio and displays a selection of striking paintings.

P.141 ▶ NORTH FROM PARNELL SQUARE

Shoppers' Dublin

Dublin boasts some excellent book and CD shops, the most notable of them specializing in Irish literature and music. Fashionistas are well catered for too, with plenty of boutiques, jewellery shops and department stores stocking the best of Irish and global design. On a fine day, consider heading for a food market or an artisan deli and picnicking in one of the city's attractive squares.

▲ Moore Street market

Browse amongst the stalls and shops at this eclectic, esoteric and, nowadays, fundamentally ethnic market.

P.135 ▸ AROUND O'CONNELL STREET

▲ Claddagh Records

The best traditional-music store in Dublin.

P.101 ▸ TEMPLE BAR

▶ Temple Bar food market

Saturday finds Dublin's foodies shopping here, for everything from cheese to oysters, and it's well worth joining them to pick up a take-away lunch.

P.102 ▸ TEMPLE BAR

▽ Avoca

Chic Irish clothes, woollen goods and gifts, plus a basement deli and an excellent café.

P.74 & P.76 ▸ TRINITY COLLEGE, GRAFTON STREET AND AROUND

▽ Brown Thomas

BT's is the city's flagship department store, the place to go for anything from Irish designer labels to a haircut.

P.74 ▸ TRINITY COLLEGE, GRAFTON STREET AND AROUND

▲ Hodges Figgis

Behind this ornate facade lies the city's finest bookshop, particularly strong on Irish literature, history and culture.

P.75 ▸ TRINITY COLLEGE, GRAFTON STREET AND AROUND

Children's Dublin

There's plenty in Dublin for kids to enjoy. As well as the attractions shown here, there's fun to be had exploring the delights of the National Wax Museum (see p.139) and Tara's Palace (see p.177), or venturing into the great outdoors, with trips to Phoenix Park or the seaside. Most attractions and activities offer significant discounts to children.

▲ Viking Splash

Amphibious vehicles take in the major sites by land before heading on to the river in probably the city's most exciting tour.

P.205 ▸ ESSENTIALS

▲ Dublinia

A long roster of imaginative activities, especially in the summer, to bring medieval and Viking Dublin to life.

P.114 ▸ THE OLD CITY AND SOUTH GREAT GEORGE'S STREET

▲ Lambert Puppet Theatre

High-quality puppet shows for kids throughout the year and performances for adults during the international festival in September.

P.207 ▶ ESSENTIALS

▼ Natural History Museum

Skeletons of whales and extinct giant deer, stuffed rhinos, moose and a dodo, and plenty of activities and events for children.

P.87 ▶ KILDARE STREET AND
MERRION SQUARE

▲ The Ark

Book your kids in for a performance or activity at Europe's only purpose-built cultural centre for children.

P.98 ▶ TEMPLE BAR

▶ Dublin zoo

As well as the chance to see animals as various as hippos and meerkats, Dublin's major child-friendly attraction features a City Farm specifically geared towards younger kids. The zoo's breeding programme offers the chance to see newborn arrivals.

P.153 ▶ PHOENIX PARK

Modern Irish cooking

Over the last fifteen years, the quality of local ingredients, often supplied by artisanal, organic producers, has been rediscovered in a way that has transformed Irish cooking. Irish meat has a justly famous reputation; excellent fish and all manner of seafood are freshly available; while the country's dairy produce and baking traditions are of the highest standards. The stress is on cooking techniques, whether based on traditional recipes or drawing on influences from around the world, that will allow these ingredients to speak for themselves.

▲ Eden

Traditional Irish weather permitting, sit outside on Meeting House Square and tuck into West Cork scallops with noodles.

P.103 ▶ TEMPLE BAR

▲ The Tea Room

Haute cuisine employing the best of Irish seasonal produce, in classically modernist surroundings.

P.104 ▸ TEMPLE BAR

▼ The Canteen

Well worth the short trip out to the Grand Canal, *The Canteen* is celebrated for its imaginative use of ingredients and fine seafood dishes.

P.161 ▸ ALONG THE GRAND CANAL

▲ Ely Wine Bar

An informal, good-value spot to sample dishes such as venison with spinach and oyster mushrooms.

P.95 ▸ ST STEPHEN'S GREEN TO
THE GRAND CANAL

▼ Chapter One

An acclaimed basement restaurant offering a delicious blend of Irish and French cuisines.

P.144 ▸ NORTH FROM PARNELL
SQUARE

Dublin views

Dublin has few tall buildings, so the backdrop of the Wicklow Mountains to the south is often visible from the city centre. And, if you do get up high, there aren't many obstructions to your bird's-eye view, which is often bisected by the River Liffey and its diverse bridges. The city's location at the centre of the magnificent sweep of Dublin Bay is undervalued, but can be fully appreciated by a journey on the DART, particularly to the south of the centre.

▲ O'Connell Bridge

The bridge provides one of the city's most expansive views, whether it's looking east towards the Custom House and the developing docklands, west along the Quays to the Four Courts, north up bustling O'Connell Street or south towards Trinity College – a great place to get your bearings.

P.129 ▸ AROUND O'CONNELL STREET

▲ The Guinness Storehouse

Sup your pint of the black stuff at the top of the seven-storey Guinness Storehouse tower and survey the panoramic vista of the city.

P.124 ▸ THE LIBERTIES AND KILMAINHAM

▲ A DART ride

A dramatic coastal train ride round Dublin and Killiney bays, Dalkey Hill and Bray Head.

P.163 ▶ THE SOUTHERN OUTSKIRTS

◀ Powerscourt

The pleasing geometry of the formal gardens, with their fine statues and fountain lake, is echoed in the neat triangular back-drop of Sugarloaf Mountain.

P.181 ▶ DAY TRIPS

▼ Smithfield Observation Chimney

The heart of the city captured in miniature, with stunning views looking east to Dublin Bay.

P.147 ▶ FROM CAPEL STREET TO COLLINS BARRACKS

Dublin cafés

The Irish drink even more tea per head than the English, so it's not surprising that Dublin has long had a thriving café society – strongly supported by the widespread temperance movement and the churches. Nowadays you're almost as likely to find baklava as brack (a delicious traditional Irish sweet bread with spices and dried fruits), accompanied by a delicate speciality tea or a frothy cappuccino.

▲ The Winding Stair

Views of the river, wholesome food and a great bookshop for browsing.

P.136 ▸ AROUND O'CONNELL STREET

▲ Caffe Cagliostro

This tiny Italian café serves up splendid coffee and delicious pastries with outside tables for watching the world pass by.

P.136 ▸ AROUND O'CONNELL STREET

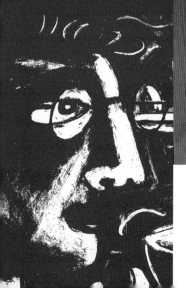

◀ Queen of Tarts

A mouthwatering display of cakes, tarts and all things yummy.

P.119 ▶ THE OLD CITY AND SOUTH GREAT GEORGE'S STREET

▲ Silk Road Café

The stylish café in the Chester Beatty Library serves mostly Middle Eastern food, from delicious moussaka and falafel to filo pies and baklava.

P.119 ▶ THE OLD CITY AND SOUTH GREAT GEORGE'S STREET

▼ The Merrion Hotel

The drawing rooms here are the place to come for sumptuous afternoon tea, sitting beneath a fine collection of Irish art, overlooking impressive gardens.

P.192 ▶ ACCOMMODATION

Theatre and film

Lovers of the theatre are spoilt for choice in Dublin where, alongside Irish classics and newer works by dramatists such as Brian Friel, numerous smaller theatres and arts centres offer more experimental productions. There are also major festivals in September and October. Film fans too are well catered for in numerous mainstream cinemas as well as a major centre for independent releases. An international film festival is held in February, and the lesbian and gay-focused Outlook, in July (see p.208).

▲ The Helix

Operating at the populist end of the spectrum, this modern theatre offers everything from musicals and ice shows to rock bands and ballet.

P.175 ▸ THE NORTHERN OUTSKIRTS

▲ Irish Film Institute

Dublin's best cinema, showing the pick of releases from around the world, and a busy social hub.

P.101 ▸ TEMPLE BAR

▲ Gate Theatre

The Abbey's main rival also stages a range of striking theatrical productions of European drama.

P.139 ▸ NORTH FROM PARNELL SQUARE

▼ Dublin Fringe Festival

Ireland's biggest performing arts festival features all manner of music, dance, street theatre, comedy and children's events.

P.209 ▸ ESSENTIALS

▲ Abbey Theatre

Ireland's most renowned theatre offers a varied programme of classic and contemporary drama.

P.132 ▸ AROUND O'CONNELL STREET

▼ Project Arts Centre

Originating as an arts project in the foyer of the Gate Theatre, the flagship of the contemporary arts scene hosts experimental theatre, film, music and dance.

P.101 ▸ TEMPLE BAR

Dublin walks

There are some spectacular walks within a surprisingly short distance of central Dublin, whether in the Wicklow Mountains, from Howth or Bray, or at Dalkey, the easiest to access. Gentle strolls are more the order of the day back in the city, either on a lively guided tour or in the vast reaches of Phoenix Park, one of the world's largest city parks.

▲ The Grand Canal

Ideal for a gentle stroll on a sunny Sunday afternoon.

P.160 ▸ ALONG THE GRAND CANAL

▶ Walking Tours

Whether it's treading in the footsteps of James Joyce and his characters or a historical guided tour such as "Rebellious Dublin", the city offers plenty of peripatetic pleasures.

P.205 ▸ ESSENTIALS

▼ North Bull Island

A stroll along the island and its three-mile beach, Dollymount Strand, will reveal a rich diversity of birds – especially in winter – and flowers.

P.173 ▸ THE NORTHERN OUTSKIRTS

▲ Dalkey and Killiney hills

An easy walk between DART stations, offering glorious views of Killiney Bay, the Wicklow Mountains and the city.

P.167 ▸ THE SOUTHERN OUTSKIRTS

◀ Phoenix Park

There's plenty to see and do here and it's easy to pass a whole day exploring the Park and its attractions.

P.153 ▸ PHOENIX PARK

Festivals

Dublin stages numerous festivals during the year. The arts are particularly well catered for, with major events devoted to theatre, film, music and literature an established part of the calendar. There's plenty for children to enjoy as well, such as the St Patrick's festival and numerous events in Temple Bar.

▲ St Patrick's Day

Six days of fun and frolics centred around March 17, featuring a parade on the day itself and a *ceili mor* day of traditional dancing.

P.208 › ESSENTIALS

▲ Summer events in Temple Bar

Diversions is Temple Bar's summer series of free events, and includes outdoor film shows and live music.

P.208 › ESSENTIALS

▲ Dublin Horse Show

This five-day show-jumping event in August features top international stars.

P.209 › ESSENTIALS

▶ Bray Jazz Festival

Jazz and Ireland may not be synonymous, but this lively festival features the cream of the local scene as well as well-known international acts.

P.208 › ESSENTIALS

▼ Docklands Maritime Festival

Tall ships visit Dublin and there's lots of quayside enjoyment too such as a street market as well as plenty of events for children.

P.208 › ESSENTIALS

Free Dublin

Though Dublin is an expensive city, there are plenty of free attractions that won't burden your pocket or purse. Some major sites, such as the National Gallery (see p.85) and National Museum (see p.83), charge no entrance fee except for special events. There's also plenty of street and outdoor entertainment, especially in summer.

▲ The House of Lords

It's well worth coming on a Tuesday for the free guided tour, to learn the fate of the eighteenth-century Irish Parliament, now a bank.

P.72 ▶ TRINITY COLLEGE, GRAFTON STREET AND AROUND

▲ Smithfield horse sales

Smithfield has been hosting a horse fair for more than three hundred years. Catch it on the first Sunday of the month, spot a bargain and sample the *craic*.

P.147 ▶ FROM CAPEL STREET TO COLLINS BARRACKS

▲ The National Library

Richly endowed literary exhibitions and the stately and historic reading room.

P.84 ▶ KILDARE STREET AND MERRION SQUARE

▲ Grafton Street buskers

You'll as likely come across a man with a *bodhrán* as a string quartet, and it's all free – apart from a penny or two in the hat, perhaps.

P.73 ▶ TRINITY COLLEGE, GRAFTON STREET AND AROUND

▼ Farmleigh

This splendid conservatory features amongst the delights of Farmleigh mansion, one of the city's most sumptuous buildings.

P.155 ▶ PHOENIX PARK

▼ Collins Barracks

Home to the National Gallery's collection of decorative arts, Collins Barracks offers plenty to enthral and entertain.

P.150 ▶ FROM CAPEL STREET TO COLLINS BARRACKS

Places

Trinity College, Grafton Street and around

Like a walled village of scholars, Trinity College takes up a surprisingly large tract of Dublin's city centre. Visitors are free to stroll through its tranquil quads and parkland, though its overarching draw is the glorious Book of Kells. Opposite, near the site of the flat-topped mound that was Dublin's Viking assembly, sits the poignant former House of Parliament, now a particularly ornate branch of the Bank of Ireland. Just a stone's throw from these august institutions, the city's most frenetic commercial street, Grafton Street, marches off towards St Stephen's Green. Here and in the surrounding streets, you'll find Dublin's most stylish shops and boutiques, notably in the elegantly converted Georgian mansion of Powerscourt Townhouse shopping centre. With the city's best concentration of traditional pubs, as well as a wide variety of fine cafés and restaurants, the area's only marginally less lively by night.

College Green

Open fields beyond the city walls when Trinity College was founded, College Green is today one of Dublin's most frantic junctions. Hemmed in by Trinity's grandiose west front and the curving facade of the Bank of Ireland, cars

▼ EDMUND BURKE

and pedestrians flow past a fine array of monumental statuary, mostly depicting old boys of the college: from the eighteenth century, philosopher and politician Edmund Burke and writer Oliver Goldsmith stand on either side of the college's main entrance; politician Henry Grattan (1746–1820) by the bank; and, in the thick of the traffic at the top of Dame Street, nineteenth-century nationalist and poet Thomas Davis, who penned some of the most popular Irish ballads. Amongst these was *A Nation Once Again*, which explains the nickname of the fountain in front of him, depicting the heralds of the four provinces of Ireland – "Urination Once Again". Much of the pedestrian traffic heads towards the college entrance between Burke and Goldsmith, the most popular meeting place in the city.

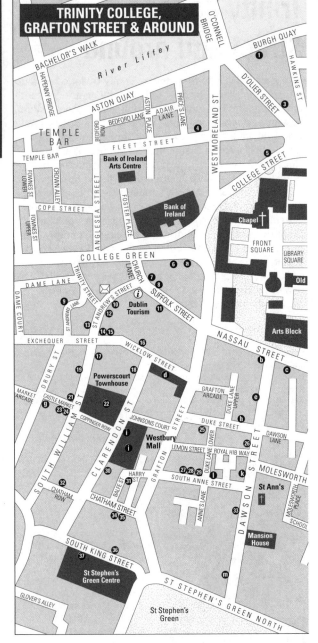

TRINITY COLLEGE, GRAFTON STREET & AROUND

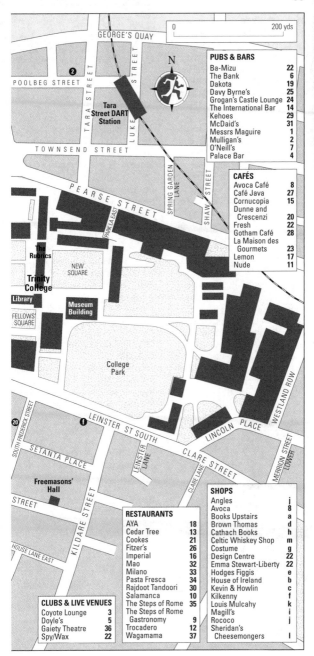

PLACES Trinity College, Grafton Street and around

GEORGE'S QUAY

0   200 yds

POOLBEG STREET

Tara Street DART Station

TOWNSEND STREET

PEARSE STREET

PARK LANE EAST

The Rubrics

Trinity College

Library

NEW SQUARE

FELLOWS SQUARE

Museum Building

College Park

LEINSTER ST SOUTH

LINCOLN PLACE

SETANTA PLACE

CLARE STREET

Freemasons' Hall

KILDARE STREET

HOUSE LANE EAST

PUBS & BARS	
Ba-Mizu	22
The Bank	6
Dakota	19
Davy Byrne's	25
Grogan's Castle Lounge	24
The International Bar	14
Kehoes	29
McDaid's	31
Messrs Maguire	1
Mulligan's	2
O'Neill's	7
Palace Bar	4

CAFÉS	
Avoca Café	8
Café Java	27
Cornucopia	15
Dunne and Crescenzi	20
Fresh	22
Gotham Café	28
La Maison des Gourmets	23
Lemon	17
Nude	11

RESTAURANTS	
AYA	18
Cedar Tree	13
Cookes	21
Fitzer's	26
Imperial	16
Mao	32
Milano	33
Pasta Fresca	34
Rajdoot Tandoori	30
Salamanca	10
The Steps of Rome	35
The Steps of Rome Gastronomy	9
Trocadero	12
Wagamama	37

SHOPS	
Angles	j
Avoca	8
Books Upstairs	a
Brown Thomas	d
Cathach Books	h
Celtic Whiskey Shop	m
Costume	g
Design Centre	22
Emma Stewart-Liberty	22
Hodges Figgis	e
House of Ireland	b
Kevin & Howlin	c
Kilkenny	f
Louis Mulcahy	k
Magill's	i
Rococo	j
Sheridan's Cheesemongers	l

CLUBS & LIVE VENUES	
Coyote Lounge	3
Doyle's	5
Gaiety Theatre	36
Spy/Wax	22

Trinity College, Grafton Street and around   PLACES

Trinity College

ⓦ www.tcd.ie. Mon–Fri 7am–midnight, Sat & Sun 8am–midnight; free. Walking tours from the main gate led by Trinity students mid-April to early Oct 9 daily; 30min; €9.50, including admission to the Old Library. An imposing architectural set-piece at the heart of the city, Trinity College was founded in 1592 by Queen Elizabeth I to prevent the Irish from being "infected with popery and other ill qualities" at French, Spanish and Italian universities. Catholics were duly admitted until 1637 when restrictions were imposed that lasted until the Catholic Relief Act of 1793. The Catholic Church, however, banned its flock from studying here until 1970 because of the college's Anglican orientation; today seventy percent of the students are Catholic. Famous alumni range from politicians Edward Carson and Douglas Hyde, through philosopher George Berkeley and Nobel-prizewinning physicist Ernest Walton, to writers such as Swift, Wilde and Beckett.

▲ STONE CARVING, MUSEUM BUILDING

The appealing eighteenth-century symmetry of Front Square, flanked by the Chapel and the Examination Hall, gives onto Library Square, which features the oldest surviving building, the Rubrics, a red-brick student dormitory dating from around 1701. In New Square beyond, the School of Engineering occupies the old Museum Building (1852), designed in extravagant Venetian Gothic style by Benjamin Woodward under the influence of his friend, John Ruskin, and awash with decorative stone-carving of animals and floral patterns.

The Old Library and the Book of Kells

June–Sept Mon–Sat 9.30am–5pm, Sun 9.30am–4.30pm; Oct–May Mon–Sat 9.30am–5pm, Sun noon–4.30pm (closed for 10 days over Christmas and New Year). €7.50; combined ticket with Dublin Experience €10.50. Trinity's most compelling tourist attraction – often with half-hour queues in summer – is the *Book of Kells*, kept in the eighteenth-century Old Library, which is entered from Fellows' Square. Beautiful pages of the *Book of Kells* (around 800 AD), the *Book of Armagh* (807) and the *Book of Durrow* (675) are on display, preceded by a fascinating exhibition "Turning Darkness into Light", which sets Irish illuminated manuscripts in context – ranging from ogham (the earlier, Celtic writing system of lines carved on standing stones) to Ethiopian books of devotions.

▼ CAMPANILE, TRINITY COLLEGE

Upstairs is the library's magnificent, barrel-vaulted Long Room. As a copyright library, Trinity has had the right to claim a free copy of all British and Irish publications since 1801; of its current stock of three million titles, 200,000 of the oldest are stored in the Long Room's oak bookcases. Besides interesting temporary exhibitions of books and prints from the library's collection, the Long Room also displays a gnarled fifteenth-century harp, the oldest to survive from Ireland, and an extremely rare original printing of the 1916 Proclamation of the Irish Republic, made on Easter Sunday in Liberty Hall.

The Douglas Hyde Gallery

ⓦwww.douglashydegallery.com. Mon–Wed & Fri 11am–6pm, Thurs 11am–7pm, Sat 11am–4.45pm. Free. In the 1980s Arts Block opposite the Old Library on Fellows' Square, right by the college's Nassau St entrance, the Douglas Hyde is one of Ireland's most important galleries of modern art. It hosts top-notch temporary shows by Irish and international artists working in a variety of media.

The Dublin Experience

Mid-May to Sept daily 10am–5pm (hourly shows). €4.20; combined ticket with Old Library €10.50. This 45-minute audiovisual show, put on in the lecture theatre of the Arts Block, gives a handy, basic introduction to the history of Dublin.

The Bank of Ireland

College Green. Mon–Fri 10am–4pm (until 5pm Thurs); guided tours Tues 10.30am, 11.30am & 1.45pm. Free. Opposite Trinity, the Neoclassical, granite Bank of Ireland was built in 1729 by Sir Edward Pearce – himself an MP – as the House of Parliament. An Irish parliament had existed in one limited form or another

▼ LONG ROOM, OLD LIBRARY

PLACES Trinity College, Grafton Street and around

The Book of Kells

Pre-eminent for the scale, variety and colour of its decoration, the **Book of Kells** probably originated at the monastery on Iona off the west coast of Scotland, which had been founded around 561 by the great Irish scholar, bard and ruler St Colum Cille (St Columba in English). After a Viking raid in 806, the Columbines moved to the monastery of Kells in County Meath, and around 1653, the manuscript was moved to Dublin for safekeeping during the Cromwellian Wars. The 340 calfskin folios of the *Book of Kells* contain the four New Testament gospels along with preliminary texts, all in Latin. It's thought that three artists created the book's lavish decoration, which shows Pictish, Germanic and Mediterranean, as well as Celtic influences.

▲ BANK OF IRELAND

since the thirteenth century, but achieved its greatest flowering here in 1782 – "Grattan's Parliament" after the prime mover behind the constitutional reform – when it was granted legislative independence from the British Parliament. Catholics were still barred from sitting, but many signs of sovereignty were established during this period, including the foundation of the Bank of Ireland; around this time, the Lords deemed it necessary to build themselves a separate entrance on Westmoreland Street, designed by James Gandon in 1785 in the Corinthian style, to distinguish it from the Ionic colonnade of what is still the main entrance. After the rebellion of 1798, however, the Irish House was persuaded and bribed to vote itself out of existence, and with the 1800 Act of Union Ireland became part of the United Kingdom, governed from Westminster. The Bank of Ireland bought the building for £40,000 in 1802, and the Commons chamber was demolished to remove a highly charged symbol of independence.

The barrel-vaulted House of Lords was also meant to be knocked down, but survives to this day to host high-level state functions and as the main attraction for visitors. Here you'll find one or two exhibits such as the Lord Chancellor's richly embroidered purse, used to carry the Great Seal of Ireland, and tapestries showing William of Orange's victories over James II and his Catholic supporters, the *Siege of Derry* and the *Battle of the Boyne*. The richly stuccoed Cash Hall – an elegant spot to do any banking chores you may have – used to be the Parliament's Hall of Requests, where constituents would petition their representatives.

The Bank of Ireland Arts Centre

Foster Place ☎01/671 2261, ⊛www .boi.ie/artscentre. Story of Banking Tues–Fri 10am–4pm; €3. Entered down a lane off College Green, the bank's former guardhouse is now an arts centre, which stages exhibitions by Irish artists, lunchtime poetry readings and classical recitals, and a variety of evening charity concerts. It's also the venue for the Story of Banking, an exhibition accessible on an engaging 45-minute guided tour which includes an audiovisual "narrated" by La Touche, the first Governor, on the bank's history, and the mace used in the former House of Commons. Sold by the descendants of the last Speaker, it was bought at Christie's of London by the bank in 1937 for £3100.

Grafton Street

Running south from College Green to St Stephen's Green, pedestrianized Grafton Street starts inauspiciously with "the tart with the cart", a gagglingly kitsch bronze, complete with wheelbarrow of cockles and mussels, of eighteenth-century street trader Molly Malone. For those who hate shopping and crowds, Grafton Street won't get any better; for people-watchers, however, it's a must, noted especially for its buskers, who range from string quartets to street poets. The street's major landmark, *Bewley's Oriental Café*, owes its beautiful mosaic facade to the mania for all things Egyptian that followed the discovery of Tutenkhamun's tomb in 1922. Founded by the Quaker Bewley family as a teetotal bulwark against the demon drink, the café was forced to close down in 2004 in the face of escalating ground rents that have made Grafton Street one of the world's five most expensive shopping streets on which to trade. As this book was going to press, the ornate premises reopened, incorporating a much-reduced Bewley's café and a branch of *Café-Bar-Deli* (see p.119).

Powerscourt Townhouse

Powerscourt Townhouse is a stylish shopping centre that incorporates the eighteenth-century Palladian mansion of Lord Powerscourt (see p.181). The house's main door, on South William Street, gives straight onto the trompe l'oeil stone floor of the entrance hall and, beyond, the central mahogany staircase, with its flighty rococo plasterwork by James McCullagh and what are thought to be the most elaborately carved balusters in Ireland. More geometrical, Neoclassical work by the house's other stuccodore, Michael Stapleton, can be seen upstairs, in what is now a suitably extravagant setting for The Town Bride. The café-bar in the atrium is notable for its location – bathed in light on sunny days – in what was once the mansion's inner courtyard.

The Solomon Gallery

Second floor, Powerscourt Townhouse Centre ☎01/679 4237, ⊛www.solomongallery.com. One of the townhouse's former living rooms, its ceiling adorned with Neoclassical stucco work, is the fitting venue for this commercial gallery for mostly Irish paintings and sculpture.

Dawson Street

Dawson Street's busy thoroughfare accommodates the city's main bookshops and several other interesting speciality shops, as well as an utterly forgettable row of over-designed "superpubs". It's also flanked by the Mansion House, built in 1705 and embellished with a stucco facade and civic coat-of-arms in Victorian times, which has been the residence of Dublin's Lord Mayor since 1715 (not open to the public).

▼ ATRIUM, POWERSCOURT TOWNHOUSE

St Ann's Church

Dawson St ☎01/676 7727.
Mon–Fri 10am–4pm. The lopsided
Romanesque style facade of
St Ann's Church is a curious
Victorian landmark at the end
of South Anne Street. Its plain,
dimly-lit, balconied interior,
however, is typical of the early
eighteenth century. Here, each
week, 120 loaves of bread are
laid out on shelves behind the
altar, according to a bequest
for the poor of the city which
has persisted since 1723.
Parishioners have included the
art collector Sir Hugh Lane
and Thomas Barnardo, founder
of the eponymous children's
homes, while Wolfe Tone (1785)
and Bram Stoker (1878) were
both married here. A stained-
glass window in the chancel
commemorates Felicia Hemans,
of 21 Dawson St, who penned
"The boy stood on the burning
deck" in her poem *Casabianca*
of 1828. It's worth calling for
details of the lunchtime and
evening concerts of classical
music given at St Ann's.

▼ ST ANN'S CHURCH

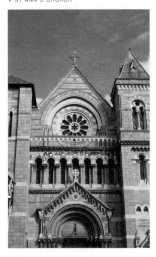

Freemasons' Hall

17 Molesworth St. Guided tours only:
June–Aug Mon–Fri 2.30pm; €2.
Behind its sombre Neoclassical
front, the headquarters of Ireland's
Grand Lodge conceals a riotous
mix of Victorian second-hand
architectural styles, from medieval
to Egyptian (complete with
sphinxes). The tour also includes
a twenty-minute video show and
a museum of Masonic regalia.

Shops

Angles

10 Westbury Mall, off Harry St
☎01/679 1964. Open Sun. Small,
friendly shop specializing in
Irish contemporary jewellery,
mainly in silver and/or with
semi-precious stones, at quite
reasonable prices.

Avoca

11 Suffolk St ☎01/677 4215. Open
Sun. Highly successful small Irish
department store, stocking its
own clothing ranges for women
and children, jewellery, beautiful
rugs and throws woven at the
original mill in Avoca, Co.
Wicklow, plus toys and chic
houseware – plenty of potential
gifts. There's a splendid deli in
the basement, and an equally
delightful café on the second
floor (see p.76).

Books Upstairs

36 College Green ☎01/679 6687.
Open Sun. Particularly strong on
Irish literature, literary criticism
and biography, as well as many
works of general Irish interest.
Also a good range of periodicals
and gay and lesbian literature,
and plenty of discounted books.

Brown Thomas

88–95 Grafton St ☎01/605 6666,
🌐www.brownthomas.com. Open Sun.

The city's flagship department store, Brown Thomas is sophisticated and pricey, featuring a long roll-call of Irish and international designer labels, and complemented by its trendier younger sibling, BT2, opposite.

Cathach Books
10 Duke St ☏01/671 8676. The place to come for first editions by Irish writers and rare Irish maps of interest, with discounted books in the basement.

Celtic Whiskey Shop
27–28 Dawson St, @www .celticwhiskeyshop.com. Open Sun. Probably the best selection of Irish whiskeys anywhere, including some rare examples from distilleries that have now closed down and familiar names at reasonable prices. The well-informed staff always have bottles open to taste and will ship around the world.

Costume
10 Castle Market ☏01/679 4188. Stylish, upmarket boutique, selling everything from jumpers and coats to evening dresses, by less familiar international designers and on its own label.

Design Centre
Top floor, Powerscourt Townhouse Centre ☏01/679 5718. An extensive showcase for Irish designers of women's fashion, such as Michelle Molloy, Louise Kennedy, John Rocha and Patrick Casey, as well as diverse clothes and accessories by international names.

Emma Stewart-Liberty
First floor, Powerscourt Townhouse Centre ☏01/679 1603. Attractive modern jewellery, much of it made in-house – the plain gold and silver bangles and earrings are particularly striking. Specially commissioned work undertaken.

Hodges Figgis
56–58 Dawson St ☏01/677 4754. Open Sun. A Dublin institution since the eighteenth century, behind an ornate, multistoreyed Dutch-style facade. Books on Ireland are on the ground floor, with everything covered from fiction and history to language and travel. Book bargains are on offer in the basement.

House of Ireland
37–38 Nassau St ☏01/677 7949. Open Sun. Upmarket tourist shop selling Waterford and Tipperary crystal, attractive Belleek ceramics and Aran jumpers.

Kevin & Howlin
31 Nassau St ☏01/677 0257. Nothing but Donegal tweed, with off-the-peg jackets and suits for men and women – allow about seven weeks for tailor-made – as well as the ubiquitous caps and hats.

Kilkenny
6 Nassau St ☏01/677 7066. Open Sun. A varied collection of fine Irish crafts: Newbridge silver cutlery; John Rocha's elegant collection for Waterford Crystal; mostly blue Belleek ceramic bowls and lamps; and an extensive range of clothes and jewellery by contemporary designers.

Louis Mulcahy
46 Dawson St ☏01/670 9311. Beautiful household objects, including vases, lights and crockery, by one of Ireland's most famous potters, plus a selection of scarves and other woollen items.

▲ MAGILL'S

Magill's

Clarendon St, next to Westbury Mall. The helpful staff at this traditional deli have all you need to compile a fine picnic: County Mayo smoked salmon, a good selection of Irish cheeses, tubs of *antipasti*, tempting breads and all manner of specialities from around the world.

Rococo

Westbury Mall ☎01/670 4007. Open Sun. Eclectic outfits in ornate designs and colours, by designers such as Noa Noa and Nougat.

Sheridan's Cheesemongers

11 South Anne St ☎01/679 3143, ⓦwww.sheridanscheesemongers .com. Fantastic, pungent array of cheeses, mostly by Irish artisan producers, sold by knowledgeable staff.

Cafés

Avoca Café

11 Suffolk St. On the top floor of this department store (see p.74), the bright, buzzy café is thronged at lunchtimes. Out of the open kitchen comes everything from shepherd's pie to delicious smoked salmon bruschetta with rocket and

tzatziki, as well as a tempting array of desserts and cakes, and a fine choice of wines and soft drinks (notably home-made lemonade), all beautifully presented and courteously served.

Café Java

5 South Anne St. Popular, modern café with tables outdoors on this quiet side street, serving breakfasts, light meals and sandwiches, plenty of cakes, wine and a huge range of coffees and teas.

Cornucopia

19–21 Wicklow St. Mon–Sat 8.30am–8pm, Sun noon–7pm. A small, friendly buffet café that's been popular with veggies for many years. On a menu which changes daily and is labelled for special diets, there's an excellent range of salads, soups and main courses such as moussaka and Thai curry, as well as cakes, breads, juices and organic wine.

Dunne and Crescenzi

14 & 16 South Frederick St. Mon–Sat 8.30am–11pm, Sun noon–6pm. A cosy Italian café, deli and wine shop, with cakes and spot-on coffee for breakfast, and, for the rest of the day, all manner of Italian sandwiches and excellent plates of *antipasti*, as well as salads and one or two daily special main courses. Packed at lunchtime, with the outside tables at a particular premium in summer.

Fresh

Second floor, Powerscourt Townhouse Centre. Closed Sun. A great setting, overlooking the shopping centre's glassed-in Georgian courtyard, and a marvellous vegetarian and vegan menu, using organic ingredients wherever possible: soups, salads, sandwiches, pasta, veggie tarts, curries, pulse dishes and hotpots; various breads, cakes and desserts; and wines, fresh juices and smoothies.

Gotham Café
5 South Anne St. Open daytime & evening. This lively café with outside tables, just off Grafton Street, does a global menu that includes great pizzas and salads, and dishes such as Louisiana crab cakes and Thai vegetable curry.

La Maison des Gourmets
15 Castle Market. Closed Sun. Chic *salon de thé* above a French patisserie. Perch on the high red banquettes to tuck into light meals such as barbecued smoked salmon salad – which will leave just enough room for a delicious cake and coffee.

Lemon
South William St. Mon–Wed, Fri & Sat 8am–7.30pm, Thurs 8am–9.30pm, Sun 10am–6.30pm. Tiny, hyperactive modern café, with one or two heated outdoor tables, dishing up a huge range of very good, inexpensive savoury and sweet crêpes, to eat in or take away – try the delicious banana maple delight with almonds.

Nude
21 Suffolk St. Mon–Fri 8am–9pm, Sat 11am–9pm, Sun 11am–7pm. Funky canteen-style café with a big open kitchen, serving up hot

▼ NUDE

and cold wraps, panini, bagels, salads, pastas, soups and some weird and wonderful juices and smoothies, to eat in or take away. Organic ingredients are used wherever possible, and there is ample choice for vegetarians.

Restaurants

AYA
48 Clarendon St ☎01/677 1544. Just behind Brown Thomas department store, the focus here is Dublin's first conveyor-belt sushi bar. There are regular tables, too, for more substantial and expensive Japanese dishes.

Cedar Tree
11 St Andrew's St ☎01/677 2121. Evenings only. In a lively cellar opposite the landmark *International Bar*, you can feast on a delicious and moderately priced array of Lebanese meat, seafood and vegetarian meze dishes – all the more tempting if you can get here before 7.30pm for the early-bird menu.

Cookes
14 South William St ☎01/679 0536. Chic new restaurant with very good service, where echoing tiled floors and large windows facing Powerscourt Townhouse magnify the buzz. There are plenty of delicious salads to start you off, while the mains feature seafood, though you'll also find appealing pasta options and meaty fare such as venison with chestnuts and juniper berries. Reasonably priced set lunch and early-bird menus.

Fitzer's
51 Dawson St ☎01/677 1155. Part of a reliable

chain of moderately priced restaurants, offering tempting standards such as Thai fishcakes and meatball linguini, as well as several daily specials and plenty of choices for vegetarians. This branch is adorned with colourful modern art and high leather banquettes, and there are tables outside in the summer.

Imperial

12A Wicklow St ☎01/677 2580. A thumbs-up from loyal Chinese customers, who generally rate it the best restaurant in the city centre. Specialities include butterfly prawns with orange sauce and crispy shredded eels with spicy sauce. Excellent dim sum, served daily until 5.30pm, is especially popular on Sundays.

Mao

2–3 Chatham Row, Chatham St ☎01/670 4899. Slick, trendy spot decorated with Warhol posters of the Chairman himself and fronted by outdoor seating. The reasonably priced menu follows a successful formula: great dishes from around Asia, including such mouthwatering temptations as tamarind tiger prawns.

Milano

38 Dawson St ☎01/670 7744. Branch of the established pizza chain (see p.104).

Pasta Fresca

3 Chatham St ☎01/679 2402. Large, informal, warmly decorated restaurant with a few tables and chairs outside, and a good-value menu of varied *antipasti*, fresh pasta, grills, salads, pizzas and daily specials.

Rajdoot Tandoori

26–28 Clarendon St ☎01/679 4274. Plush Indian restaurant with

excellent service, cooking up specials such as makhani chicken in yoghurt and plenty of options for vegetarians. Cheaper menus at lunchtime and pre- and post-theatre.

Salamanca

St Andrew's St. A huge range of good-value tapas – try the very tasty and substantial house paella – accompanied by friendly service, soft lighting, warm decor and, on Sun evening, live Spanish guitar music.

The Steps of Rome

1 Chatham Court, Chatham St ☎01/670 5630. Tiny, simple restaurant, serving cheap and excellent pizza, alongside variations such as focaccia, as well as pasta, salads and a few meat dishes. If you can't get a table, there's pizza by the slice to take away.

The Steps of Rome Gastronomy

St Andrew's Lane ☎01/672 9857. Much larger branch of the above, with a few outdoor tables, offering a far longer menu of authentic Italian dishes at very reasonable prices: as well as *antipasti*, pastas and salads, there are mains such as pork fillet in white wine sauce, or just

▼ TROCADERO

plump for a bottle of red and a cheese plate for two.

Trocadero

3 St Andrew's St ☎01/677 5545. Evenings only, closed Sun. A welcoming haven, done out with plush booths, signed photos of showbiz visitors and yards of red velvet. Excellent, though predictable, food (mostly Italian), whether à la carte or on the reasonably priced set menus, which include a good-value pre-theatre option (you need to vacate the table by 8pm).

Wagamama

South King St ☎01/478 2152. Basement branch of the well-known, good-value chain, with an open kitchen knocking out healthy Japanese meat and vegetarian dishes to punters sharing long bench tables. Best for noodle soups, dumplings and a wide variety of wholesome juices; takeaway service available.

Pubs and bars

Ba-Mizu

Powerscourt Townhouse Centre. Low-lit modern bar with comfy leather furniture in the vaulted stone cellars of Lord Powerscourt's former mansion. There's a popular food menu, featuring dishes such as caramelized pear and goat's cheese tart, a seafood bar, and outdoor tables on South William Street.

The Bank

College Green. Behind its distinctive Scottish sandstone facade, the former Belfast Bank has been sensitively converted in all its Victorian splendour as one of Dublin's most luxurious bars: mosaic floors, stained glass

▲ DAKOTA

ceiling, beautiful plaster rosettes and porphyry columns, all best admired from the projecting mezzanine. More prosaic sustenance is provided by a good selection of beers, wines and cocktails, as well as salads, sandwiches and main meals, but who needs the latest stock market prices flashed above the bar?

Dakota

9 South William St. Thurs till 2am, Fri & Sat till 2.30am. A stylish conversion, in chocolate and brick, of a fabric warehouse. Table service at the dark leather booths and armchairs is aimed at pulling in a late-twenties and early-thirties crowd, who duly cram the place at weekends.

Davy Byrne's

21 Duke St. After extensive redecoration as a lounge bar, in a mix of Art Deco and other vaguely modernist styles, you'll have your work cut out to imagine Davy Byrne's "moral pub" where Bloom takes a break for a Gorgonzola sandwich and

a glass of Burgundy in *Ulysses*. All the same, it's a good place for a quiet drink and perhaps a plate of oysters, a sandwich or a scone.

Grogan's Castle Lounge
15 South William St. Lively, eccentric traditional pub where works for sale by local artists hang on the walls, and budding writers and artists take colourful inspiration from the stained-glass memorial to famous *Grogan's* regulars.

The International Bar
23 Wicklow St ☎01/677 9250. Sociable, old-fashioned pub that heaves congenially at weekends. The ground floor with its stained glass and ornate woodcarving is particularly sought after, so you may have better luck finding space in the basement bar. Upstairs is the lively venue for comedy (Mon, Thurs, Fri & Sat), jazz (Tues)

and Lazybird, a club night with live bands on Sun.

Kehoes
9 South Anne St. Characterful meeting place, where Dubliners tend to settle in if they can get a seat, especially in either of the cosy snugs. The low mahogany bar, with its old-fashioned till and drawers, used to double up as a grocery, while upstairs, where the last resident publicans in the city centre formerly lived, still feels like a comfortable sitting room.

McDaid's
3 Harry St. This literary landmark was the home-from-home of writer Brendan Behan (see p.15), who would spend his days drinking, entertaining, sleeping it off and drinking again here. Despite now selling its own T-shirts, the bright, high-ceilinged pub is still highly popular with locals, with pleasant overspill seating upstairs for when the crush gets too mighty.

Messrs Maguire
1–2 Burgh Quay. Mon–Wed & Sun till 12.30am, Thurs–Sat 2.30am. Though not quite as classy as the *Porterhouse* (see p.105), this microbrewery pub overlooking the river, with countless floors and mezzanines off a grand, winding staircase, is well worth trying out. There's a varied food menu featuring dishes such as Wicklow

▼ THE INTERNATIONAL BAR

▲ THE PALACE BAR

rack of lamb with rosemary and red wine sauce.

Mulligan's

8 Poolbeg St. A little off the beaten track, this large no-nonsense pub remains a favoured watering hole for journalists and workers at the nearby *Irish Times*. Vies with *Ryan's* (see p.157) and of course *The Gravity Bar* (see p.125) as home of "the best pint in Dublin".

O'Neill's

2 Suffolk St. Huge, disorientating old pub adorned with acres of oak panelling and green leather where, despite the throngs of Trinity students, you should be able to find yourself a quiet corner. Renowned for its long and varied food menu, including a lunchtime carvery.

The Palace Bar

21 Fleet St. Relaxing, sociable Victorian pub famed both for the quality of its pint and for its handsome decor of mirrored screens and ornate woodcarving. The overflow bar upstairs hosts regular sessions of traditional music.

Clubs and live venues

Coyote Lounge

21 D'Olier St ☎01/671 2089, ⊛www .xlmedia.com. As much for lounging and ligging as dancing, this cavernous underground club serves as both a mid-evening bar and as a place for a late night danceathon. Friday's funk night with Shortee and The Goat is the one to head for.

Doyle's

9 College St ☎01/571 0616. Famed for being the place to spot up-and-coming singer-songwriters at its Ruby Sessions (Tues 9pm), *Doyle's* pub also hosts other live musical events and late D-Basement club nights (Wed–Sat until 2.30am).

Gaiety Theatre

King St South ☎01/679 5622, ⊛www .gaietytheatre.ie. The *Gaiety* transforms itself each Friday and Saturday night from theatre into a hotbed of dance, trance and, possibly, romance, claiming to be the latest-opening club in the city. With five bars, and up to four DJs spinning discs in different rooms, there's plenty to entice and invigorate.

Spy/Wax

Powerscourt Townhouse Centre ☎01/677 0014, ⊛www.pod.ie. *Spy* is an astonishingly extravagant DJ bar, the modern decor of its four contemporary bars fully complementing its Georgian setting, while bright young things ogle their surroundings. *Wax* downstairs hosts a range of club nights, usually focused on the funky side of House.

PLACES Trinity College, Grafton Street and around

Kildare Street and Merrion Square

Ireland's political and cultural Establishments have their power bases in the tight confines of Kildare Street and Merrion Square. Leinster House and its grounds, home of Ireland's parliament, straddles the two locations, surrounded by the unmissable treasures of the National Museum, the National Library and its impressive literary exhibitions, the National Gallery's trove of European art and the charmingly unreconstructed displays of the Natural History Museum. Former residences of a historical Who's Who of Ireland, from O'Connell to the Wildes, Merrion Square's Georgian terraces are now occupied by such diverse organizations as the Arts Council and the Football Association of Ireland, while its quiet, tree-shaded lawns lighten the heavy, stately feel. There are no pubs or restaurants on Merrion Square itself, but Kildare Street supports one or two places to refuel and most of the cultural institutions have a café.

Leinster House

Kildare St ⊛ www.irlgov.ie. Now the seat of the Oireachtas (the Irish Parliament), Leinster House was built in 1745 as a mansion on the edge of town for James Fitzgerald, Earl of Kildare (later the Duke of Leinster). The architect, Richard Castle, designed the impressive pedimented frontage to be viewed along Molesworth Street, and employed the Swiss Lafranchini brothers to adorn the ceilings with baroque stucco work. After serving as the headquarters of the Royal Dublin Society from 1815, the house was acquired by the government of the newly formed Irish Free State in 1924.

The Oireachtas has two chambers: elected by proportional representation, the Dáil (or House of Representatives, who are known as *teachtaí Dála* or

TDs) sits in the nineteenth-century former lecture theatre of the Royal Dublin Society; members of the Seanad (Senate), who are either nominated by the Taoiseach (prime minister) or elected from various panels or by the universities, meet in a semicircular eighteenth-century room that was the mansion's picture gallery. Parliament usually sits from mid-January to early July (breaking for Easter), and October until Christmas, on Tuesday afternoons, Wednesdays and Thursdays. Overseas visitors should write as far as possible in advance to the Captain of the Guard (or go through their embassy in Dublin) to arrange a free guided tour; visits are possible year round (indeed, you're likely to see more of the building itself when the Oireachtas isn't in session), and tend to be busiest in the summer.

The National Museum

Kildare St ⓦ www.museum.ie. Tues–Sat 10am–5pm, Sun 2–5pm; free. Guided tours Tues–Sat 3.30pm, Sun 2.30pm and at other variable times posted up in the entrance rotunda each day; 40min; €2. The National Museum on Kildare Street is the finest of a portfolio of jointly run museums – including the Natural History Museum (see p.85) and Collins Barracks (see p.150), which focuses on the decorative arts – and is a must-see for visitors to Dublin. Undoubted stars of the show here are a stunning hoard of prehistoric gold and a thousand years' worth of ornate ecclesiastical treasures, but the whole collection builds up a fascinating and accessible story of Irish archeology and history. The shop in the beautiful entrance rotunda sells a range of high-quality crafts inspired by works in the museum, and there's a small café.

Prehistoric gold (ór), much of it discovered during peat-cutting, takes pride of place on the ground floor of the main hall. From the Earlier Bronze Age (c. 2500–1500 BC) come *lunulae*, thin sheets of gold formed into crescent-moon collars. After around 1200 BC, when new sources of the metal were apparently found, goldsmiths could be more extravagant, fashioning chunky torcs, the spectacular Gleninsheen collar and the Tumna Hoard of nine large gold balls, which are perforated, suggesting a huge necklace. Further prehistoric material is arrayed around the walls of the main hall, including the fifteen-metre-long Lurgan Logboat, dating from around 2500 BC, which was unearthed in a Galway bog in 1902.

The adjacent Treasury holds most of the museum's better-known ecclesiastical exhibits, notably the ornate, eighth-century Ardagh Chalice and the Tara Brooch, decorated with beautiful knot designs. Also on the ground floor is the small Road to Independence exhibition, which comprises such artefacts as the death mask

PLACES Kildare Street and Merrion Square

▲ READING ROOM, NATIONAL LIBRARY

Kildare Street and Merrion Square

PLACES

of revolutionary Robert Emmet (1778–1803).

Upstairs, Viking-age Ireland (c. 800–1150) features models of a house and the layout of Dublin's Fishamble Street, while an adjoining room displays some famous Christian objects from the same period, notably the beautiful Crozier of St Tola and the Cross of Cong, created to enshrine a fragment of the True Cross given to the king of Connacht by the pope in 1123. The museum's most recent exhibit moves on to medieval Ireland (1150–1550), to cover the first English colonists, their withdrawal to the fortified area around Dublin known as "the Pale" after 1300, and the hybrid culture that developed across the period – you can listen to recordings of poetry written in Ireland in Middle Irish, Middle English and Norman French. Unmissable here is a host of small, ornate shrines, made to hold holy relics or texts, such as the Shrine of the Cathach, containing a manuscript written by St Columba of Iona, legendary bard, scholar, ruler and evangelizer of Scotland.

The National Library

Kildare St ⓦ www.nli.ie. Mon–Wed 10am–9pm, Thurs & Fri 10am–5pm, Sat 10am–1pm. Free. The National Library was opened in 1890, shortly after the National Museum, whose design it mirrors across the courtyard of Leinster House. Its main draw are the long-term temporary exhibitions, on subjects such as Joyce and W.B. Yeats, that are mounted in a beautiful, new, high-tech space on the lower ground floor. Visitors are also allowed up to the hushed domed Reading Room on the first floor, decorated with ornate bookcases and an incongruously playful frieze of cherubs. It is in the office here that Stephen Daedalus engages the librarians – who appear under their real names – in literary talk in the "Scylla and Charybdis" episode of *Ulysses*. On the way up, on the mezzanine landing, look out for the curious stone plaques representing, from left to right, Asia, Europe, America and Africa. In the Genealogy Room (Mon–Fri 10am–4.45pm, Sat 10am–12.30pm; free), professional genealogists can give advice to anyone researching their family history on how to access the records here and elsewhere in Dublin, as well as in Belfast. The library's ground floor shelters a very attractive café and a small bookshop.

The Heraldic Museum

2–3 Kildare St ⊛www.nli.ie.
Mon–Wed 10am–8.30pm, Thurs &
Fri 10am–4.30pm, Sat 10am–1pm.
Free. A few doors down from
the National Library, by which
it is administered, the Heraldic
Museum contains such items
as Sir Roger Casement's Order
of St Michael and George,
the Lord Chancellor's purse,
and the mantle and insignia of
the Order of St Patrick. And
if your mantelpiece just isn't
complete without an Irish
coat-of-arms, the attached
Office of the Chief Herald is
the place to come – it'll cost
you around €3000 and take up
to a year to complete. These
august establishments occupy
a mid-nineteenth-century
brick edifice in Venetian
style that used to house the
deeply conservative, Anglo-
Irish Kildare Street Club,
which novelist George Moore
– himself a leisured member
of the landed class – lambasted
in *Parnell and His Island* in
1887: "a sort of oyster-bed into
which all the eldest sons of the
landed gentry fall as a matter
of course . . . drinking sherry
and cursing Gladstone in a
sort of dialect, a dead language
which the larva-like stupidity
of the club has preserved". The
O'Shea brothers, who executed

the whimsical stone carving
on the facade, may well have
shared Moore's view – look out
for the three monkeys playing
billiards on one of the ground-
floor windows.

The National Gallery

Access from Merrion Square West or
from Clare St via Millennium Wing.
⊛www.nationalgallery.ie. Mon–Sat
9.30am–5.30pm, Thurs till 8.30pm,
Sun noon–5.30pm; free (€3 donation
suggested). Free guided tours Sat
3pm & Sun 2pm, 3pm & 4pm; meet in
the Shaw Room (Dargan Wing Level
1, near Merrion Square entrance).
The National Gallery hosts
a fine collection of Western
European art dating from the
Middle Ages to the twentieth
century. The gallery's old
building, divided into Beit,
Milltown and Dargan wings,
has now been joined by the
Millennium Wing, which
hosts temporary exhibitions
around its striking atrium. The
resulting layout of the gallery,
however, can be confusing, so
the first thing to do when you
go in is to pick up a floor plan
leaflet (free). As well as classical
and contemporary concerts,
the gallery offers lectures and
workshops (detailed in the
monthly *Gallery News*, available
in the foyer), some of which
are intended for children and
people with
disabilities.
    Level 1 is
chiefly given
over to Irish
art from the
seventeenth
century onwards,
including a large
gallery in the
Millennium
Wing devoted
to the twentieth
century. The real

▼ MONKEYS PLAYING BILLIARDS, HERALDIC MUSEUM

stand-out in the Irish collection, however, is the Yeats Museum (below the National Portrait Gallery), which traces the development of Jack B. Yeats (1871–1957), younger brother of the writer W.B., from an unsentimental illustrator of everyday scenes to an expressive painter in abstract, unmixed colours.

▲ THE NATIONAL GALLERY

Highlights of Level 2 include a fine selection of works from the Early Renaissance; Caravaggio's dynamic *The Taking of Christ*, and a characteristic Vermeer nearby, *Woman Writing a Letter*, one of only 35 accepted works by the artist; outstanding works by Velázquez, Rubens and Mantegna; a fascinating room devoted to art in eighteenth-century Rome; and an excellent survey of French art from Poussin to the Cubists. In the mezzanine Print Gallery, as well as temporary exhibitions throughout the year, watercolours by Turner are exhibited every January, when the light is low enough for these delicate works.

Merrion Square

Begun in 1762, Merrion Square represents Georgian town-planning at its grandest. Its long, graceful terraces of red-brown brick sport elaborate doors, knockers and fanlights, as well as wrought-iron balconies (added in the early nineteenth century) and tall windows on the first floor, where the main reception rooms would have been. The north side of the square was built first and displays the widest variety of design.

The broad, manicured lawns of the square's gardens themselves are a joy, quieter than St Stephen's Green, and especially agreeable for picnics on fine weekends. Revolutionary politician Michael Collins is commemorated with a bronze bust on the gardens' south side, near a slightly hapless stone bust of Henry Grattan (see p.67 & p.72), while writer, artist and mystic George Russell ("AE") stands gravely near the southwest corner and his former home at no. 74. But the square's most remarkable and controversial statue is at the northwest corner: here, opposite his childhood home (see p.89), Oscar Wilde reclines on a rock

▼ SUNDAY, MERRION SQUARE

in a wry, languid pose that has earned the figure the nickname "the fag on the crag". In front of him, a male torso and his wife Constance, pregnant with their second child, stand on plinths inscribed with Wildean witticisms: "This suspense is terrible. I hope it will last", "I drink to keep body and soul apart". Nearby on the railings opposite the back of Leinster House, dozens of artists hang their paintings for sale every Sunday.

The Merrion Square South terrace, which has the greatest concentration of famous former residents, gives a particularly vivid sense of the history of the place. Politician Daniel O'Connell bought no. 58 in 1809, the Nobel Prize-winning Austrian physicist Erwin Schrödinger occupied no. 65, and Gothic novelist Joseph Sheridan Le Fanu died at no. 70, which is now the Arts Council building. At no. 39 stood the British Embassy, burnt down by a crowd protesting against the Bloody Sunday massacre in Derry in 1972.

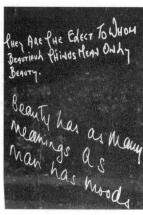

▲ WILDEAN WITTICISMS, MERRION SQUARE

The Natural History Museum

Merrion Square West ⊛ www.museum .ie. Tues–Sat 10am–5pm, Sun 2–5pm; free. For information on guided tours and children's activities, go to the website or ☎ 01/648 6453.
Billing itself as "a museum of a museum", the Natural History Museum has evolved remarkably little since its inauguration in 1856. The tone is set on the lawn outside, by a heroic bronze of Surgeon-Major T.H. Parke with his foot on an animal skull and a rifle in his hands – born in Roscommon, Parke went with Stanley on his 1887 expedition to the Congo River

and was the first Irishman to cross Africa. The museum's display of around ten thousand animals, out of a holding of two million specimens, would be impressive in any age, however. Guarding the ground-floor Irish Room stand three skeletons of giant Irish deer which, despite intimidating rivals and impressing females with the largest antler span – ten feet – of any deer ever, became extinct around 9000 BC.

Upstairs, the World Collection concentrates on the zoology of Africa and Asia, but includes the Barrington collection of birds, many of which were hapless enough to crash into Irish lighthouses. The lower gallery here, the last resting place of a stuffed dodo, is the best spot to view the skeletons of two whales stranded on Irish shores, one of them a sixty-foot fin whale. The upper gallery deals with invertebrates, including the Blaschka Collection, beautiful glass models of marine creatures; look out also for a pair of cosy golden gloves, knitted from threads secreted by the fan mussel.

PLACES Kildare Street and Merrion Square

▲ THE NATURAL HISTORY MUSEUM

Government Buildings

Merrion St Upper. Guided tours Sat
10.30am, 11.30am, 12.30pm, 1.30pm
& 2.15pm; 40min. Free tickets from
the National Gallery on the day.
Next to the Natural History
Museum rises the Neoclassical
pile of Government Buildings,
headquarters of the civil service
and their ministers. Erected
between 1904 and 1922 as
the Royal College of Science,
this was the last great building
work by the British – and was
promptly commandeered by
the ministers of the Free State
as a secure base during the
Civil War of 1922–23. Tours
of the stylishly refurbished
complex will take you into the
Cabinet room, decorated with
portraits of Irish heroes, and the
Taoiseach's office, which has its
own lift to the rooftop helipad.
On the ceremonial staircase
look out for Evie Hone's *My
Four Green Fields*, a striking
modernist representation of
the four provinces of Ireland in
stained glass.

The Yeats House

82 Merrion Square ☎01/676 1173.
Mon–Fri 9.30am–1pm & 2–5pm. Free.
The grandiosely proportioned
residence of W.B. from 1922 to
1928 will appeal mostly to Yeats

buffs. It was restored
from a ruin in the late
1990s, using gorgeous
marble fireplaces
and chandeliers
rescued from similar
houses on Merrion
Square. Still the most
imposing room is the
former drawing room,
decorated with richly
coloured cornices,
where Yeats would
entertain and host
plays. As the rooms are
now working offices,
it's better, though not essential,
to phone ahead.

No. 29 Fitzwilliam Street Lower

☺www.esb.ie/education. Tues–Sat
10am–5pm, Sun 2–5pm, closed last
three weeks of Dec. €4.50. This
townhouse at the southeast
corner of Merrion Square has
been carefully reconstructed in
the style of a middle-class home
of the period 1790–1820 by the
Electricity Supply Board, using
furniture from the National
Museum's collection. The
ESB may sound like a strange
curator for such a venture, but
the house was rebuilt as an act
of homage after the Board had
knocked down 26 Georgian
houses here to build its
adjoining offices in the 1960s.
Entertaining guided tours bring
to life the details of bourgeois
Georgian life, both below stairs
and in the elegant living rooms
upstairs, which benefited from
such gadgets as a lead-lined
wine cooler and a belly-warmer
for soothing gastric complaints.
From this corner of the square
there's a fine view down
Mount Street Upper of the
"peppercanister" church of St
Stephen's, a Greek Revival work
dating from 1824.

The Oscar Wilde House

Mon, Wed & Thurs tours at 10.15am & 11.15am. €2.50. No. 1, at the northwest corner of Merrion Square, was the home from 1855 to 1876 of Sir William, surgeon and polymath, and Lady Jane Wilde, society hostess and polemical poet under the pseudonym "Speranza", as well as their more famous son, Oscar. It's been heavily restored and converted into the base of the American College Dublin and several of the rooms are open to public visits, but it's really only for Wilde freaks.

Shops

Cleo

18 Kildare St ☎01/676 1421, ⊛www .cleo-ltd.com. Small clothes shop specializing in traditional Irish designs and natural fibres, including Aran sweaters, linen shirts and woollen coats, scarves and other accessories.

Greene's

16 Clare St ☎01/676 2554. Characterful landmark of a bookshop – and post office – selling new and secondhand stock, particularly of Irish interest, much of it displayed outside under its wrought-iron canopy.

Cafés and restaurants

Fitzer's

Millennium Wing, National Gallery, Clare St entrance. Restaurant daily noon–3pm, café same hours as gallery (see p.85). In a sleek, modern location under the new wing's glass roof, *Fitzer's* is a well-presented self-service restaurant, offering dishes such as Cajun salmon, salads and plenty for vegetarians. The café upstairs stretches to lasagne, quiches and sandwiches, as well as tempting cakes, scones and cookies.

Patrick Guilbaud

Merrion Hotel, 21 Merrion St Upper ☎01/676 4192, ⊛www .restaurantpatrickguilbaud.ie. Closed Sun. One of Dublin's finest and most expensive, a classic French restaurant that makes the most of Irish seasonal produce. Formal and showy in the evenings, "Paddy Giblets" loosens his collar just a little at lunchtime, when the €33 set menu (two courses plus coffee and petits fours) represents very good value.

Town Bar & Grill

21 Kildare St ☎01/662 4724. Closed Sun. Cavernous cellar, decorated simply and elegantly, where the very high standards of cooking match the complex menu and extensive wine list. To reflect the informality of its name, *antipasti* and pastas are available in two sizes, and a bar menu operates in the afternoons.

▼ GOVERNMENT BUILDINGS

St Stephen's Green to the Grand Canal

As well as being a major landmark and transport hub, St Stephen's Green is central Dublin's largest and most varied park, whose statuary provides a vivid history lesson in stone, wood and bronze. Among the diverse minor attractions in the vicinity, the main sightseeing draws are the Georgian splendours of Newman House and the elegant streets and squares to the east of the Green, which are also home to some fine upmarket eateries. Two nightlife strips that run off the Green are worth making time for: the hallowed Baggot Street crawl of traditional pubs to the east; and the vibrant, studenty trail of DJ bars and live venues down Camden and Wexford streets, culminating in the stylish and varied offerings of the old Harcourt Street station.

St Stephen's Green

Mon–Sat 7.30am–dusk, Sun 9.30am–dusk. The largest of central Dublin's squares, St Stephen's Green preserves its distinctive Victorian character, with a small lake, bandstand, arboretum and well-tended flower displays. It was originally open common land, a notoriously dirty and dangerous spot and the site of public hangings until the eighteenth century. In 1880, however, it was turned into a public park with funding from the brewer Lord Ardilaun (Sir Arthur Guinness), who now boasts the grandest of the Green's many statues (see also p.91), seated at his leisure on the far western side. Over-anxious locals make exaggerated complaints that drunks and ne'er-do-wells are returning the Green to its former unsavoury nature, but it's actually a pleasant, popular spot to take a break in the very heart of the city centre. From the Green's northwest corner, by the top of Grafton Street, you can hire a horse and carriage, either as a grandiose taxi or for a tour of the sights, which will typically set you back €50 for thirty minutes.

St Stephen's Green North

Known as the "Beau Walk" in the eighteenth century, St Stephen's Green North is still the most fashionable side of the square. The *Shelbourne Hotel* here claims to have been the best address in Dublin since its establishment in 1824, but is currently closed for major renovation. It's due to reopen in late 2006, when the pleasures of afternoon tea in the Lord Mayor's Lounge, drinks with politicos and celebs in the *Horseshoe* and *Shelbourne* bars, as well of course as accommodation, will once again be available. Beyond the hotel at the start of Merrion Row, the tiny, tree-shaded Huguenot

A monumental tour of St Stephen's Green

A short stroll around the monuments of St Stephen's Green gives you a vivid sense of the city's history, of diverse episodes and characters that are each firmly rooted in their location; maps at the main entrances will help you find your way. Probably the most striking of the Green's statues is a piercing bronze bust of **James Joyce**, gazing intently over his bony hand towards his alma mater, Newman House, just across the road on St Stephen's Green South. At the southeast corner, the **Three Fates fountain** was presented to Dublin by the German government in recognition of the help given to refugee children after World War II.

An uninspiring bust on the south side of the central floral display does scant justice to the remarkable **Countess Markiewicz**, dynamic socialist and feminist, who was second-in-command of the insurgents at St Stephen's Green during the Easter Rising of 1916. On the west side of the flower display, a tiny plaque inlaid in a wooden park bench commemorates the so-called "fallen women" – mostly unmarried mothers or abused girls – who were forced to live and work in severe conditions in Ireland's **Magdalen laundries**; the last of them, in Dublin, wasn't closed down until 1996. *Knife Edge*, beyond, a memorial by Henry Moore to **W.B. Yeats** is more spiritually uplifting. On the far west side of the Green, an animated bronze of **Robert Emmet** looks proudly across towards the site of his birthplace, now demolished.

Facing Grafton Street from the northwest corner, **Fusiliers' Arch**, which remembers Royal Dublin Fusiliers killed in the Boer War, is still known to some as "Traitors' Gate". Humour resurfaces at the northeast corner, where a row of granite monoliths in honour of eighteenth-century nationalist **Wolfe Tone** is nicknamed "Tonehenge". Behind it stands a moving commemoration of the **Great Famine**.

Cemetery was opened in 1693 for Protestant refugees fleeing religious persecution in France, many of whom settled in The Liberties (see p.123). A large plaque inside the gates gives a roll-call of Huguenot Dubliners, among whom the most famous have been writers Dion Boucicault and Sheridan Le Fanu.

Newman House

85–86 St Stephen's Green South. Guided tours only: June–Aug Tues–Fri noon, 2pm, 3pm & 4pm. €5. Newman House boasts some of the finest Georgian interiors in Dublin, noted especially for their decorative plasterwork. The house is named after John Henry Newman, the famous British convert from Anglicanism, who was invited to found the Catholic University of Ireland here in 1854 as an alternative to Anglican Trinity College and the then recently established "godless" Queen's Colleges in Belfast, Cork and Galway. James Joyce and Éamon de Valera were educated here at what became University College Dublin (UCD), now relocated to a large campus in the southern suburbs.

Newman House began life as two houses: no. 85 is a Palladian mansion built by Richard Castle in 1738 and adorned with superb baroque stucco work by the Swiss Lafranchini brothers, while the much larger no. 86

▼ HENRY MOORE, *KNIFE EDGE*

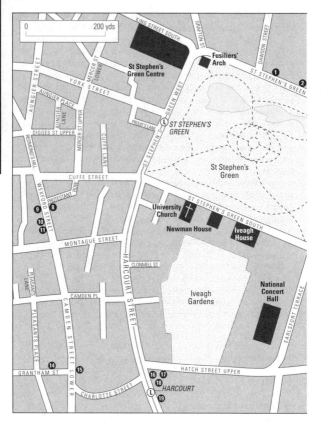

was added in 1765. On the top floor of the latter are a lecture room, done out as in Joyce's student days (1899–1902), and the bedroom of the English poet Gerard Manley Hopkins. Having converted from Anglicanism, Hopkins became a Jesuit priest and then Professor of Classics here in 1884; after five wretched years in Dublin, he died of typhoid and was buried in an unmarked grave in Glasnevin Cemetery.

The University Church and Iveagh House

Next to Newman House stands the Byzantine-style curiosity of the 1850s University Church, complete with ornately carved capitals and extravagant painting and gilding. It got a hostile reception when it was first built, in the style of

▼ THE UNIVERSITY CHURCH

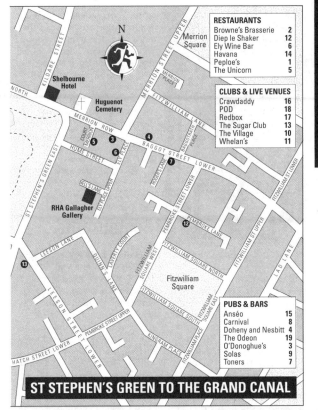

RESTAURANTS

Browne's Brasserie	2
Diep le Shaker	12
Ely Wine Bar	6
Havana	14
Peploe's	1
The Unicorn	5

CLUBS & LIVE VENUES

Crawdaddy	16
POD	18
Redbox	17
The Sugar Club	13
The Village	10
Whelan's	11

PUBS & BARS

Anséo	15
Carnival	8
Doheny and Nesbitt	4
The Odeon	19
O'Donoghue's	3
Solas	9
Toners	7

ST STEPHEN'S GREEN TO THE GRAND CANAL

an eleventh-century Italian basilica, but is now a fashionable venue for weddings. Along the street stands Iveagh House, the first building Richard Castle designed in Dublin (1730) but now much altered as the home of the Department of Foreign Affairs.

Iveagh Gardens

Mon–Sat 8am–6pm, Sun 10am–6pm, closes at dusk in winter. Free. Accessible through a gate behind the National Concert Hall (see p.206) on Earlsfort Terrace, or from Clonmell Street (off Harcourt Street), the little-known Iveagh Gardens are a perfect place to recharge your batteries in the heart of the city. Designed as a pleasure ground in 1863, this secret garden unveils a grotto, a cascade, fountains, a maze and a rosarium.

Fitzwilliam Square and around

The area to the east of St Stephen's Green is the most rewarding in the city for a Georgian architectural tour: an aimless wander will reveal plenty of wrought-iron balconies and much-photographed doorways

▲ GEORGIAN FRONT DOOR, FITZWILLIAM SQUARE

is one of the country's leading contemporary art venues. Where once stood the home of Oliver St John Gogarty, wit, writer and the model for Buck Mulligan in *Ulysses*, this discreet 1970s building now lies at the end of a quiet Georgian cul-de-sac. Its well-designed viewing spaces are home to the RHA Annual Exhibition every May and June – which celebrated its 175th anniversary in 2005 – and include the ground-floor Ashford Gallery, devoted to introducing new Irish artists.

sporting elegant knockers and fanlights. At its centre lie the still-private lawns of the small but well-preserved Fitzwilliam Square (1825). W.B. Yeats lived here, at no. 42, from 1928 to 1932, while his brother, the painter Jack B., had a house and studio round the corner at no. 18 Fitzwilliam Place. Together with its continuation Fitzwilliam Street, this forms a – now much-interrupted – half-mile terrace of Georgian houses, marching off towards the magnificent backdrop of the Wicklow Mountains.

The RHA Gallagher Gallery

Ely Place ☎01/661 2558, ⊛www .royalhibernianacademy.com. Tues–Sat 11am–5pm, Thurs till 8pm, Sun 2–5pm; free. Guided tours (45min) of the current exhibition Wed 1.15pm; free. Hosting major temporary shows by Irish and international artists, the Royal Hibernian Academy of Arts' Gallagher Gallery

Restaurants

Browne's Brasserie

22 St Stephen's Green North ☎01/638 3939, ⊛www.brownesdublin.com. Closed Sat lunchtime. Elegant Georgian townhouse, where you can bask in the opulent decor of a former gentlemen's club and enjoy classy cooking and service. Carpaccio of beef with wild mushroom and truffle vinaigrette will get you off to a good start, while the main courses emphasize seafood, with the likes of chargrilled swordfish with aubergine caviar. Expensive, but more manageable on the lunchtime set menu.

Diep le Shaker

55 Pembroke Lane, off Pembroke St Lower ☎01/661 1829, ⊛www .diep.net. Closed Sat lunchtime & Sun. Dublin's best and most

▼ THE RHA GALLAGHER GALLERY

expensive Thai restaurant. The surrounds are bright and swanky, and the menu, strong on fish and seafood, offers imaginative takes on thoroughly authentic dishes: try the scallops with garlic and soy and oyster sauces, the chargrilled beef sirloin with fish sauce, chilli and lime dressing, or the stir-fried spinach with yellow bean sauce and tofu.

Ely Wine Bar

22 Ely Place ☎01/676 8986, ⊛www .elywinebar.ie. Closed Sun. Popular, congenial and moderately priced wine bar that offers wholesome food, using carefully sourced, mostly organic Irish ingredients, to accompany over seventy wines by the glass. Choose either a simple dish such as bread and dips or a plate of cheeses and cold meats, or something more substantial like venison with spinach and oyster mushrooms.

Havana

3 Camden Market, Grantham St ☎01/476 0046, ⊛www.havana .ie. Congenial, laid-back bar-restaurant where, surrounded by eccentric decor and cool Cuban sounds, you can graze on tasty and cheap tapas.

Peploe's

16 St Stephen's Green North ☎01/676 3144. Closed Sun. Styling itself a "wine bistro", this chic basement restaurant and wine bar offers well-prepared dishes, from linguini with clams in white wine to venison with figs and chocolate-flavoured sauce, served by affable, smartly dressed staff.

The Unicorn

12B Merrion Court, off Merrion Row ☎01/662 4757. Characterful, upmarket Italian trattoria,

▲ BROWNE'S BRASSERIE

buzzing with politicians and media types tucking into authentic fare such as *involtini alla saltimbocca* – pockets of veal stuffed with Parma ham, mozzarella and sage. In summer, the buzz tends to move out from the stylish interior to the tables set out in the secluded alley.

Pubs and bars

Anséo

18 Camden St. Unpretentious venue with plenty of velour banquettes to chill out on, but one of the bars of the moment for its easy-going atmosphere and roster of DJs from Wednesday to Saturday. Tuesday is open mike night for singer-songwriters.

Carnival

Wexford St. Open till 2.30am Fri & Sat. Popular DJ bar – hung with a desultory few Venetian masks to justify the name – with mellow lighting, a few comfortable booths and a large, graffitied yard out the back.

Doheny and Nesbitt

5 Baggot St Lower. Don't be dismayed if the tiny front bar of this famous old pub, all dark wood and cut-glass partitions, is packed: there's a spacious back bar – a good place to catch TV sport – where the interior courtyard for smokers is almost

as coveted these days as the atmospheric snugs.

The Odeon

Old Harcourt Street Station, Harcourt St. Late opening with DJ Fri & Sat (till 2.30am, cover charge Sat after 10pm). Palatial and sophisticated bar in the old railway station, sporting Art Deco fittings, comfy armchairs and an ornamental bar salvaged from a South African bank. One of Dublin's few gastropubs, serving good, modern food such as smoked haddock and fennel pie, with a separate restaurant area if you want a little more formality. Heaving most nights, it's chilled out on Sunday for brunch. The outdoor seats under the station portico now fittingly overlook the new LUAS stop.

O'Donoghue's

15 Merrion Row. The centre of the folk and traditional music revival that began in the late 1950s, *O'Donoghue's* will forever be associated with ground-breaking balladeers The Dubliners. Nightly sessions from about 8.30pm draw a considerable crowd, partly because the pub is a notable landmark on the tourist trail. Earlier in the day,

however, the simple, flagstoned bar and sizeable heated yard are good spots to appreciate a quiet pint of Guinness.

Solas

31 Wexford St. Open till 1.30am Fri & Sat, 12.30am Sun–Thurs. Handy for *The Village* and *Whelan's* (see p.97), this loud and lively bar offers bright, simple booths, good DJs most nights of the week, and a striking mural of photos of Dublin.

Toners

139 Baggot St Lower. The sign outside, "TONERS – A PUB", says it all: plain, stone floors, a cosy snug and mirrored partitions, where despite the crowds you'll never have to wait too long for a pint.

Clubs and live venues

Crawdaddy

Old Harcourt Street Station, Harcourt St ☎01/478 0166, ✆www.pod.ie. Named after a famed London blues club, this recent arrival is fast stealing a march on its older local contenders with

▼ O'DONOGHUE'S

▲ TONERS

also renowned as a major club – its Basics session (Fri 11pm–3am) features star international DJs.

its imaginative programme of international acts, ranging from jazz and reggae to world music.

POD

Old Harcourt Street Station, Harcourt St ☏01/478 0166, ⊛www.pod.ie. Housed in the station's vaults, *POD* ("Place of Dance") has enjoyed many a makeover during its ten-year-plus existence. It's currently sporting black granite walls, overhead amoebic inflatables and rich mandarin booths – all guaranteed to enhance the lighting, whose vibrancy matches the intense House rhythms supplied by resident and international guest DJs. Friday's H.A.M. has returned as one of the city's most upfront gay nights while Saturday's Pogo is also a major draw.

Redbox

Old Harcourt Street Station, Harcourt St ☏01/478 0166, ⊛www.pod.ie. This sizeable two-floored venue with four bars fills the space once occupied by the former station's turntables, yet its deft use of booths means it retains a degree of intimacy lacked by other comparable venues. Big names often play here (past bookings include Public Enemy, Stereophonics and Faithless), but the place is

The Sugar Club

8 Leeson St Lower ☏01/679 7188. A lush and plush Southside venue, just off St Stephen's Green, *The Sugar Club* hosts a diverse and often left-field variety of entertainment (bands, torch-singers, comedy, cabaret) – some divine, others innately terrible – but the atmosphere is always unquestionably on the button.

The Village

26 Wexford St ☏01/475 8555, ⊛www.thevillagevenue.com. Startlingly successful since its arrival a couple of years back, Whelan's bigger sister has double the capacity (around 750) and consequently books bigger names while following its sibling's eclectic booking policy. DJs spin sounds in the hyper-cool bar nightly and *The Village* also operates late clubs (Thurs–Sat 11pm–late) with guests at the turntables.

Whelan's

25 Wexford St ☏01/478 0766, ⊛www.whelanslive.com. Featuring a popular front bar too, *Whelan's* has recently celebrated fifteen years as one of the city's most successful live venues, thanks to an extensive programme of the old and the new – a blend of traditional music, renowned folk acts, emerging talent and occasional one-off performances by major names.

Temple Bar

Sandwiched between the busy thoroughfare of Dame Street and the Liffey, Temple Bar is marketed, with a fair dose of artistic licence, as Dublin's "Left Bank" (inconveniently, it's on the right bank as you face downstream). Its transformation into the city's main cultural and entertainment district came about after a 1960s plan for a new central bus terminal here was abandoned after much procrastination. Instead, the area's narrow cobbled streets and old warehouses, by now occupied by short-lease studios, workshops and boutiques, began to be sensitively redeveloped as an artistic quarter in the 1980s. Nowadays, as well as more galleries and arts centres than you can shake a paintbrush at, Temple Bar shelters a huge number of restaurants, pubs and clubs, engendering a notoriously raucous nightlife scene that attracts more outsiders than Dubliners.

Sunlight Chambers

At the bottom of Parliament Street, which runs up from Grattan Bridge to the Neoclassical portico of City Hall, stand the Sunlight Chambers, whose curious

▼ TEMPLE BAR

facade merits a short detour. Built in the early twentieth century in the style of an Italian Renaissance palace by the Sunlight soap company, the Chambers sport colourful ceramic friezes on their exterior on the theme of hygiene; underneath the soot you can make out farmers and builders getting their clothes dirty on the upper tier, and women washing them below.

The Ark

11A Eustace St ☎01/670 7788, ⓦwww.ark.ie. The Ark is Europe's only custom-built cultural centre for children (aged 4–14), housing theatres, galleries and a workshop. Get in touch for details of its plays, exhibitions, workshops, festivals, concerts,

Temple Bar information

Temple Bar has its own, friendly information centre on Essex Street East (Mon–Fri 9am–6pm, Sat 10am–6pm; ☎01/677 2255, ⓦwww.temple-bar.ie).

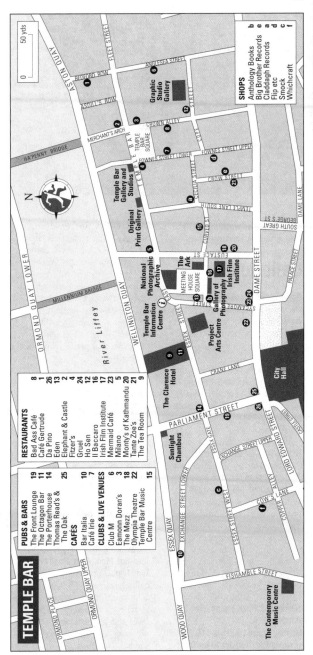

TEMPLE BAR

0 50 yds

PUBS & BARS

The Front Lounge	19
The Octagon Bar	11
The Porterhouse	14
Thomas Read's &	
The Oak	25

CAFES

Bar Italia	10
Café Irie	7

CLUBS & LIVE VENUES

Club M	6
Eamonn Doran's	3
The Mezz	18
Olympia Theatre	22
Temple Bar Music	
Centre	15

RESTAURANTS

Bad Ass Café	8
Café Gertrude	1
Da Pino	26
Eden	13
Elephant & Castle	2
Fitzer's	4
Gruel	24
Ho Sen	12
Il Baccaro	16
Irish Film Institute	17
Mermaid Café	23
Milano	5
Monty's of Kathmandu	20
Tante Zoe's	21
The Tea Room	9

SHOPS

Anthology Books	b
Big Brother Records	e
Claddagh Records	a
Flip etc	d
Smock	c
Whichcraft	f

▲ SUNLIGHT CHAMBERS

readings, opera, dance and multimedia programmes.

Galleries

Gallery of Photography

Meeting House Square ☎01/671 4654, ⊚www.irish-photography.com. Tues–Sat 11am–6pm, Sun 1–6pm. Free. It's well worth checking out what's on at this gallery, which stages some great exhibitions of contemporary photographs from Ireland and around the world, in smart, well-lit rooms above a good photographic bookshop.

Graphic Studio Gallery

Cope Street ☎01/679 8021, ⊚www .graphicstudiodublin.com. Mon–Fri 10am–5.30pm, Sat 11am–5pm. In an attractive converted warehouse down a small alley, this commercial gallery hosts exhibitions by contemporary, mostly Irish, printmakers, including those who have been invited to work at its nearby print studio.

National Photographic Archive

Meeting House Square ☎01/603 0200, ⊚www.nli.ie. Mon–Fri 10am–5pm,

Sat 10am–2pm. Free. From the photographic collections of the National Library – around 300,000 photographs, mostly on Irish historical subjects, from political events to early tourist snaps – the archive mounts a series of often fascinating temporary exhibitions. The attached shop sells popular postcards and prints from the collections.

Original Print Gallery

4 Temple Bar ☎01/677 3657, ⊚www.originalprint.ie. Tues–Fri 10.30am–5.30pm, Sat 11am–5pm, Sun 2–6pm. A commercial gallery, where you can catch changing exhibitions of contemporary prints by both up-and-coming and established Irish and international artists.

Temple Bar Gallery and Studios

5–9 Temple Bar ☎01/671 0073, ⊚www.templebargallery.com. Tues–Sat 11am–6pm, Thurs till 7pm. Free. This publicly funded gallery, purpose-built in the 1990s with thirty artists' studios attached, exhibits cutting-edge Irish and international artists working in a wide range of media.

Arts centres

The Contemporary Music Centre

19 Fishamble St ☎01/673 1922,
🌐www.cmc.ie. The national
archive and resource centre
for new music, which is open
to the public free of charge,
also hosts salon concerts, talks
and workshops. Opposite once
stood Neal's Music Hall, where
Handel conducted the combined
choirs of Christ Church and St
Patrick's cathedrals in the first
performance of his *Messiah* in
1742. In a private garden on the
site, the composer's reward is
a statue of himself conducting
in the nude, perched on a set
of organ pipes. Every April 13,
on the anniversary of the first
performance, Our Lady's Choral
Society performs excerpts from
the *Messiah* here – contact
Temple Bar Information Centre
(see p.98).

Irish Film Institute

6 Eustace St ☎01/679 3477, 🌐www
.irishfilm.ie. In a converted
eighteenth-century Quaker
meeting house, the IFI, though
principally an art-house cinema,
has evolved into a stylish and
sociable all-round venue, whose
bar-restaurant (see p.103) is a
fashionable meeting-place and
holds events such as Friday late-
night salsa sessions.

Project Arts Centre

39 Essex St East ☎01/881 9613 or
881 9614, 🌐www.project.ie. The
bright-blue flagship of the
Dublin contemporary arts scene
– which began life as an art
project in the foyer of the Gate
Theatre – Project hosts theatre,
dance, film, comedy and live
music as well as challenging
visual and performance art.

Shops

Anthology Books

Meeting House Square ☎01/635 1422,
🌐www.anthologystore.com. Tues–Sat
10am–9pm, Sun noon–6pm. Eclectic
range of small-press, progressive
and alternative literature,
including a wide selection of
literary and artistic periodicals,
as well as a programme of
readings and other literary
events.

Big Brother Records

4 Crow St ☎01/672 9355, 🌐www
.bigbrotherrecords.com. Basement
trove of vinyl and CDs,
focussing on hip-hop, funk,
soul and deep house; check
out the noticeboard's fliers for
the city's newest club nights.
Selectah upstairs specializes in
drum'n'bass, techno and reggae
on vinyl.

Claddagh Records

2 Cecilia St ☎01/677 0262,
🌐www.claddaghrecords.com.
Unquestionably the finest
traditional-music emporium
in Dublin. You can find just
about every currently available
recording here and, if you're not
sure what you're looking for,
the helpful and knowledgeable
staff can point you in the
right direction. Also stocks
contemporary Irish music,
Scottish and English folk, world
music, country and blues.

Cow's Lane Market

Cow's Lane, with an extension in
the nearby St Michael and John's
Banqueting Hall on Essex St West in
winter. Sat 10am–5.30pm, closed Jan.
Stalls on this pedestrianized alley
concentrate on contemporary
women's clothes, bags and
jewellery – generally sold by the
designers themselves – but you'll

also find interesting ceramics, paintings and photographs.

Flip, Helter Skelter, Sharp's Ville and The Real McCoy

4–6 Fownes St Upper ☎01/671 4299. Quartet of small shops, selling second-hand and new street clothes, much of it retro, as well as caps, bags and other accessories.

Smock

20–22 Essex St West ☎01/613 9000. Sophisticated party and smart fashions for a slightly older market by international designers such as Dries van Noten.

Temple Bar Food Market

Meeting House Square. Sat 10am–5pm. A magnet for Dublin's foodies, but also one of your best bets to grab Saturday lunch. As well as organic meat, fruit and veg, stalls sell tapas, Mexican food, hot dogs, burgers, breads, cakes and a huge variety of cheeses, and there's a West Clare oyster bar.

Whichcraft

Cow's Lane ☎01/474 1011 & Lord Edward St ☎01/670 9371, ⓦwww .whichcraft.com. The Whichcraft Store on Lord Edward Street stocks all manner of jewellery, vases and objets d'art by contemporary Irish craft designers, while the Whichcraft Gallery, down the lane opposite, sells larger and more conceptual works – furniture, larger batiks, statuary – as well as housing Designyard, an outlet for predominantly Irish modern jewellery.

Cafés

Bar Italia

Essex Quay. Closed Sun. Small, Italian-run café in a good corner location with outdoor tables on the tiny piazza in front. Croissants, Danish pastries and very good coffee for breakfast; tasty panini, soups, plates of antipasti and pastas – including vegetarian choices and a daily special such as wild boar pappardelle – for lunch.

Café Irie

11 Fownes St Lower. Grungy café offering cheap sandwiches, bagels, panini, wraps and pitta with a tempting variety of copious fillings – "build your own" (one meat, one cheese and salad leaves) gives the flavour of it. Salads are available if that all sounds too starchy.

Restaurants

Bad Ass Café

9–11 Crown Alley ☎01/671 2596, ⓦwww.badasscafe.com. Popular, cheery restaurant – where Sinéad O'Connor once worked as a waitress – serving all kinds of pizzas, burgers, salads and pastas at reasonable prices.

Café Gertrude

3–4 Bedford Row ☎01/677 9043. Congenial, moderately priced

▼ EDEN

▲ IL BACCARO

bistro serving unpretentious dishes such as pizzas, spinach cannelloni, shepherd's pie and Dublin sausages with red wine, bacon and mushrooms, as well as cheap daily specials. Lighter meals are served at lunchtime, and there is a good-value early-bird menu daily (4–8pm). Wine is available by the carafe.

Da Pino
38–40 Parliament St ☎01/671 9308. Keenly priced, informal Italian restaurant, offering simple, cheery decor and traditional dishes such as *saltimbocca*, fish, pasta and pizza; there's a cheap two-course lunch menu Monday to Friday.

Eden
Sycamore St/Meeting House Square ☎01/670 5372. Stylish, upmarket but convivial restaurant, with much-coveted tables out on the square in summer. Excellent modern Irish cuisine with a global twist, in dishes such as Castletownbere scallops with noodles and organic steak Béarnaise.

Elephant & Castle
18 Temple Bar ☎01/679 3121. Ever-popular, cosy, pine-furnished diner, dishing up all-day brunch and eggs anyhow – much sought-after on Sundays – as well as gourmet burgers, salads, sandwiches and late-night meals.

Fitzer's
Temple Bar Square ☎01/679 0440. Landmark branch, with modern minimalist decor, of the ever-reliable chain of restaurants – see p.77.

Gruel
67 Dame St. Wholesome, inexpensive food from an open kitchen. At lunchtime, soups, roast meat rolls, salads and pizza are prepared to take away. In the evening, it's an excellent-value, no-frills restaurant (no bookings and just one house wine), doling out dishes such as linguini with chorizo and clams and curried lamb chop with sweet potatoes, as well as plenty of veggie options.

Ho Sen
6 Cope St ☎01/671 8181. Bright, friendly Vietnamese restaurant, preparing authentic dishes such as a tasty beef salad, fresh spring rolls and *goy* – coleslaw Vietnamese style.

Il Baccaro
Meeting House Square ☎01/671 4597. Closed lunchtimes (except Sat). Friendly, reasonably priced trattoria, serving up good versions of Italian standards and wine from the barrel, in an atmospheric cellar.

Irish Film Institute
6 Eustace St. Great for an inexpensive lunch or dinner before the show, or just a drink, whether sitting in the cosy bar

▲ NEW ENGLAND CRAB CAKES, *THE MERMAID CAFÉ*

or the echoing atrium. Simple meals ranging from burgers, fish and chips and lasagne to fish cakes and goat's cheese salad, with lots of vegetarian options.

The Mermaid Café
69–70 Dame St ☎01/670 8236. Chic restaurant with unfussy modern decor, where the emphasis is on helpful service and great global-influenced food, with an equally well-travelled wine list. The short menu, which always includes their signature New England crab cakes with piquant lime mayonnaise, is augmented by daily specials such as chargrilled swordfish with basil butter. Though expensive, it's more manageable at lunchtime when there are set menus Monday to Saturday, and brunch on Sunday.

Milano
19 Temple Bar ☎01/670 3384. British visitors will be on familiar ground in this Dublin chain, the Irish version of *Pizza Express*: the tried-and-trusted formula of well-prepared pizzas, salads and pastas in smart casual settings.

Monty's of Kathmandu
28 Eustace St ☎01/670 4911, ⊛www .montys.ie. Closed Sun lunchtime. Excellent, authentic Nepalese restaurant where bright, simple decor and microbrewed lager complement some deliciously refreshing starters and main courses such as succulent tandoori tiger prawns and chicken gorkhali, cooked with yoghurt, chilli, coriander and spices. If you get your act together, order the momo dumplings stuffed with lamb 24 hours in advance.

Tante Zoe's
1 Crow St ☎01/679 4407, ⊛www .tantezoes.com. Dublin's only Cajun-Creole restaurant, a lively place dishing up shrimp in spicy tomato sauce and other authentic New Orleans favourites in smart, seductive surroundings. Moderately priced with a cheaper menu at lunchtime.

Bono - U-2
The Tea Room
The Clarence Hotel, 6–8 Wellington Quay ☎01/670 7766, ⊛www .theclarence.ie. Closed Sat lunchtime. In Dublin's most stylish hotel, *The Tea Room* is one of the city's most elegant, airy restaurants, with a spectacular balcony bar. The menu features Irish produce in season, given Continental treatment in dishes like duck breast with rosti potato in endive and lentil sauce. One to save up your cents for.

Pubs and bars

The Front Lounge
33 Parliament St. Open till 2.30am Fri & Sat. Behind an Art-Deco frontage, a sophisticated and relaxing interior of polished wood floors and comfy red

armchairs and sofas, with contemporary art exhibitions on the walls. A big hit with both gay and straight Dubliners, not least for its range of entertainment, including karaoke and a drag show on Tuesdays and DJs at the weekend. Good cocktails and cappuccinos.

The Octagon Bar

owned by Bonov - 2

The Clarence Hotel, 6–8 Wellington Quay. The octagonal bar of *The Clarence* (see p.193), bathed in artificial daylight and panelled with light oak, is one of Dublin's coolest hangouts, though by no means feels exclusive. The unusual snug – like an enclosed church pew – is perfect for making and breaking confidences, while the open fire draws small crowds in winter.

The Porterhouse

16 Parliament St ⊛www .porterhousebrewco.com. Open till 1am Thurs & Sun, 2am Fri & Sat. Excellent microbrewery-bar, sporting huge brass vats in its rambling but cosy interior. For €5 you can sample three stouts, including the oyster stout – not a joke, and tastes a lot better than it sounds. Live music every night, traditional sessions on Saturday and Sunday afternoons and good food.

Thomas Read's and The Oak

1 Parliament St. Open till 2.30am Fri & Sat. Two contrasting, interconnected bars. *Thomas Read's* is a high-ceilinged café-bar, packed with a youngish crowd at weekends; quieter by day, it's perfectly located for people-watching, on the corner of Dame Street just opposite the beautifully refurbished City Hall. *The Oak* next door is a more introverted spot, cosy

and traditional, with much of its dark panelling filched from deconsecrated churches.

Clubs and live venues

Club M

Bloom's Hotel, 6 Anglesea St ☎01/671 5622, ⊛www.blooms.ie. Closed Sun. Very much one for the younger and more boisterous set, *Club M* features three floors, five bars and a laser lightshow. Nights such as Crunchie (Friday) and Storm (Saturday) feature stalwart local DJs blending dance, chart and R'n'B sounds.

Eamonn Doran's

3A Crown Alley ☎01/679 9114. *Doran's* cemented its reputation as the place to catch both hopeless wannabes and potential contenders a long time ago, and its basement continues to host an eclectic range of bands and singers, plus regular club nights.

▼ THE OCTAGON BAR

The Mezz

23 Eustace St. Raucous, grungy bar that lays on a very popular roster of live music and DJs: Monday is open mike night; Tuesday, funk, soul, salsa and blues; Wednesday, reggae; Thursday, soul; and Sunday is blues night. From Thursday (sometimes Wednesday) to Sunday you can go on to *The Hub* nightclub downstairs, which usually has a live band – anything from traditional Irish to punk – then a DJ.

▲ THE MEZZ

Olympia Theatre

Dame St ☎01/677 7744. An old and much esteemed venue, the *Olympia* continues to stage a variety of musical events, featuring major Irish names such as Paul Brady and Luka Bloom, as well as international stars. For much of the summer it turns over to the Ragus traditional music and dance show.

Temple Bar Music Centre

Curved St ☎01/670 5202, ⊛www.tbmc.ie. Brash and determinedly modernist, *TBMC*'s booking policy is decidedly left field, focussing mainly on art-house and indie bands. The bar area is often used for free concerts showcasing emerging acts and the place transforms itself into a late club (until 3pm) at weekends – Sunday's reggae night is probably the best.

The old city and South Great George's Street

On a ridge above the Liffey, where previously the Vikings had established themselves, the Anglo-Norman invaders rebuilt Dublin in the thirteenth century with Christ Church Cathedral at its centre and highest point. Several other remnants of British hegemony are still dotted the site of the old city: Dublin Castle, whose star attraction is now the Chester Beatty Library, a world-class collection of books and objets d'art from around the globe; the beautifully restored rotunda of City Hall; and St Patrick's Cathedral, with its intriguing array of memorials. Much of the area of the old city is now modern, residential and uneventful, but South Great George's Street, on the castle's east side, is a vibrant, diverse strip of restaurants and bars, flanked by the high and low fashions, book and record stalls of the Market Arcade.

City Hall

Cork Hill, Dame St. Mon–Sat 10am–5.15pm, Sun 2–5pm. Free. Under the gleamingly restored rotunda of City Hall, creamy Portland stone columns, interspersed with statues of Daniel O'Connell (the city's first Catholic Lord Mayor) and other notables, bathe in wonderful natural light from the dome. The sumptuous Neoclassical building was constructed between 1769 and 1779 as the Royal Exchange, but fell into disuse after the Act of Union of 1800 passed governance of Ireland back to London; Dublin Corporation bought it in 1851, and it's still the venue for city council meetings. Among the Arts and Crafts murals under the dome that trace Dublin's history, look out for one Lambert Simnel – 10-year-old pretender to Henry VII's throne – being carried through the streets after his mock coronation in Christ Church Cathedral in 1487; the ill-starred Simnel ended up enslaved as the king's kitchen-scullion. The colourful floor mosaic shows the civic coat

▼ CITY HALL

The old city and South Great George's Street

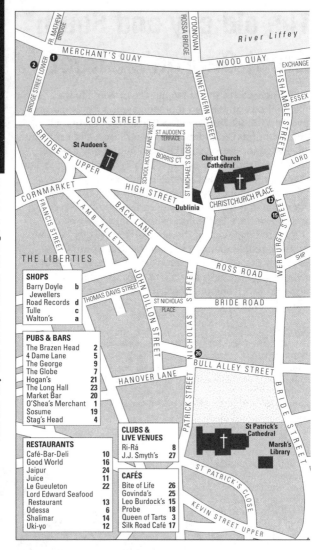

River Liffey

FR MATHEW BRIDGE
ROSSA BRIDGE
O'DONOVAN
MERCHANT'S QUAY
WOOD QUAY
EXCHANGE
BRIDGE STREET LOWER
WINETAVERN STREET
FISHAMBLE STREET
ESSEX
COOK STREET
ST AUDOEN'S TERRACE
BRIDGE ST UPPER
St Audoen's
SCHOOL HOUSE LANE WEST
BORRIS CT
ST MICHAEL'S CLOSE
Christ Church Cathedral
LORD
CORNMARKET
HIGH STREET
CHRISTCHURCH PLACE
FRANCIS STREET
LAMB ALLEY
BACK LANE
Dublinia
CHRISTCHURCH PLACE 13
WERBURGH STREET
15
SHIP
THE LIBERTIES
ROSS ROAD

SHOPS

Barry Doyle Jewellers	**b**
Road Records	**d**
Tulle	**c**
Walton's	**a**

THOMAS DAVIS STREET
JOHN DILLON STREET
ST NICHOLAS PLACE
NICHOLAS STREET
BRIDE ROAD

PUBS & BARS

The Brazen Head	2
4 Dame Lane	5
The George	9
The Globe	7
Hogan's	21
The Long Hall	23
Market Bar	20
O'Shea's Merchant	1
Sosume	19
Stag's Head	4

HANOVER LANE
26
BULL ALLEY STREET
BRIDE STREET
PATRICK STREET

CLUBS & LIVE VENUES

Ri-Rá	8
J.J. Smyth's	27

St Patrick's Cathedral
Marsh's Library

RESTAURANTS

Café-Bar-Deli	10
Good World	16
Jaipur	24
Juice	11
Le Gueuleton	22
Lord Edward Seafood Restaurant	13
Odessa	6
Shalimar	14
Uki-yo	12

CAFÉS

Bite of Life	26
Govinda's	25
Leo Burdock's	15
Probe	18
Queen of Tarts	3
Silk Road Café	17

ST PATRICK'S CLOSE
KEVIN STREET UPPER
ST KEVIN STREET

of arms, three castles topped by flames, which apparently represent the zeal of the citizens to defend Dublin – reinforced by the city motto *Obedientia Civium Urbis Felicitas* ("Happy the City whose Citizens Obey").

The Story of the Capital

Cork Hill, Dame St ⊛ www.dublincity.ie /cityhall. Mon–Sat 10am–5.15pm, Sun 2–5pm. €4. The vaults beneath City Hall now shelter The Story of the Capital, a fascinating multimedia journey through Dublin's history and politics

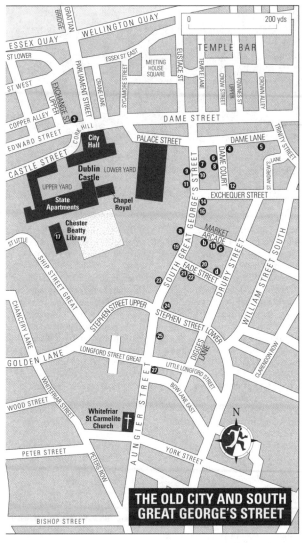

– with occasional hints of self-promotion for the exhibition's sponsors, the city council. The story is told through exhaustive display panels, slick interactive databases and a series of videos, complemented by an entertaining audioguide narrated by Irish actress Sinead Cusack with snippets from leading historians. There are few exhibits as such, a notable exception being the intricate city seal and its strongbox, which, instituted after the seal was stolen in 1305, required the presence of all

▲ DUBLIN COAT OF ARMS, CITY HALL

six keyholders. To make up for the lack of hard evidence on show, however, the enterprising curators have commissioned a series of artworks, including *Utopian Column*: a stack of glass plates engraved with historical scenes and flooded with light.

Dublin Castle

You're free to walk around the courtyards (and the Chapel Royal) of Dublin Castle, an architectural mish-mash that's home to police and tax offices, as well as various tribunals set up to investigate political corruption over the last ten years. The castle was the seat

▼ DUBLIN CASTLE

of British power in Ireland for seven hundred years, after its establishment by the Anglo-Normans in the early thirteenth century as the main element of their walled city, and successfully withstood all attempts to take it by force. It did, however, succumb to a major fire in 1684 and was rebuilt during the eighteenth century as a complex of residential and administrative buildings over two quadrangles, giving a sedate, collegiate appearance.

Looming over the Lower Yard, the Record Tower was built in 1258 but heavily renovated and Gothicized in the early nineteenth century; it was originally a prison and now, fittingly but not at all compellingly, hosts the Garda Síochaná Museum, stuffed with musty memorabilia of the Irish police force. It is worth looking in on the adjacent Chapel Royal, however, an ornate Gothic Revival gem; note especially the viceroys' coats of arms carved on the balcony rail and around the altar. Behind the tower and chapel, overlooked by the Chester Beatty Library, lies the pretty castle garden:

now adorned with a swirling motif taken from the passage grave at Newgrange (see p.184), it marks the site of the "black pool" (*dubh linn*) which gave the city its English name. The Upper Yard follows the outline of the medieval castle. Above its original main gate, the Cork Hill State Entrance, stands a statue of Justice, wearing no blindfold and turning her back on the city – a fitting symbol of British rule, locals reckon.

The State Apartments and Undercroft

Dublin Castle ☎01/677 7129, ⊛www.dublincastle.ie. Guided tours only Mon–Fri 10am–4.45pm, Sat & Sun 2–4.45pm; 45min; €4.50. It's advisable to ring ahead, as tours don't run on state occasions, when a tour of the Chapel Royal and the Undercroft may be substituted. Built as the residence of the English viceroy and entered from the castle's Upper Yard, the State Apartments now host major Irish state occasions – including the signing of the ground-breaking Anglo-Irish Agreement by Taoiseach Garrett Fitzgerald and Prime Minister Margaret Thatcher in 1985. The Grand Staircase leads up to the east wing of bedrooms and drawing rooms, which had to be refurbished after a major fire in 1941, and were restored to their original eighteenth- and nineteenth-century style. The bedrooms served as a Red Cross hospital during World War I, and here the wounded James Connolly, one of the leaders of the 1916 Easter Rising, was treated before being carted off to a firing squad at Kilmainham Gaol. The tour's artistic highlight is *The Countess of Southampton* by van Dyck, a keenly wrought, restrained – apart from the shimmering dress – portrait of the 17-year-old Elizabeth Leigh, painted for her wedding.

The brass chandelier in the Throne Room, with its shamrock, rose and thistle emblems, commemorates the 1801 Act of Union, while the Picture Gallery beyond is lined with viceroys, including – hiding ignominiously behind the door – the first Marquis of Cornwallis, who not only lost the American colonies, but also faced rebellions as viceroy first of India then of Ireland (1798). St Patrick's Hall, formerly a ballroom which hosted investitures of the Knights of St Patrick, is now used for the inaugurations and funerals of Irish presidents. Its overblown, late-eighteenth-century ceiling paintings show St Patrick converting the Irish, Henry II receiving the submission of the Irish chieftains, and George III's coronation.

The tour finishes at the excavations of the Undercroft beneath the Lower Yard, which have revealed the base of the gunpowder tower of the medieval castle and steps leading down to the moat, fed

▼ FIGURE OF JUSTICE, DUBLIN CASTLE

▲ CHESTER BEATTY LIBRARY

by the old River Poddle on its way down to the Liffey, as well as part of the original Viking ramparts.

The Chester Beatty Library

Dublin Castle ☎01/407 0750, ⊛www.cbl.ie. Tues–Fri 10am–5pm, Sat 11am–5pm, Sun 1–5pm, plus May–Sept Mon 10am–5pm; free. Free guided tours Wed 1pm & Sun 3pm & 4pm. Housed in the eighteenth-century Clock Tower Building at the back of Dublin Castle, the Chester Beatty Library preserves a dazzling collection of books, manuscripts, prints and *objets d'art* from around the world. Superlatives come thick and fast here: as well as one of the finest Islamic collections in existence, containing some of the earliest manuscripts from the ninth and tenth centuries, the library holds important Biblical papyri, including the earliest surviving examples in any language of Mark's and Luke's Gospels, St Paul's Letters and the Book of Revelations. Elegantly displayed in high-tech galleries, the artefacts are used to tell the story of religious and artistic traditions across the world with great ingenuity, a formula which justifiably won the CBL the European Museum of the Year award in 2002.

The collection was put together by the remarkable Sir Alfred Chester Beatty, an American mining magnate who moved himself and his works to Dublin in the early 1950s, after cutting a deal with the Irish government on import taxes and estate duties. In 1957 he was made the first honorary citizen of Ireland, and when he died in 1968, he bequeathed his collection to the state and was given a state funeral.

Most of the CBL's vast holding is accessible only to scholars via the reference library, with less than two percent on show in the public galleries at any one time – though that's more than enough to keep you occupied for a few hours. It makes sense to start with the second-floor gallery, which covers Sacred Traditions, while the first floor deals with Artistic Traditions (alongside a space for fascinating temporary exhibitions), with each divided into Western, Islamic and Eastern sections; exhibits range from sixteenth-century biblical engravings by Albrecht Dürer to books carved in jade for the Chinese emperors, and from gorgeously illustrated collections of Persian poetry to serene Burmese statues of the Buddha.

Christ Church Cathedral

☎01/677 8099, ⊛www.cccdub.ie. Mon–Fri 9.45am–5pm, Sat & Sun

▼ MUMMIFIED CAT, CHRIST CHURCH CATHEDRAL

▲ STRONGBOW'S TOMB

10am–5pm; €5, discounted to €3 with a ticket for Dublinia (see p.114). Choral Evensong Tues–Thurs 6pm, Sat 5pm, Sun 3.30pm, Sung Eucharist Sun 11am. Hemmed in by buildings and traffic, Anglican Christ Church appears as an unexceptional neogothic hulk, but its interior reveals its long history as the seat of the Archbishop of Dublin. In about 1030, the Viking king of Dublin, Sitric Silkenbeard, built a wooden cathedral here, which was replaced by the Normans between 1186 and 1240 with a magnificent stone structure. Of this, the crypt (see below), the transept, which retains some eroded Romanesque carvings, and the remarkable leaning north wall can still be seen – as the church was built over a bog, the roof and south wall collapsed in 1562 and the north side was pulled eighteen inches out of the perpendicular. In the 1870s, distiller Henry Roe lavished the equivalent of €30 million on the heavy-handed restoration you can see today, and bankrupted himself.

Near the entrance, you'll find the tomb of Strongbow, the Norman leader who captured Dublin in 1170. The original tomb, around which Dublin's landlords had gathered to collect rents, was destroyed by the roof collapse, and had to be replaced with an effigy of the Earl of Drogheda so that business could proceed as usual. The half-figure alongside is probably a fragment of the original tomb, though legend maintains that it's an effigy of Strongbow's son, hacked in two by his own father for cowardice in battle.

The chapels off the choir show the Anglo-Normans celebrating their dual nationality. To the left stands the Chapel of St Edmund, the ninth-century king of East Anglia who was martyred by the Vikings, while on the right is the Chapel of St Laud, the sixth-century bishop of Coutances in Normandy. The floor tiles here are original – they were replicated throughout the cathedral in the 1870s – while on the wall you can see an iron box containing the embalmed heart of twelfth-century Laurence O'Toole, Dublin's only canonized archbishop.

Treasures of Christ Church

Christ Church Cathedral. Mon–Fri 9.45am–5pm, Sat 10am–3.15pm, Sun 12.30–3.15pm; free with cathedral admission. If you descend the stairs by the south transept of Christ Church, you'll reach the crypt, the least changed remnant of the twelfth-century cathedral; formerly a storehouse for the trade in alcohol and tobacco, it's one of the largest crypts in Britain and Ireland, extending under the entire cathedral for 175 feet. Here you'll find the Treasures of Christ Church exhibition, which includes an interesting twenty-minute audiovisual presentation on the history of the cathedral, as well as a miscellany of manuscripts and church crockery. Look out for a ropey-looking tabernacle and pair of candlesticks made for James II on his flight from England in 1689, when, for three months only, Latin Mass was again celebrated at Christ Church (the existing cathedral paraphernalia was hidden by quick-thinking Anglican officials under a bishop's coffin). In extravagant contrast is a chunky silver-gilt plate, around three-foot wide, presented by King William III in thanksgiving for his victory at the Battle of the Boyne in 1690.

Dublinia

High St ☎01/679 4611, ☜www .dublinia.ie. April–Sept daily 10am–5pm; Oct–March Mon–Sat 11am–4pm, Sun 10am–4.30pm. €6, children €3.75, family ticket €16. Housed in the former Synod Hall of the Church of Ireland, Dublinia provides a lively, hands-on portrait of medieval Dublin that's especially good fun for kids (phone for details of falconry and archery displays in the summer months). Themes such as the plague and the medieval fair are explored via walk-through tableaux of streets and houses, sound effects and lots of fun, interactive possibilities, such as throwing balls at a criminal in the stocks. The first floor's centrepiece is

a fascinating model of Dublin in about 1500, showing the walled city dominated by Christ Church. The excavations of the Viking and medieval settlements at nearby Wood Quay are shown in the next rooms; highlights include the thigh of a stone effigy from Fishamble Street, which may have come from the original tomb of Strongbow at Christ Church. On the second floor, the Great Hall, where the Anglican bishops met until 1982, is now the long-term temporary home of Viking World, which uses a near-life-size ship, demonstrations of coin-minting and the chance to try on slave chains to convey Viking life. Before crossing the graceful, much-photographed bridge over to Christ Church Cathedral, it's worth climbing St Michael's Tower, a remnant of the seventeenth-century Church of St Michael and All Angels, for fine views over the city.

St Audoen's

Church of Ireland St Audoen's, Cornmarket, High St ☎01/677 0088. June–Sept daily 9.30am–5.30pm, last admission 4.45pm. Free. The two contrasting churches to the west of Dublinia are dedicated to St Audoen (in French, Ouen), seventh-century bishop of Rouen and the patron saint of Normandy. The forbidding edifice of Catholic St Audoen's was raised in 1846, while the Church of Ireland version, built by the Anglo-Normans around 1190, is now an intriguing tourist site, though there are still services every Sunday – the church has been continuously

▼ DUBLINIA

▲ "BRIDGE OF SIGHS", CHRIST CHURCH

used for worship longer than any other in Dublin.

The appeal of St Audoen's lies in the fascinating physical evidence showing how its fortunes waxed and waned over the centuries. As it prospered through association with the city's guilds, the original church, with its deeply moulded Romanesque doorway, was augmented by a chancel and St Anne's Guild Chapel, making a two-aisled nave. The latter is now the main exhibition area, with interesting displays on the parish, the guilds and the church's architecture. By the fifteenth century, St Audoen's was the top parish church among Dublin's leading families, and the addition in 1455 of the Portlester Chapel marked the zenith of its fortune. After the Reformation, however, many members of the Guild of St Anne refused to become Protestant, and by the nineteenth century St Audoen's had retreated to its original single nave. You can now poke around the roofless chancel and Portlester Chapel where, before the building was declared a national monument, locals would hang their washing out to dry.

It's worth going down the steps behind the Protestant church to Cook Street to see the thirteenth-century St Audoen's Arch and a heavily restored two-hundred-yard stretch of the Norman city walls.

St Patrick's Cathedral

ⓦ www.stpatrickscathedral .ie. March–Oct daily 9am–6pm; Nov–Feb Mon–Fri 9am–6pm, Sat 9am–5pm, Sun 10am–3pm; €4.20. St Patrick's history is remarkably similar to that of its fellow Anglican rival Christ Church: it was built between 1220 and 1270 in Gothic style, but its roof collapsed in 1544, leading to a decline that included its ignominious use as a stable by Cromwell's army in 1649. Its Victorian restoration, however, by Sir Benjamin Guinness in the 1860s, was more sensitive than Christ Church's, and it has a more appealing, lived-in feel, thanks largely to its clutter of quirky funerary monuments.

To the right of the entrance in the harmoniously proportioned nave are diverse memorials to Jonathan Swift, the cathedral's dean for 32 years, including his and Stella's graves, his pulpit and table, and a cast of his skull – both his and Stella's bodies were dug up by Victorian phrenologists, studying the skulls of the famous. In the south transept, look out for the marble monument to Archbishop Marsh (see p.117), the finest work by sculptor Grinling Gibbons in Ireland. The Door of Reconciliation, by the north transept, recalls a quarrel between the earls of Kildare and Ormond in 1492. Ormond sought sanctuary in the cathedral's chapterhouse, but Kildare cut a hole in the door and stretched his arm through

Jonathan Swift

"Here is laid the body of Jonathan Swift . . . where fierce indignation can no longer rend the heart. Go, traveller, and imitate if you can this earnest and dedicated champion of liberty."

Swift's epitaph in St Patrick's Cathedral, penned by himself and translated here from the Latin, conveys not only his appetite for political satire and campaigning, but also perhaps a certain prescience about the longevity of his popular literary fame. Born in Dublin in 1667 and educated at Trinity College, Swift went to England in 1689 to work as secretary to the retired diplomat Sir William Temple. Here he met Esther Johnson, nicknamed **Stella**, the daughter of Temple's housekeeper, who became his close companion – whether platonic or sexual, no one knows – until her death in 1728. Swift was ordained in the Church of Ireland in 1695, and anonymously wrote his first major work, **A Tale of a Tub**, in 1704, satirizing the official churches and the unscrupulous "modern" writers of his day. Sent to London to lobby the government for the relief of church taxes, from 1710 he was at the centre of England's political and literary life, a friend of Tory ministers as well as of Alexander Pope and John Gay. When the Tories fell, however, instead of the English bishopric he had hoped for, he was made Dean of St Patrick's, in 1713. Here he turned his caustic wit on Irish injustices, writing a series of pamphlets in the 1720s and 1730s including **A Modest Proposal**, one of the most admired works of irony in the English language, which suggests that the Irish poor sell off their children to the rich as "a most delicious, nourishing and wholesome food". At this time too, he wrote his most famous work, the gloriously imaginative satirical novel, **Gulliver's Travels** (1726). Swift's later years were blighted by a progressive mental illness causing dizziness, and when he died in 1745, he left his estate to build St Patrick's on James's Street, the first psychiatric hospital in Ireland.

to shake Ormond's hands – so giving us the phrase "chancing your arm".

In the northwest corner of the nave stands a slab carved with a Celtic cross that once marked the site of a well next to the cathedral, where St Patrick baptized converts in the fifth century. Back near the entrance, you can't miss the extravagant Boyle monument, which Richard Boyle, Earl of Cork, erected in 1632 in memory of his wife, Katherine, who had borne him fifteen children, including the famous physicist Robert Boyle (shown in the bottom centre niche). Viceroy Wentworth, objecting to being forced to kneel before a Corkman, had the monument moved here from beside the altar, but Boyle exacted revenge in later years by engineering Wentworth's execution.

▼ ST PATRICK'S CATHEDRAL

Marsh's Library

St Patrick's Close, ⊛ www.marshlibrary .ie. Mon & Wed–Fri 10am–1pm & 2–5pm, Sat 10.30am–1pm; €2.50.

The oldest public library in Ireland, Marsh's Library has remained delightfully untouched since it was built by Sir William Robinson, the architect of Kilmainham Hospital, in 1701, and still functions as a research and conservation library. Its founder, Archbishop Narcissus Marsh, was particularly interested in science, mathematics and music, and oversaw the first translation of the Old Testament into Irish. His books form one of the library's four main collections, totalling 25,000 works relating to the sixteenth, seventeenth and early eighteenth centuries. They're housed in beautiful rows of dark-oak bookcases, each with a carved and lettered gable (for cataloguing purposes) topped by a bishop's mitre, and three screened alcoves, or "cages", where readers were locked in with rare books. The library mounts regular exhibitions from its collections on subjects such as astronomy, and displays a death mask of its former governor, Jonathan Swift (see opposite), as well as a cast of Stella's skull.

Whitefriar Street Carmelite Church

Aungier Street. Re-established in 1827 on the site of a dissolved Carmelite priory, Whitefriar Street Carmelite Church caters to a wide cross-section of Catholic worshippers with a panoply of shrines and statues. Our Lady of Dublin, a fifteenth-century carved-oak Madonna and Child, takes pride of place by the entrance, the only wooden image to have survived the dissolution of Ireland's monasteries. Used as a pig trough after the Reformation, it was rescued in the 1820s by

Father Spratt, the priest who re-founded the church, from a pawn shop near St Mary's Abbey, where the statue had probably originally stood. There was no sign, however, of the image's silver crown, which was said to have been used for the mock coronation of the pretender Lambert Simnel in Christ Church Cathedral in 1487 (see p.107). Whitefriar Street is also the scene of many romantic pledges, as a casket on the north side of the church supposedly enshrines the remains of St Valentine, the third-century Roman martyr, donated by Pope Gregory XVI in 1835.

Shops

Barry Doyle Jewellers

Upstairs, 30 Market Arcade, South Great George's St ☎01/671 2838, ⓦwww.barrydoyledesign.com. Stylish contemporary designs, including many sophisticated silver necklaces, in all price ranges. Commissions undertaken.

▼ ST VALENTINE, WHITEFRIAR STREET CARMELITE CHURCH

The Market Arcade

Between South Great George's St
and Drury St. Some shops open Sun.
Laid-back indoor market with
an alternative edge to it, offering
second-hand books and records,
upmarket and street clothing,
jewellery and speciality foods.
There's also the excellent *Probe*
café (see opposite).

Road Records

16B Fade St ☎01/671 7340, ⓦwww
.roadrecs.com. Open Sun. Tucked
away off South Great George's
Street, Road is the ultimate
indie, alternative and alternative
country specialist, stocking vinyl,
CDs and DVDs. Certainly the
best place to find new releases, it
also offers an extensive range of
left-field Irish recordings.

Tulle

28 Market Arcade, South Great
George's St ☎01/679 9115. This hip
boutique stocks everything from
T-shirts and two-piece skirts
to evening dresses and one-off
designs for special occasions,
by rising Irish stars like Joanne
Hynes and small international
designers.

▼ THE MARKET ARCADE

Walton's

69 South Great George's St ☎01/475
0661. Summer music school ☎01/478
1884, ⓦwww.newschool.ie. Dublin's
leading music shop sells the
full range of Irish traditional
instruments from tin whistles
to harps, as well as teaching
aids, sheet music and CDs and
cassettes of Irish artists. In the
summer the attached music
school offers two-hour crash
courses for absolute beginners
in the tin whistle or bodhrán,
the two most popular – and
easiest to learn – instruments of
Irish music.

Cafés

Bite of Life

55 Patrick St. A cosy,
welcoming café with
fresh flowers on the table,
newspapers to peruse and a
chilled jazz soundtrack, *Bite
of Life* also offers excellent
food, including fresh ciabatta
rolls with imaginative fillings,
homemade soups and cakes
– the chocolate biscuit cake is
particularly feted – and great
coffee, tea and freshly made
fruit juices.

Govinda's

4 Aungier St ⓦwww.govindas.ie.
Mon–Sat noon–9pm. Excellent
Hare Krishna-run vegetarian
café, serving cheap and filling
samosas, salads, pizzas and
burgers, as well as daily specials
such as pasta and vegetables
au gratin. They also offer great
juices and lassis, as well as cakes
and other desserts.

Leo Burdock's

2 Werburgh St. Closed Sun
lunchtimes. Dublin's most famous
fish-and-chipper (takeaway
only) is all gleaming surfaces

and friendly service. The multi-award-winning menu now stretches to Japanese tiger prawns, but otherwise there are no surprises. Expect to queue lunchtimes and evenings.

Probe

Market Arcade, South Great George's St. Funky little spot with wooden booths and cheerful staff, serving inexpensive Mexican food, Irish stew, falafels, baked potatoes, salads, sandwiches and all-day breakfasts, with plenty of choices for vegetarians.

Queen of Tarts

4 Cork Hill, Lord Edward St. Small, laid-back patisserie-cum-café with an overflow branch in the vaults of City Hall opposite. Bagels and croissants for breakfast; chicken, spinach and cheese tarts, Greek salad and all sorts of sandwiches for lunch; and yummy cakes baked fresh on the premises to keep you going between times.

Silk Road Café

Chester Beatty Library, Dublin Castle. Same hours as museum (see p.112). Stylish and good-value museum café, spilling over into the Library's sky-lit atrium, that's well worth a journey in its own right. The chef (who's from Jerusalem, one of Chester Beatty's favoured hunting grounds) rustles up mostly Middle Eastern food – lamb moussaka and Lebanese chicken, falafels, spinach and feta filo pie and plenty of other veggie options, as well as very good salads, creative panini and a special kids' menu. To round off, as you'd expect, there's great coffee and titbits such as Turkish delight and baklava.

Restaurants

Café-Bar-Deli

12–13 South Great George's St. A former *Bewley's Café* that's been smartly updated without losing its character: comfy red booths, bentwood furniture, brass rails and coathooks. The reasonably priced menu of simple food well done is a winner, too, with some interesting starters; pastas such as rigatoni with gorgonzola, spinach and cream; Mediterranean salads; thin, crispy pizzas; and mouthwatering desserts. No bookings.

Good World

18 South Great George's St ☎01/677 5373. Open daily until 2.30am. Daytime dim sum (12.30–6pm) is especially popular on Sundays, while in the evenings regular customers – sometimes raucous after pub closing – come for a varied menu that specializes in seafood and sizzling dishes, with enough options to keep vegetarians happy.

Jaipur

41 South Great George's St ☎01/677 0999, ⊛www.jaipur.ie. Colourful modern decor is the setting for a wide range of richly flavoured Indian food, notably a delicious Goan seafood curry and a full menu for vegetarians, backed up by considerate service and a decent wine list.

Juice

73–83 South Great George's St ☎01/475 7856. Stylish and moderately priced vegetarian and vegan restaurant. The chef is more creative in the evenings, rustling up dishes such as stir fries, Thai curries, mushroom Wellington and aduki bean

▲ SILK ROAD CAFÉ, CHESTER BEATTY LIBRARY

Juiceburgers; simpler and cheaper lunchtime dishes might include tabouleh and scrambled tofu. To drink, choose from juices, smoothies and organic wines. The early-bird menu (Mon–Fri 5–7pm) is great value.

Le Gueuleton

1 Fade St ☎01/675 3708. Closed Sun. A recent instant hit on Dublin's restaurant scene, serving great French bistro food from an open kitchen at very reasonable prices. Well-executed dishes such as rigatoni with braised oxtail and blanquette of lamb, accompanied by good-value French wine, are followed by some novel desserts and fine coffee.

Lord Edward Seafood Restaurant

23 Christchurch Place ☎01/454 2420. Closed Sat lunchtime & Sun. Established in 1890, and apparently little changed since, the *Lord Edward* offers an old-fashioned combination of fresh and simple seafood dishes – fish stew a speciality – traditional hospitality from bow-tied waiters, and manageable prices, from its second-floor perch with fine views of Christ Church Cathedral. The congenial bar and lounge of the eponymous pub below also serve decent food.

Odessa

13–14 Dame Court, off Dame St ☎01/670 7634, ⊛www.odessa.ie. Closed Mon–Fri lunchtimes. Friendly service and cool sounds and decor, whether you sink into the big velour bench seats on the ground floor or the leather armchairs downstairs. The wide-ranging menu features dishes such as Moroccan spiced filo parcel as well as a fish of the day; brunch is offered at weekends and there's a good-value, two-course early-bird menu from Sunday to Thursday 6–7pm.

Shalimar

17 South Great George's St ☎01/671 0738, ⊛www.shalimar.ie. Open till midnight Fri & Sat. Long-established Punjabi restaurant where you can choose between the more formal ground floor, offering some unusual dishes such as roast quail, and the simpler menu of the balti house downstairs. There are plenty of veggie dishes on offer, and a cheap two-course lunch menu.

Uki-yo

7–9 Exchequer St ☎01/633 4071. Open till 2.30am Thurs, Fri & Sat. Chic oriental bar-restaurant with a novel take on the Dublin snug: karaoke boxes out the back for €25 per hour (available until 3.30am at weekends). Out front, you can graze at the bar on what they call Korean and Japanese "tapas", such as tasty beef dumplings, or tuck into something more substantial at the sturdy, dark-wood tables, including salmon teriyaki, lamb curry and noodle soup. To wash it down, there's a wide selection of wine and sake.

Pubs and bars

The Brazen Head

20 Bridge St Lower ☏ 01/679 5186.
Established in 1189 and laying
claim to the title of Ireland's
oldest pub, *The Brazen Head*'s
many rooms ramble round a
large courtyard. Traditional
musicians play every night,
though the quality of the
sessions can be extremely
variable.

4 Dame Lane

4 Dame Lane ☏ 01/679 0291. Open
till 2.30am Mon–Sat, 1am Sun.
Announced by burning braziers
just along the lane from *The
Stag's Head*, this airy, minimalist
bar-club probably has the
stylistic edge over its bare-
brickwork-and-wood rivals.
Good tunes, too: anything from
hip-hop to jazz, with a DJ every
night, either in the upstairs or
ground-floor bar.

The George

89 South Great George's St ☏ 01/478
2983. Open till 2.30am Wed–Sat, 1am
Sun. Ireland's longest-established
gay bar, which still draws huge
crowds at weekends. The outside
is painted a gaudy purple
with a neon-lit sign offering
"Bona Polari" (gay-adopted
Romany slang meaning "good
chat"), while the inside, full
of character, is spread across
two distinct sections: a lushly
decorated main venue on two
floors, and a quieter, more
traditional pub to the right.
Entertainment includes cabaret,
game shows, DJs and Sunday-
night bingo with drag queen,
Shirley Temple-Bar.

The Globe

11 South Great George's St. Lively
watering-hole that's much
favoured by students and
twenty-somethings, perhaps
for its lack of a design concept:
just long, wooden tables,
exposed bricks and low lighting.
Tapas is available Tuesday to
Friday evenings and Saturday
afternoons.

Hogan's

35 South Great George's St. Open
till 2.30am Fri & Sat. Another
favourite of the cheery, beery
under-thirties, especially hectic
during weekend late opening.
It's a rambling, easy-going bar,
with huge picture windows
onto the street, an eclectic
range of music and a tempting
assortment of sofas and
armchairs.

The Long Hall

51 South Great George's St. Old-
time classic that's hanging on
tenaciously in the midst of a
building site. Inside it's business
as usual, blissfully unperturbed:
ornate plasterwork, mirrors and
dark-wood panelling, a suitably
long bar, friendly staff and a
good pint of Guinness.

The Market Bar

Fade St. Closed Sun lunchtime.
Civilized "superpub" in a huge,
simply furnished red-brick
space (a former abbatoir) that's
particularly appealing during the
day when lit through the glass
roof. Better for a drink than
its food menu, which ventures
global tapas.

O'Shea's Merchant

12 Bridge St Lower. Opposite the
more famous *Brazen Head*,
the *Merchant* nurtures the
atmosphere of a homely, good-
natured country pub in the
centre of the city, providing
sanctuary for "culchies" from
any county, but especially

Kerrymen. Traditional sessions are hosted every night around 10pm, including set dancing on Mondays and Wednesdays, and it's a good place to watch a GAA game.

Sosume

64 South Great George's St. Open till 1.30am Wed, 2.30am Thurs–Sat. Generations of tellers who worked in this lofty former bank are no doubt turning in their graves at its oriental-themed reincarnation – and the drunken antics of their besuited successors. Its punning name belongs firmly to the modern Celtic Tiger, but the theme, with its Buddhas, dragons and botanical prints, is attractive and not too in-your-face.

The Stag's Head

1 Dame Court. Closed Sun. Pretty Victorian bar, all dark woods and stuffed, tiled and stained-glassed stags, that attracts a hugely varied crowd. You'll have to come early to grab a seat in the snug, but later in the evening you might be lucky under the large windows upstairs, or else you'll just have to join the throngs outside on the pavement. The hunting theme is not continued on the menu, which just offers cheap, unpretentious pub grub: cod and chips, boiled bacon and cabbage, soup and sandwiches, all served Monday to Friday 12.30–3.30pm and 5–7pm, Saturday 12.30–2.30pm.

Clubs and live venues

Rí Rá

13 Dame Court ☎01/677 4835. Though nowadays more institution than innovator, there's still plenty to thrill at *Rí Rá*, especially when the redoubtable Dandelion is unleashing the beat at Monday's Strictly Handbag – great sounds and a unique atmosphere.

J.J. Smyth's

12 Aungier St ☎01/475 2565. *The* place in Dublin to catch blues and jazz-fusion bands, this pub's intimate upstairs room rocks most nights to the sound of the city's finest 12-bar and "let's try that again in 7/4 time" merchants.

The Liberties and Kilmainham

While the impact of Ireland's recent economic boom is clearly visible in other areas of the city, the predominantly working-class Liberties district remains for the most part decidedly untouched. Its main appeal lies in wandering its bustling streets and markets, perhaps picking up a bargain amongst the antiques shops of Francis Street. The area takes its name from the various freedoms, such as low rents and freedom of passage, granted by charter to the residents of its several separate districts. After the arrival of the Huguenots in the seventeenth century, it became a thriving mercantile area, largely dependent upon textiles, but as trade fell away in the nineteenth century, decline set in and the area's name became synonymous with poverty. Such conditions formed a hotbed for republicanism and, later, trades unionism. To the west of the Liberties, the Guinness Brewery, one of Ireland's most profitable enterprises, is celebrated in its towering Storehouse museum. Further west still, the district of Kilmainham is home to the innovative Irish Museum of Modern Art and Kilmainham Gaol, a former prison indelibly associated with the struggle for Irish freedom.

Francis Street

Currently undergoing piecemeal rejuvenation, Francis Street is a major centre for Dublin's antiques trade and home to some cosy local pubs. The street takes its name from the Franciscan abbey, founded in 1235, whose site is nowadays occupied by the Neoclassical church of St Nicholas of Myra which was constructed in 1830 to celebrate Catholic Emancipation in Ireland. Just to the north stands the Iveagh Market Hall, financed by the then Lord Iveagh, Edward Cecil Guinness. The building has been closed for some years, but its facade is still adorned by a number of carved heads of Moorish and oriental traders. The rather cheeky, bearded one is said to be E.C. Guinness himself.

Maternity Hospital Gateway

On The Coombe, one of the city's oldest thoroughfares, stands the only vestige of the old Coombe Maternity Hospital. Founded in 1826 by a Mrs Boyle in response to the fate of a young woman who died in childbirth trying to reach the Rotunda Hospital across the river, the hospital has long left this site. However, its gateway offers testament to a number of Dublin eccentrics whose nicknames have been etched into the stone. While Nancy Needle Balls was presumably keen on knitting, it's harder to fathom what Stab the Rasher or Johnny Wet Bread were up to.

Thomas Street West

At the junction of the busy thoroughfare of Thomas Street West and St Catherine's Lane stands St Catherine's Church, outside whose impressive facade Robert Emmet (see p.35) was hanged, along with his co-conspirators in the doomed rising of 1803. Heading there from the top of Meath Street, you'll pass a plaque on the *IAWS* pub, commemorating the arrest of one of the leaders of the earlier 1798 Rebellion, Lord Edward Fitzgerald, who subsequently succumbed to the wounds he received during the struggle.

Guinness Storehouse

Off Belleview ☎01/458 4800, ⊛www .guinness-storehouse.com. Daily: July & Aug 9.30am–8pm, Sept–June 9.30am–5pm. €14. The seven-storey Guinness Storehouse occupies a mere fraction of the 64-acre St James's Gate Brewery, a complex so massive that at one time it ran its own railway system, surviving tracks of which are still visible in the surrounding streets. You'll certainly get a whiff of the brewing process as you approach.

The Storehouse's self-guided tour is an exploration of the first three floors of this high-tech temple to the black stuff. Things start off with an explanation of the brewing process – a whirl of water (not from the Liffey, despite the myth) and a reek of

▼ GUINNESS STOREHOUSE

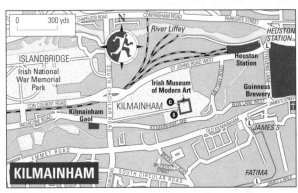

SHOPS				CLUBS & LIVE VENUES	
Final Vinyl	b	The Wicked Chef	3	Vicar Street/Shelter	1
IMMA Bookshop	c	**BARS**		**ACCOMMODATION**	
The Liberty Market	a	The Fountain	5	Brewery Hostel	A
CAFÉS		The Liberty Belle	2		
Grass Roots Café	6	Silken Thomas	4		

barley, hops and malt – before progressing to the storage and transportation areas, the latter featuring a surviving railway engine. A huge barrel dominates the section on the lost art of coopering.

The remainder of the tour consists of a staggering array of marketing memorabilia, supported by plenty of facts and figures about the Guinness empire. There is a newly installed gallery on John Gilroy, an esteemed painter also employed as a commercial artist for the company, who was responsible for the original Guinness insignia – initially

a pelican, until changed by another employee, the novelist Dorothy L. Sayers.

Right at the top of the tower is the tour's highlight, where you can savour your complimentary pint of perhaps the best Guinness in Dublin while absorbing the superb panorama of the city and the countryside beyond.

Irish Museum of Modern Art

Royal Hospital, Military Rd ☎01/612 9900, ⊛www.imma.ie. Tues–Sat 10am–5.30pm, Sun & public holidays noon–5.30pm. Guided tours of the exhibitions Wed, Fri & Sun 2.30pm; free. Guided tours of the Royal

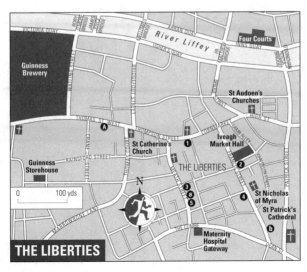

THE LIBERTIES

▲ IRISH MUSEUM OF MODERN ART

Hospital July to mid-Sept Wed & Fri 2.30pm, Sun 12.15pm; free; to book places call ☎01/612 9967. Occupying the former Royal Hospital, the Irish Museum of Modern Art (IMMA) has a justifiable reputation for its imaginative exhibitions, covering both selections from its own permanent collection and loaned works. All shows are temporary and can range from retrospectives of major international artists to new works by modern Irish painters and sculptors. Recent examples include installations by Laurie Anderson and another devoted to Jasper Johns. Some of IMMA's most exciting exhibitions draw upon the museum's Outsider Art collection – works, largely paintings, by unschooled artists that explore the psyche's complexity.

The Royal Hospital itself was built between 1680 and 1684 by William Robinson (also responsible for the restoration of Dublin Castle) at the behest of the Duke of Ormonde, who had been inspired by Louis XIV's Les Invalides in Paris. Set around a courtyard, the Hospital is externally a model of grey stone symmetry, while its interior includes an impressive

banqueting hall featuring seventeenth- and eighteenth-century portraits, and a Baroque chapel with a reconstructed papier-maché ceiling and woodcarvings by the Huguenot James Tarbery. A small heritage exhibition next to IMMA's reception in the south wing is devoted to the Hospital's history and includes a short, informative video.

Kilmainham Gaol

Inchicore Rd ☎01/453 5984, ⊛www .heritageireland.ie. April–Sept daily 9.30am–5pm; Oct–March Mon–Sat 9.30am–4pm, Sun 10am–5pm. Guided tours every 45min until 1hr 15min before closing; €5; Heritage Card. Kilmainham Gaol has an iconic place in the history of Ireland's struggle for independence and, during its latter years, came to symbolize both Irish political martyrdom and British oppression. Opened in 1796,

▼ KILMAINHAM GATE

the gaol became the place of incarceration for captured revolutionaries, including the leaders of the 1916 Easter Rising, who were executed here. Even after the War of Independence Republicans were imprisoned here, though it closed in July 1924 after the release of its last inmate, Eamon de Valera – later to become Ireland's Taoiseach and president.

Guided tours of the prison provide a chilling impression of the prisoners' living conditions and the gaol's Spartan regime. Its single cells ensured that prisoners were forced into solitary contemplation, and since the building was constructed on top of limestone, their health was often sorely affected by damp and severe cold in winter.

Before embarking on the tour, it's well worth visiting the exhibition galleries. The ground floor's galleries display includes a mock-up of a cell and an early mug-shot camera. Here too is a small side gallery containing paintings by Civil War internees and a huge self-portrait of Constance Gore-Booth (better known as the Countess Markiewicz, see p.91) as the Good Shepherd. The upstairs gallery provides an enthralling account of the struggle for independence with numerous mementoes, old cinematic footage of Michael Collins (see p.171) and the letter ordering the release of Charles Stewart Parnell.

Irish National War Memorial Park

Con Colbert Rd, Islandbridge ⊛ www .heritageireland.ie. Mon–Fri 8am–dusk, Sat & Sun 10am–dusk. Free. Designed by Sir Edwin Lutyens and opened in 1939, a date that subsequent events would prove

▲ 1916 PROCLAMATION OF THE IRISH REPUBLIC, KILMAINHAM GAOL

poignant, the park's pavilions, monuments, fountains and pools pays tribute to the 50,000 Irishmen who died on the fields of Belgium and Northern France fighting for the British army during World War I. Their names are inscribed on granite memorial books kept in the pair of pavilions found at each end of the park. A tranquil place, with views across the Liffey to Phoenix Park, the gardens are also a horticultural pleasure, particularly in spring.

Shops

Final Vinyl

73 Francis St ☎ 01/402 0660. Mon–Sat 11am–7pm. Probably stocking Dublin's best selection of second-hand vinyl records, the shop's CD range covers everything from punk to jazz, via soul and metal, and there are plenty of bargains on offer.

Francis Street

There's no one place to pick out, but the antiques shops here are a great place to explore, with the chance to pick up a bargain on furniture, cast iron fireplaces, old lamps, stained glass, and any number of knick-knacks and *objets d'art*.

IMMA Bookshop

Royal Hospital, Kilmainham. Open Sun noon–5.30pm. The best place to head not only for books on modern art and paraphernalia related to the museum's exhibits, but also for its extensive collection of works on modern architecture too.

The Liberty Market

Meath St. Thurs–Sat 10am–5pm. A higgledy-piggledy indoor maze of stalls retailing everything from cheap clothes and footwear to Westlife posters and replica football gear.

Cafés

Grass Roots Café

IMMA, Royal Hospital, Kilmainham. Serving everything from snacks to reasonably priced full lunches, IMMA's basement café also offers a potent cup of coffee.

The Wicked Chef

73 Meath St. Mon–Sat 8am–11pm, Sun 9am–10pm. Don't be deterred by its fast-food joint exterior – this is a real jewel in the Liberties' crown. Apart from a range of filling breakfasts, the delights on offer include exceptional-value Irish dishes such as Dublin stew and bacon and cabbage, which is much more enjoyable than you might imagine.

Pubs and bars

The Fountain

63–64 Meath St. A typical old-fashioned locals' bar, popular with local traders.

The Liberty Belle

35 Francis St. Cheap by Dublin standards, this plain but cosy local offers the chance to eavesdrop on Liberties gossip and maybe catch an antiques dealer on a magnanimous day.

Silken Thomas

121 Francis St. Named after Thomas Fitzgerald, leader of the abortive 1534 rising against Henry VIII, the pub is a standard but pleasant Southside boozer.

Clubs and live venues

Vicar Street/Shelter

58–59 Thomas St West ☎0818 713 390, ⊛www.vicarstreet.com. Arguably the city's premier small live music venue, this 300-seater has an estimable programme of live music, comedy and other events, featuring major names. The attached intimate and stylish *Shelter* club opens its doors at weekends (from 11pm until late) to local promoters, so many events are one-offs. The first Friday of each month, however, is Static night, featuring top international DJs.

Around O'Connell Street

Running due north from O'Connell Bridge, broader than it is long, to Parnell Square, O'Connell Street is the main artery of Dublin's Northside. Lined with numerous impressive memorials and the remarkable four-hundred-foot high stainless steel "Spike" sculpture, this bustling thoroughfare was originally laid out in the fashion of the grand Parisian boulevards. Poorly redeveloped since the damage caused by the 1916 Easter Rising, nowadays the street is very much a mishmash of modern shop frontages, though glancing at the upper storeys reveals some of its former glory. The streets around, however, represent a consumer's paradise and, particularly on Liffey Street Lower and in the burgeoning new Italian quarter centred on Bloom Lane, you'll find plenty of stylish bars and cafés. Notable cultural landmarks east of O'Connell Street include the Abbey Theatre, centre of the twentieth-century revival in Irish theatre, and, along The Quays, the impressive, opulent, eighteenth-century Custom House.

Ha'penny Bridge

Dublin's most renowned crossing, the cast-iron Ha'penny Bridge is the oldest of the pedestrian river crossings, with great views of the river along the Quays in both directions. It began life in 1816 as the Wellington Bridge but soon acquired its nickname thanks to a halfpenny toll, levied until 1919.

O'Connell Street

O'Connell Street has a remarkable number of monuments, mostly positioned in its broad central reservation. Crossing O'Connell Bridge you'll first encounter the imposing figure of Daniel O'Connell, "The Liberator", who played a major role in nineteenth-century political campaigns to secure independence. The winged figures by his side represent O'Connell's bravery, patriotism, fidelity and eloquence while the smaller female figure nearby symbolizes Ireland unchained. At the Abbey Street junction stands Oisín Kelly's statue of Jim Larkin, a key trades union activist during the first half of the twentieth century, caught in the act of addressing a crowd.

Further up, by the junction with Earl Street North, the city's latest landmark stands on the spot occupied

▼ HA'PENNY BRIDGE

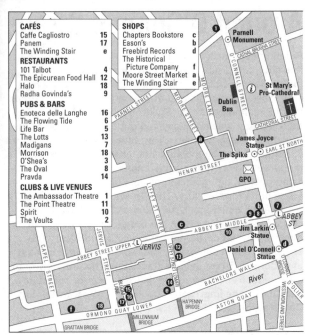

CAFÉS	
Caffe Cagliostro	15
Panem	17
The Winding Stair	e
RESTAURANTS	
101 Talbot	4
The Epicurean Food Hall	12
Halo	18
Radha Govinda's	9
PUBS & BARS	
Enoteca delle Langhe	16
The Flowing Tide	6
Life Bar	5
The Lotts	13
Madigans	7
Morrison	18
O'Shea's	3
The Oval	8
Pravda	14
CLUBS & LIVE VENUES	
The Ambassador Theatre	1
The Point Theatre	11
Spirit	10
The Vaults	2

SHOPS	
Chapters Bookstore	c
Eason's	b
Freebird Records	d
The Historical Picture Company	f
Moore Street Market	a
The Winding Stair	e

by Nelson's Pillar until it was blown up in 1966 – the frankly astonishing Dublin Spire, or "Spike" as it's colloquially known, which was constructed

▼ LIFFEY STREET LOWER

to celebrate the city's entry into the new millennium. Designed by Ian Ritchie, this four-hundred-foot high stainless-steel needle, surmounted by a beacon, is easily the tallest structure in the city centre. Just over three-feet wide at its base, it tapers to a mere six inches at its summit. In the early morning or at dusk its surface takes on an ethereal blue colour while at night it seems to loom ominously over the city. What the ghost of the author James Joyce whose adjacent, somewhat rakish statue stands just down Earl Street North would make of it all is open to question.

Near the very top of O'Connell Street stands a monument to Charles Stewart Parnell, one of the major figures in Ireland's nineteenth-century Home Rule movement.

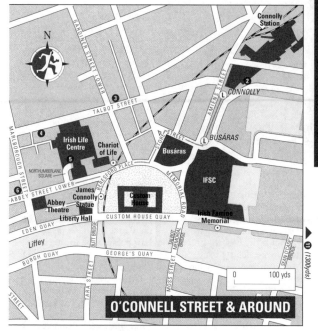

O'CONNELL STREET & AROUND

▲ STATUE OF JIM LARKIN, O'CONNELL STREET

General Post Office

O'Connell St Lower. Mon–Sat 8am–8pm. Free. The General Post Office is a building of crucial significance in Ireland's political history. On Easter Monday, April 1916, Pádraig Pearse (see p.163) strode from its doors to read a proclamation on behalf of the Provisional Government of the Irish Republic declaring Ireland's independence from Britain. The rebels held on to the GPO for six days, one of several buildings seized that day, during which much of the surrounding area was badly damaged by the fighting. Eventually, however, the weight of British Army artillery fire proved too much to withstand and the insurgents set the GPO ablaze before fleeing. Most, including Pearse himself, were however either captured or surrendered in nearby streets.

Initial public reaction to the Rising was profoundly hostile. Much of central Dublin was in ruins and more than 1300 people had been

▲ NORMAN TEELING, *THE EASTER RISING*, GPO

killed or seriously wounded. Nevertheless, Britain's execution of all the Rising's leaders (barring Éamon de Valera, who was not of Irish birth) proved utterly miscalculated and sparked increasing demands for Home Rule.

The GPO itself, which dated back to 1818, did not survive the Rising, except for its Ionic portico which still bears the marks of gunfire. Displayed on the walls inside are paintings by the Irish artist Norman Teeling portraying scenes from the Rising, though these are sometimes obscured by temporary exhibits relating to postal services. Part of the Proclamation has also been reproduced, but the most enthralling sight is Oliver Sheppard's intricately wrought bronze statue *The Death of Cúchulainn*, representing a key moment in the Irish legend *Táin Bó Cúailnge*.

The Abbey Theatre

26 Abbey St Lower ☎01/878 7222, ⓦwww.abbeytheatre.ie. Backstage tours Thurs 11am; €6; call ☎01/887 2223 to book. Ultimately the focal point for Ireland's twentieth-century cultural revival, the Abbey Theatre first opened its doors in December 1904 to present three plays, two by the poet and dramatist W.B. Yeats and the other by his patron Lady Gregory. The theatre's company turned professional in 1906 and Yeats and Gregory, along with J.M. Synge, became its first directors. The staging of Synge's tragi-comic *Playboy of the Western World* the following year, with its frank language and suggestion that Irish peasants would condone a murder, provoked riots on its opening night. Later, in 1926, Seán O'Casey's *The Plough and the Stars* incited bitter outrage, the audience regarding its view of the Easter Rising as derisive, not least because the theatre had begun to receive state funding the previous year.

The original Abbey burnt to the ground in 1951 and its more modern, outwardly grim replacement opened in 1966. Informative guided tours – a must for anyone interested in the link between Ireland's culture and politics – take in both back- and front-stage areas and recount key moments in the Abbey's history. The

▼ *THE DEATH OF CÚCHULAINN*, GPO

▲ THE CUSTOM HOUSE

theatre's programme continues to include a range of drama, blending revivals of Irish classics with new works by established writers such as Hugh Leonard and Brian Friel while the much smaller Peacock Theatre in the basement is devoted to new experimental works. In 2005, however, financial mismanagement almost caused the Abbey's closure; there are plans to relocate the theatre into a newly built development in the docklands.

St Mary's Pro-Cathedral

Marlborough St ☎ 01/874 5441, ⓦ www.procathedral.ie. Mon–Fri 7.30am–6.45pm, Sat 7.30am–7.15pm, Sun 9am–1.45pm & 5.30–7.45pm, public holidays 10am–1.30pm. Free. With a six-columned facade modelled on the Temple of Theseus in Athens, St Mary's is the city's principal Catholic church. Its side-street position resulted from Protestant opposition to plans to locate the building on Sackville Street (now O'Connell Street), a site which instead became occupied by the General Post Office. St Mary's opened in 1825 but did not adopt its full title as Pro-Cathedral until the end of the nineteenth century, when its status "standing in" for a Catholic cathedral (which the city had lacked since the Reformation) was sanctioned by the then archbishop of Dublin, Dr Walsh. The current archbishop continues to serve as the church's parish priest.

Despite its impressive frontage, there's little of attraction inside, and the Pro-Cathedral is nowadays best-known for its male Palestrina Choir, founded in 1903 and named after the sixteenth-century Italian composer. The choir can be heard singing Latin Mass every Sunday at 11am from September and June, and at vespers on Fridays at 5.20pm year-round. During July and August its place on Sundays is taken by visiting choirs.

Custom House Visitor Centre

Custom House Quay ☎ 01/888 2538. Mid-March to Oct Mon–Fri 10am–12.30pm, Sat, Sun & public holidays 2–5pm. €1. Opened in 1791, the imposing Custom House is one of several notable Dublin landmarks designed by the English architect James Gandon (others include the Four Courts and the O'Connell Bridge). Constructed on a submerged mudflat that required covering with a layer of solid pine planks, and showing off Gandon's fabulously intricate architectural detail, the Custom House cost the then unearthly sum of £500,000 sterling, a figure that proved even more extravagant when the Act of Union transferred customs and excise to London in 1800. The building's grandiose Neoclassical exterior, more than a hundred yards in length, features sculptures by Gandon's contemporary Edward Smyth, with cattle heads symbolizing Ireland's beef trade, and others representing Ireland's rivers, including the Liffey above the main entrance.

A small section of the building's interior now houses a visitor centre. Its ground-floor displays depict how, after 1801, the Custom House became the administrative centre for the city's work on public hygiene and Poor Law relief, the latter demonstrated by an enormous Famine pot, used to prepare meals for those at risk of dying. The building suffered a major fire in 1833 and was completely gutted in 1921 after being set alight by the IRA. Subsequently restored, though with significant changes to its internal structure and facade, it housed various government departments – one ground-floor room in the visitor centre houses pictures showing some of its more illustrious employees, including Brian O'Nolan, better known as the comic novelist Flann O'Brien, and the songwriter Percy French.

Upstairs is devoted to Gandon's career and designs, though the building's undoubted highlight is the 115-foot-high dome, based on Christopher Wren's Greenwich Hospital. Look out for the intricately egg-and-dart ornamented pillars, perfect cornices and scrolled brackets, all using cut stone rather than plasterwork.

Around the Custom House

Just around the corner from the Custom House on Beresford Place, and facing Liberty Hall, the headquarters of SIPTU, Ireland's largest trade union, stands, appropriately, a statue of James Connolly – socialist theorist, trade union activist and one of the leaders of the Easter Rising. Nearby, at the junction with Abbey Street Lower, Oisín Kelly's remarkable *Chariot of Life* sculpture shows a charioteer struggling to control his horses, meant to represent the conflict between passion and reason. The mammoth forty-acre site of the International Financial Services Centre dominates the eastern edge of Beresford Place, a symbol of the Celtic Tiger boom of the 1990s.

Irish Famine Memorial

Custom House Quay. Set between the looming presence of the IFSC and the Liffey, these six life-size bronze figures were designed and cast by the Dublin sculptor Rowan Gillespie to mark the 150th anniversary of the worst year of the Great Famine (1845–49), or Black '47 as it is sometimes

▼ JAMES CONNOLLY STATUE, BERESFORD PLACE

known. Over the course of the famine more than a million people died of starvation and another million and a half emigrated, while the British government adopted a laissez-faire approach and continued to export food from Ireland around the world. That these stark, beseeching figures are staring eastwards is not coincidental.

▲ MOORE LANE

Shops

Chapters Bookstore

108 Abbey St Middle. Open Thurs until 8.30pm and Sun noon–6pm. "Stack 'em high and sell 'em cheap" seems to be the ethic of this long-standing Northside bookshop, and delving into the extensive fiction section will uncover many bargains. The store's basement is crammed with second-hand books, while upstairs houses racks of cheap CDs and DVDs.

Eason's

40 O'Connell St Lower. Open Thurs until 8.45pm and Fri until 7.45pm, plus Sun noon–5.45pm. The largest general bookshop on the Northside, Eason's also stocks a vast range of newspapers and magazines. There's a branch of Tower Records on the first floor and a café on the second.

Freebird Records

Downstairs, 1 Eden Quay. Open Thurs & Fri until 7.30pm. Freebird crams an astonishing range of new and second-hand CDs into its racks, covering every genre from rock to hip-hop, via reggae, jazz, blues and folk, with an extensive section on Irish indie bands and singers.

The Historical Picture Company

5 Ormond Quay Lower ☎01/872 0144. With its vast selection of nostalgic, historical and just plain beautiful photographs from every county in Ireland, organized by town and village, this is *the* place to track down that picture of grandfather's cottage in Cooraclare. Photos come ready-mounted or can be framed on the spot.

Moore Street Market

Moore St. Mon–Sat 10am–6pm. This lively street market, a long-standing Dublin institution, and its adjacent shops nowadays reflects the city's changing ethnicity. The traditional butchers, fishmongers and greengrocers are still present, though you're bound to see price tags in Cantonese too, and there are also a number of Afro-Caribbean stalls.

The Winding Stair

40 Ormond Quay Lower. The ground floor of this bookshop and café (see below) is chock-full of second-hand titles, with particularly good sections on Irish literature and biography.

Cafés

Caffe Cagliostro

Bloom Lane. A splendid, tiny Italian café serving arguably the Northside's premier coffees and delicious pastries, with newspapers for perusal. There are tables outside on a fine day.

Panem

21 Ormond Quay Lower. Closed Sun. Petite but perfectly formed, *Panem* dishes up a worthy range of good-value snacks and savouries, including freshly-made soups, strikingly good focaccia and a variety of pasta dishes.

The Winding Stair

40 Ormond Quay Lower. Closed Sun. The bookshop's upstairs café, overlooking Ha'penny Bridge, offers excellent coffee, a delicious range of light snacks, crêpes and pastries, and more substantial lunches, including daily specials at €5.99.

▼ THE WINDING STAIR

Restaurants

101 Talbot

100–101 Talbot St ☎01/874 5011. Closed all day Sun & Mon and lunchtimes Tues–Sat. Wise diners make advance bookings at this upstairs establishment. The imaginative starters, including stuffed roast flat mushrooms and Thai beef salad, are but a prelude to the delightful Mediterranean-influenced dishes, such as chicken stuffed with mozzarella and chorizo or Moroccan bean cakes, presented with style and served with élan. It's worth taking advantage of the three-course early bird menu (€21), served until 8pm.

The Epicurean Food Hall

13–14 Liffey St Lower. Open until 10pm daily. You're spoilt for choice in this dedicated food mall, wondering which of the dozen or so eateries (and a bar) to plump for. Options include *Leo Burdock's* fish and chips, tempting Chinese street food and *Christophe's* superb-value boeuf bourgignon.

Halo

Morrison Hotel, Ormond Quay Lower ☎01/887 2421, ⊛www.morrisonhotel .ie. Brilliantly designed modern decor married to faultlessly presented cuisine makes *Halo* a gourmet's dream. The menu combines natural Irish ingredients with a cosmopolitan range of herbs, spices and delicacies. Starters include boneless quail served in black truffle sauce, or pumpkin and celeriac soup; main courses cover fish and meat dishes, such as fillet of sea bass served with sautéed pak-choi, or loin of venison with garlic spinach. Expect to pay around €50 (plus wine) for a three-course meal.

Radha Govinda's

84 Abbey St Middle. Open till 9pm Mon–Sat; closed Sun. This bright, breezy and inexpensive south Indian vegetarian restaurant has added some culinary variety to the Northside. The menu includes a range of tasty soups and dishes such as cauliflower, potato and carrot curry, served with fresh dill yoghurt, dhal and rice – in generous helpings. Treat yourself to the *malpoora* (small fried doughnuts) and don't miss the lemon lassi.

Pubs and bars

Enoteca delle Langhe

Bloom Lane. A focal point of Dublin's new Italian quarter, the *Enoteca* brings all the flavours of a Neapolitan bar to the city, serving up an astonishingly wide range of wines and a small, but still intriguing menu of antipasti and other dishes.

The Flowing Tide

9 Abbey St Lower. Long connected with the Abbey Theatre opposite, this pub features tasteful stained-glass windows, a mural celebrating the theatre's history and a horseshoe-shaped bar. A good spot for a decent pint and a filling lunchtime sandwich.

Life Bar

Northumberland Square. Tucked away next to the back entrance of the Irish Life shopping mall, the *Life Bar* is a stylish place to relax during the day; at night, however, its two floors come alive, especially between Thursday and Saturday when DJs spin a broad range of tunes. Decently priced food – a range of salads, wraps and pasta – is served between noon and 8.30pm.

The Lotts

9 Liffey St Lower. It's often standing-room only at this friendly corner bar, which lays claim to being the Northside's smallest. It offers a tasty selection of Mediterranean-inspired meals in its fashionable café-bar upstairs.

Madigans

4 Abbey St Lower. A straightforward, pleasant, wood-panelled bar serving well-kept stout, *Madigans* never seems to get crowded, despite its proximity to O'Connell Street.

The Morrison

Morrison Hotel, Ormond Quay Lower. Chic and stylishly modern, with good views of the river, this hotel bar is one of the city's mellowest places to pass the time. Don't be deterred by the apparent ultra-hip exterior for inside you'll find broad mix of locals and guests enjoying their pints or sampling the range of tempting cocktails.

O'Shea's

19 Talbot St. Hugely popular, thanks to its first-rate service and very reasonably priced meals, *O'Shea's* also hosts occasional traditional-music sessions and gigs.

The Oval

78 Abbey St Middle. In former days this calm, friendly, atmospheric bar was often packed with

newshounds from the adjacent *Irish Independent*. The paper has since moved its HQ, though the bar's international clocks remain in place.

Pravda

Liffey Street Lower. Thurs open till 1.30am, Fri & Sat till 2.30am. A real oddity, this late-opening Soviet-influenced theme bar sports revolutionary murals in the "noble worker" style and, appropriately, serves Russian and Polish lagers in addition to the standard pint. Standard fare such as burgers and chilli and tuna melts is served during the day.

Clubs and live venues

The Ambassador Theatre

O'Connell Street Upper ☏01/872 7000, ⊛www.mcd.ie. An old but well-regarded venue at the very northern end of O'Connell Street, the *Ambassador's* programme is decidedly eclectic, focusing very much on middle-ranking, left-field indie and rock bands.

The Point Theatre

East Link Bridge Rd, North Wall Quay ☏01/836 3633, ⊛www.thepoint.ie.

Once a railway depot, the cavernous *Point*, a mile east of O'Connell Bridge, is Ireland's largest dedicated music venue with a capacity of 7500 (half of this for seated gigs). Unsurprisingly, it hosts major international names with high prices to boot.

Spirit

57 Abbey St Middle ☏01/877 9999, ⊛www.spiritdublin.com. Wed–Sun 10.30pm–5am. One of the city's largest clubbing venues, *Spirit's* three floors are devoted to, respectively, mind, body and soul, with appositely named nights to match, such as Rapture (Thurs), Revelation (Fri) and Redemption (Sat). Entry prices can be steep at weekends (around €20).

The Vaults

Harbourmaster Place ☏01/605 4700. Tucked away under Connolly Station, this spacious cellar bar hosts popular club nights at weekends (Fri & Sat 11pm–3am), with a house and funk focus. More sedately, there's a regular Sunday afternoon jazz session (3–6pm; free).

North from Parnell Square

Situated at the northern end of O'Connell Street, Parnell Square might lack the subtle allure of its Georgian equivalents on the Southside, but still possesses a certain charm. Three of the square's sides are busy thoroughfares, the southern part dominated by the prominent cupola of the eighteenth-century Rotunda Maternity Hospital, the first of its kind in Europe, and the prestigious Gate Theatre. The northern side, however, is more peaceful, and worth making for in its own right. Here you'll find the Garden of Remembrance, devoted to the memory of those who died in the struggle for Ireland's independence, while other highlights include one of Dublin's premier art galleries, the Hugh Lane, and the Dublin Writers Museum, an excellent place to learn more about the city's literary history. Away from Parnell Square, nearby attractions include Dublin's version of Madame Tussaud's, and an informative centre devoted to the works of the writer James Joyce. To the northeast, across the Royal Canal, stands Croke Park, a major sports arena and home to the innovative GAA Museum.

The Gate Theatre

1 Cavendish Row, Parnell Square East ☎01/874 4045 or 01/874 6042, ⓦwww.gate-theatre.ie. The Gate Theatre has been a home for quality dramatic productions since it was founded in 1928 by two Englishmen, life-long lovers Hilton Edwards and Michael Wilmore. In a strong tradition continuing today, The Gate showcased modern European and American theatre, as well as classic and new Irish works, and its enduringly powerful programme saw it quickly become a contender to the Abbey's crown (see p.132). Both Orson Welles and James Mason began their careers here.

National Wax Museum

Granby Row, Parnell Square ☎01/872 6340. Mon–Sat 10am–5.30pm, Sun noon–5.30pm. Adults €7, children €5. Puppet shows daily 11.30am (except Sun), 12.30pm, 2pm, 3pm and 4.40pm. Fronted by an enormous model

▼ ROTUNDA MATERNITY HOSPITAL, PARNELL SQUARE

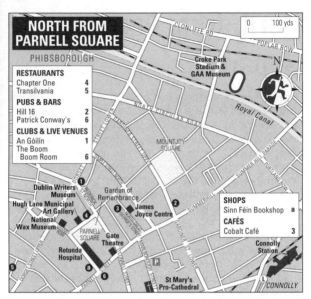

NORTH FROM PARNELL SQUARE

PHIBSBOROUGH

RESTAURANTS	
Chapter One	4
Transilvania	5
PUBS & BARS	
Hill 16	2
Patrick Conway's	6
CLUBS & LIVE VENUES	
An Góilín	1
The Boom Boom Room	6

Croke Park Stadium & GAA Museum

Royal Canal

MOUNTJOY SQUARE

Dublin Writers Museum

Hugh Lane Municipal Art Gallery

National Wax Museum

PARNELL SQUARE

Rotunda Hospital

Gate Theatre

Garden of Remembrance

James Joyce Centre

SHOPS	
Sinn Féin Bookshop	a
CAFÉS	
Cobalt Café	3

Connolly Station

St Mary's Pro-Cathedral

CONNOLLY

of the legendary giant Fionn Mac Cumhaill, the mythical creator of Giant's Causeway and Lough Neagh, the wax museum is an entertaining way to pass an hour or so, especially if you have children in tow. More than three hundred exhibits cover everyone from a gathering of Taoisigh (prime ministers) to musicians,

▼ FIONN MAC CUMHAILL, NATIONAL WAX MUSEUM

such as Ronan Keating and U2, sporting heroes and movie stars, with sections on *Star Wars*, *The Simpsons* and *Teletubbies*. There are crawl-through tunnels for younger children, Punch and Judy shows and a somewhat fiendish chamber of horrors featuring various nasties such as Vlad the Impaler. A more surprising exhibit is the actual Popemobile used by the late John Paul II when he visited Ireland in 1979.

Garden of Remembrance

Parnell Square East. April–Sept 8.30am–6pm, Oct–March 9.30am–4pm. Free. A tranquil spot, the Garden of Remembrance was created in 1966 on the fiftieth anniversary of the Easter Rising, and commemorates those who died in the cause of Irish independence. The garden's railings are replete with Celtic and Christian symbols, including a cruciform-shaped

▲ *CHILDREN OF LIR*, GARDEN OF REMEMBRANCE

pond. At its western end stands Oisín Kelly's arresting *Children of Lir* statue, based on the complex legend of the lord of the sea whose children by his first wife were transformed into swans by her resentful sister whom Lir had subsequently married. The statue portrays Lir's anguish at the moment of metamorphosis.

The Hugh Lane Municipal Art Gallery

Parnell Square North ☎01/874 1903, ⊛www.hughlane.ie. Tues–Thurs 9.30am–6pm, Fri & Sat 9.30am–5pm, Sun 11am–5pm. Entrance to gallery free; Francis Bacon studio €7. The elegant, Georgian, stone-clad Charlemont House, with its curved outer and inner walls and Neoclassical interior has provided a permanent home for the Hugh Lane Gallery since 1933. Sir Hugh, a nephew of Lady Gregory (see p.132), wanted Dublin to house a major gallery of Irish and international art. He amassed a considerable collection by persuading native artists to contribute their work and purchasing many other paintings himself, particularly from the French Impressionist school and Italy.

The gallery holds around half of the Lane collection (the rest is in London's National Gallery) and only a fraction is on display here at any one time, though you're likely to see works by Renoir, Monet and Degas, as well as Pissarro and the Irish painter Roderic O'Connor. Simultaneously, there are usually other temporary exhibitions of more modern artworks. Regular Sunday lunchtime classical music concerts are also held here (noon; free).

Part of the gallery is devoted to a recreation of Dublin-born painter Francis Bacon's studio, transported from its original location at Reece Mews in South Kensington, London, where the artist lived and worked for the last thirty years of his life. After his death in 1992, his studio was donated to the gallery by his heir, John Edwards, and reconstructed here with astonishing precision – more than seven thousand individual items were catalogued and placed here with verisimilitude in the reconstruction. The studio can only be viewed through the window glass but amongst the apparent debris are an old Bush record-player,

▼ THE HUGH LANE MUNICIPAL ART GALLERY

▲ DUBLIN WRITERS MUSEUM

empty champagne boxes and huge tins of the type of matt vinyl favoured by Bacon, the fumes of which exacerbated his asthma. The surrounding rooms hold displays of memorabilia, such as photographs and correspondence, but the crowning glory is unquestionably his five unfinished paintings. Characteristically stark, warts-and-all they convey the sense of overriding despair that pervaded Bacon's work. The subject of one, *Study after Velazquez 1950*, bears an uncanny resemblance to Ronald Reagan.

Dublin Writers Museum

18 Parnell Square North ☎01/872 2077, ⊛www.writersmuseum.com. Mon–Sat 10am–5pm (July & Aug until 6pm), Sun & public holidays 11am–5pm. €5.50. If you want to know more about Dublin's rich literary history, then this museum makes the ideal starting point. With a wealth of anecdote and information, the audio-guide (available from reception) helps to illuminate literature's pivotal role in Irish society, particularly in terms of politics

and national identity. The displays covers not only giants such as Wilde, Shaw, Joyce and Beckett, but also lesser known figures like Sheridan Le Fanu and Oliver St John Gogarty (see p.94 and p.166).

The ground floor of the museum contains a plethora of displays on particular writers or literary schools, covering first or early editions, playbills, programmes and memorabilia.

Downstairs, the hall is hung with a varied and changing selection of modern paintings of writers and leads to a pleasant outdoor Zen garden where you can contemplate works you've purchased in the museum's well-stocked ground-floor bookshop, or head for the café at the rear.

On the first floor of the museum is the Gallery of Writers, an elegant salon featuring decorative plasterwork by Michael Stapleton, renowned as the finest stuccodore of the Georgian era, James Joyce's piano and more paintings, of which the most impressive is a portrait of the author George Moore by John B. Yeats, father of the poet and dramatist William B. and the painter Jack B. Yeats. The Gorham Library, next door, features numerous rare editions.

The James Joyce Centre

35 North Great George's St ☎01/878 8547, ⊛www.jamesjoyce.ie. Mon–Sat 9.30am–5pm, Sun & public holidays 12.30–5pm. €5. Walking tours Tues, Thurs & Sat 2pm; €10; 1hr. The James Joyce Centre aims to illuminate the work of perhaps Ireland's most imaginative yet most complex writer, who spent part of his life living in the inner Northside, and drew upon his experiences in the creation of his characters and the settings

for his works. The centre occupies a grand eighteenth-century townhouse, restored in the 1980s, that features decorative stucco mouldings by Michael Stapleton. The ground floor houses a small shop full of Joyceiana, such as books and prints, and an airy courtyard which includes the actual period door of 7 Eccles Street, the fictional home of Leopold and Molly Bloom, two of the main protagonists in *Ulysses*, as well as a somewhat enigmatic large-scale Joyce-inspired sculpture of a cow. On the way upstairs you'll pass prints and paintings based on the writer's work, while the first-floor rooms themselves house a small library of Joyce's publications and related works, some of which may be browsed. Also displayed are photographs of people and places associated with *Ulysses*, and a time-line to trace the development of the novel's plot. The centre's walking tour, which begins here, is well worth taking if you want to learn more about Joycean connections with the surrounding area.

▲ THE GAA MUSEUM

The GAA Museum

Croke Park, St Joseph's Ave ☎01/819 2323, ⊚www.gaa.ie. Mon–Sat 9.30am–5pm (July & Aug until 6pm), Sun & public holidays noon–5pm. Stadium tours: April–Sept Mon–Sat 12.30pm & 3pm, Sun 1pm, 2.15pm & 3.30pm (except match days) and less frequently in winter – call to check availability. Museum only €5.50; museum and stadium tour €9.50. Bus #123 from O'Connell St. Croke Park is the home of the Gaelic Athletic Association (GAA). It's a magnificent and, after much redevelopment, now very modern stadium, its capacity of 82,000-plus putting it amongst the largest in Europe. Inside the stadium, under the Cusack Stand, is the GAA Museum, one of the finest in Dublin. The creatively designed exhibits, and imaginative multimedia displays provide an enthralling account of the sports of hurling and Gaelic football (see box, p.144), as well as lesser known games such as handball and camogie (the women's variant on hurling).

Historical and political contexts are explored too, in a thoroughly engaging manner – since its foundation in 1884,

▼ FRONT DOOR, 7 ECCLES STREET, JAMES JOYCE CENTRE

Gaelic football and hurling

Two of the world's fastest and most physical sports, Gaelic football and hurling have roots in the distant past, but were revived during the general Irish process of cultural renewal which began in the nineteenth century. Gaelic football combines elements of both rugby and soccer, but predates both games. Players can kick, catch and pass to each other by striking the ball with the hand or fist. Hurling bears more similarities to hockey, with participants using a curved wooden stick (a hurley or *camán*) to hit the ball (*sliotar*).

the GAA has always been irrevocably linked with Irish Nationalism. Thus the museum does not shirk from recounting key politically sensitive events such as Bloody Sunday, when British troops fired on the crowd attending a match in 1920, killing twelve people in the process. On a lighter note, upstairs you can have a go at whacking a hurling ball or test your balance and reactions via various simulations.

Taking the stadium tour is highly recommended, not just to view this remarkable arena at first hand, but to learn more about key events in its history – including, not least, the momentous decision in April 2005 to suspend the GAA's constitution to allow professional Rugby Union and Association Football international matches to take place here while Lansdowne Road stadium (see p.207) undergoes redevelopment – previously only games of Irish origin, played by amateurs, could be staged here.

Shops

Sinn Féin Bookshop

44 Parnell Square West. Closed Sun. The Republican party's literature outlet stocks a compact range of historical and political tomes, including some you're unlikely

to find anywhere else in Dublin, as well as CDs (including some hard-to-find Christy Moore releases), videos and DVDs.

Cafés

Cobalt Café

16 North Great George's St. Closed Sun. A relaxing haven in an area with a dearth of cafés, the *Cobalt* offers a range of coffees as well as light snacks, all of which can be enjoyed while admiring the original artworks displayed on its walls.

Restaurants

Chapter One

18–19 Parnell Square North ☎01/873 2266. Closed all day Sun & Mon and Sat lunchtime. Housed in the cellars of the Dublin Writers Museum, this Northside culinary gem specializes in French-inspired modern Irish food. Starters include salmon gravadlax and braised venison, while main courses might feature loin of boar or civet of rabbit. Carnivores can also opt for selections from the charcuterie trolley. The restaurant offers a pre-theatre special dinner (6–7pm, €31 for three courses).

Transilvania

7A Henrietta Place ☎01/873 4375. Closed all day Mon and Tues–Fri

▲ EASTER RISING PLAQUE, *PATRICK CONWAY'S* PUB

Patrick Conway's

70 Parnell St. Running since 1745 (when it was known as *Doyle's*), *Conway's* is the oldest pub on the Northside. It's also famous since Pádraig Pearse surrendered to the British on the corner outside after the Easter Rising. As well as its historical associations, the pub offers filling bar meals (including massive baguettes, served with chips and salad) and *The Boom Boom Room* upstairs (see below).

Club and live venues

An Góilín

Upstairs, *Tom Maye's* pub, corner of Dorset St Upper and Frederick St North ☎086/815 0946, ⊛www.goilin.com. The city's longest-standing traditional singers' club opens its doors every Friday from 9.30pm. For the ridiculously cheap minimum contribution of €2, you can hear some of Dublin's finest, singing unaccompanied, at the regular club nights, or catch guests drawn from across Ireland. Sometimes the latter includes *sean-nós* ("old-style") singers from Irish-speaking areas such as Connemara.

The Boom Boom Room

Patrick Conway's, 70 Parnell St ☎01/873 2687, ⊛www.theboomboomroom.tv. The *Boom Boom* hosts a diverse range of live gigs, the genre depending on the night of the week: experimental jazz (Thurs); aspiring singer-songwriters (Fri); and a mix of blues, fusion, world music and electronica (Sat). Gigs last from around 9 or 10pm until closing time.

lunchtimes. Probably Ireland's only Romanian restaurant, the reasonably priced menu here includes an intriguing range of traditional soups including spicy chicken, as well as main courses featuring dishes such as *tocitura* – various meats in a red wine source – and *sarmale* – pork, beef and rice wrapped in a cabbage leaf – and delicious homemade cheeses. A cosy place, the atmosphere is sometimes enlivened by Romanian musicians.

Pubs and bars

Hill 16

Gardiner St Middle. Named after Croke Park's most popular stand, the bar is a magnet for GAA devotees, particularly those who follow the fortunes of Dublin's Gaelic football team. Naturally, it's busiest on match-days, though service remains impeccable, when the chance to share the *craic* and banter with fans is the main draw.

From Capel Street to Collins Barracks

Much redeveloped in recent years, the traditionally working-class area west along the Quays from Capel Street is a focus for Dublin's nightlife, with two of the city's finest traditional-music establishments and several more modern, fashionable bars. There's also a small but vibrant gay scene on Capel Street itself. From Grattan Bridge, at the street's southern end, views west along the river are dominated by the arresting Four Courts. North from here, the renovated Smithfield area, home to the Old Jameson Distillery, is renowned for its 300-year-old monthly horse fair, while the crypt of the Northside's oldest church, St Michan's, holds the ghoulish attraction of several mummified bodies from as long ago as the Crusades. To the west, the striking Collins Barracks houses the delights of the National Museum decorative arts collection.

The Four Courts

Inns Quay. Public court galleries
Mon–Fri 11am–1pm & 2–4pm
(closed Aug & Sept). Free. Fronted
by Corinthian columns and
surmounted by an impressive
dome, this imposing riverside
structure has seen many a legal
hearing since it first opened
its doors in 1802. Like the
Custom House (see p.133) the
building was designed by James
Gandon, and took some sixteen
years to complete at a cost of
£200,000 sterling. The four
courts embodied in its name
were those of the Chancery,
Common Pleas, Exchequer and
Kings Bench, though somehow
a fifth, the Judicature, was
forgotten when naming the
building. The Four Courts was
seized by Republicans opposed
to the Anglo-Irish Treaty in
1921, and heavily bombarded
by Free State forces during the
subsequent Civil War using,
ironically, howitzers borrowed
from the British. However,
before the siege came to its
inevitable end, the
rebels accidentally
set off explosives
inside the building,
destroying the Public
Records Office
and innumerable
irreplaceable historic
documents. After
rebuilding, the Four
Courts reopened in
1931 and nowadays

▼ THE FOUR COURTS

▲ MUMMIES, ST MICHAN'S CRYPTS

houses the High Court of Justice. A better – and often more entertaining – bet, though, is to take a seat in the District Court, entered via Chancery Place, which deals with less salubrious local matters.

St Michan's Church

Church St ☎01/872 4154. March–Oct Mon–Fri 10am–12.30pm & 2–4.30pm, Sat 10am–12.45pm; Nov–Feb Mon–Fri 12.30–3.30pm, Sat 10am–12.45pm. €3.50. Dating from 1095, St Michan's was constructed by the Vikings in honour of a Danish bishop. The church was substantially rebuilt some six hundred years later and its interior has subsequently undergone much refurbishment. Next to the church organ, reputedly once played by Handel, is the unusual Penitents' Pew, in which parishioners knelt facing the congregation to confess their errant ways.

However, it's the church's vaults that hold the most fascination. Guided tours descend an almost sheer staircase to view the contents of tiny crypts, including, most notably, a dozen bodies, some dating back some seven hundred years. These have been mummified, a process caused by two factors: the vaults' limestone walls, which absorb the air's natural moisture, and the methane produced by vegetation rotting below the floor. One of the mummies is believed to have been a Crusader, another a nun and a third, which lacks a hand, may have been a repentant thief. Another crypt contains John and Henry Sheares, executed for their role in the 1798 Rebellion, as well as the death mask of one of the Rebellion's leaders, Wolfe Tone. Two other rebels, Oliver Bond and the Reverend William Jackson, are buried in the church's graveyard, and some reckon an unmarked grave to the rear houses the body of Robert Emmet, leader of the 1803 rising.

Smithfield Village and Dublin Horse Fair

Horse Fair first Sun of each month 9am–noon. Less an identifiable community than an ongoing process of redevelopment, the centrepiece of this modern "village" is the old, broad, cobbled Smithfield itself, the city's largest civic open space. Surrounded by rising blocks of executive flats, a luxury hotel, *Chief O'Neill's* (see p.195), and new shops and restaurants Smithfield still manages to host one of Dublin's major sights. The Dublin Horse Fair draws plenty of traders and other horse-lovers

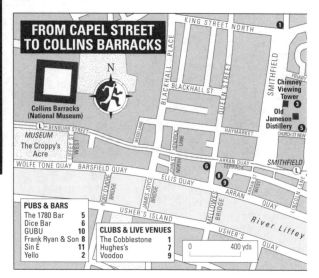

FROM CAPEL STREET TO COLLINS BARRACKS

Collins Barracks (National Museum)

MUSEUM
The Croppy's Acre

PUBS & BARS	
The 1780 Bar	5
Dice Bar	6
GUBU	10
Frank Ryan & Son	8
Sin É	11
Yello	2

CLUBS & LIVE VENUES	
The Cobblestone	1
Hughes's	7
Voodoo	9

Chimney Viewing Tower

Old Jameson Distillery

SMITHFIELD

0   400 yds

River Liffey

keen to spot a bargain, and onlookers geeing up teenagers willing to race bareback around the surrounding streets. From mid–November until early January, Smithfield also becomes host to a massive open-air ice-rink (see ⓦwww.smithfieldonice .ie for details).

The Old Jameson Distillery

Bow St, Smithfield ⓣ01/807 2355, ⓦwww.whiskeytours.ie. Daily 9.30am–6pm; last tour 5.30pm. €8.75. The

▼ THE OLD JAMESON DISTILLERY

buildings where John Jameson set up his whiskey company have long been turned over to a somewhat touristy shrine to "the hard stuff" – indeed, Jameson's has been distilled in Midleton, Co. Cork for some years. Following a short video on the history of Irish whiskey production, guided tours take visitors through the process itself, taking in factors such as milling and mashing – the "washback" mashing barrel was once cleaned by the hazardous means of lowering a worker into its innards, using a candle first to test for carbon dioxide – to the utterly essential distillation element. While the separation of water from alcohol only occurs once in bourbon and twice in Scotch, the production of *uisce beatha* (Irish for "water of life", anglicized to "whiskey") involves a three-stage process. The resulting liquid, known as "young whiskey", is diluted to 62 percent alcohol via the addition of water, and then left

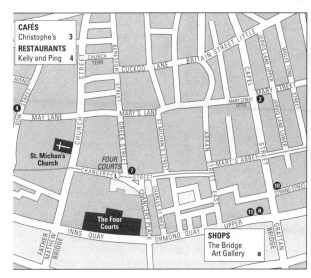

CAFÉS	
Christophe's	3
RESTAURANTS	
Kelly and Ping	4

St. Michan's Church

FOUR COURTS

The Four Courts

SHOPS	
The Bridge	
Art Gallery	a

in imported oak casks, formerly used for sherry, port or brandy. Typically, maturation lasts for five to seven years, though some rare whiskeys are left for 25 years before bottling – two percent of the alcohol disappears in the interim, known as the "angel's share". The tour ends with a tasting exercise in which three testers

▼ THE CHIMNEY VIEWING TOWER, SMITHFIELD

are requested to sample four brands of whiskey, plus one each of bourbon and Scotch before plumping for their favourite – if you want to take part, make sure to volunteer at the tour's beginning, otherwise you'll only receive a complimentary glass of Jameson's from the bar.

The Chimney Viewing Tower

Smithfield Village ☎01/817 3800, ⊛www.chiefoneills.com. June–Aug Mon–Sat 10am–5.30pm, Sun 11am–5.30pm; rest of the year call for times. €5 – tickets from the adjacent *Chief O'Neill's* hotel's shop. The former chimney of the Jameson Distillery stands somewhat distant from Smithfield's modern development. A lift attached to the chimney's side whisks passengers up the tower's 185 feet to an enclosed viewing platform at the summit. The panoramic views from here are markedly different to the vistas from the Guinness Storehouse's *Gravity Bar* (see p.125) and vividly present the city of Dublin in action.

▲ NATIONAL MUSEUM OF IRELAND, COLLINS BARRACKS

National Museum of Ireland: Decorative Arts and History

Collins Barracks, Benburb St ☎01/677 7444, ⊛www.museum.ie. Tues–Sat 10am–5pm, Sun 2–5pm; free. Guided tours daily 3.30pm; €2. Museum LUAS stop. This excellent museum gets far fewer visitors than its first-class exhibitions deserve – and there's no excuse now that it is easily accessible by LUAS. Before entering the museum, it's worth investigating the former Dún Laoghaire–Nelson's Pillar tram gracing the museum's forecourt – at one hundred paces broad and long, it was once Europe's largest regimental drilling square.

Inside, the wonderful series of galleries is devoted to the fine arts of Ireland and selections from abroad. Unquestionably, the best of these is Curator's Choice, on the first floor of the west block, which is selected by museum curators from all over Ireland. Among its draws are a medieval oak carving of St Molaise; the extravagant cabinet presented by Oliver Cromwell to his daughter Bridget in 1652; and the remarkable fourteenth-century Chinese porcelain Fonthill Vase. The Out of Storage section is another highlight,

bringing together everything from decorative glassware to a seventeenth-century suit of Samurai armour, while others focus on coinage, silverware, period furniture, costumes and scientific instruments. A recent and insightful addition covers neo-Celtic art from the 1400s onwards and there is also a variety of temporary exhibitions.

The Croppy's Acre

Wolfe Tone Quay. Many of those executed for their part in the 1798 Rebellion are buried in The Croppy's Acre, an enclosed area just below Collins Barracks. A Wicklow granite monument marks the precise location of their graves. The origins of the term "Croppy" have been much debated, though it is commonly believed to have been ascribed to Republicans who wore their hair closely cropped at the back in the style of French revolutionaries. One of the most famous songs of the 1798 Rebellion is "The Croppy Boy", which Loyalists countered with their own "Croppies Lie Down".

Shops

The Bridge Art Gallery

6 Ormond Quay Upper ☎01/872 9702. Contemporary arts and

▼ JAPANESE HEAD ARMOUR, NATIONAL MUSEUM OF IRELAND

crafts ranging from ceramics and sculpture to paintings and prints, often at prices that won't see you digging too deep into your pockets. The gallery at the rear also hosts exhibitions of innovative work.

Cafés

Christophe's

Duck Lane. Closed Sun. Set next to the Old Jameson Distillery, large, swish *Christophe's* provides everything from excellent coffee and bagels to full breakfasts, roasts and salads.

Restaurants

Kelly and Ping

Smithfield Village ☎01/817 3840 ⓦwww.kellyandping.com. Closed Sun. With its tasteful, breezy design and a flavoursome range of Thai-influenced dishes, *K&P* is one of Smithfield's major successes. The restaurant offers very popular, superb value set lunches (€13.50) and "early bird" evening meals (4–7pm, €20).

Pubs and bars

The 1780 Bar

Corner of Bow St/Church St New. A cheery and airy bar, the *1780* serves a reliable pint and has a popular lunchtime menu of excellent soups (carrot and ginger is a particular favourite), as well as a range of paninis and club sandwiches. Newspapers for browsing are also to hand.

Dice Bar

78 Queen St. Late opening Fri & Sat until 2.30am. Low-lit and compact, the *Dice Bar* is an ultra-cool New York-style joint that remains atmospheric without ever feeling too cramped. Most of the ales come from the Dublin Brewing Company and DJs play nightly, the music ranging from Johnny Cash to French hip-hop, via Beck, blues and ska.

GUBU

7–8 Capel St. The ex-Taoiseach Charles Haughey once commented that a certain political controversy was "grotesque, unprecedented, bizarre and unbelievable" and the acronym GUBU was subsequently coined. This gay but straight-friendly bar, lushly decorated with banquettes for lounging, may not always live up to that image, but its Wednesday night G-Spot cabaret, featuring Busty Lycra, comes close. Friday's Eighties-disco-inspired Kajagubu is otherwise as wild as it gets.

Frank Ryan & Son

5 Queen St. Definitely a place for respite from the city's hurly-burly, this sociable, old-fashioned bar is cosiness incarnate. The friendly staff serve a grand pint of stout.

Sin É

14–15 Ormond Quay Upper. Owned by the same team as *The Cobblestone*, this candle-lit bar appeals to a lively cosmopolitan crowd because of its wide selection of brews, including draught wheat beers and bottled Leffe and Chimay, and eclectic choice of nightly musical entertainment (sometimes live gigs, but mostly DJs), plus free finger food some evenings.

Yello

61–63 Capel St. A recent addition to Dublin's gay scene, *Yello*

▲ HUGHES'S BAR

has so far proved deservedly popular with both gay men and lesbians. There's usually a lively crowd here, especially for Friday's hilarious Kylie Karaoke.

Clubs and live venues

The Cobblestone

77 King St North. Arguably the best traditional-music venue in Dublin, this dark, cosy, wooden-floored bar is also a fine place to sample the hoppy products of the nearby Dublin Brewery Company. High-quality sessions take place nightly from around 9pm (from 7pm on Thurs), and on Sunday afternoons.

Hughes's

19 Chancery St. Tucked away behind The Four Courts, *Hughes's* attracts the cream of the city's traditional musicians to its nightly sessions (from around 9pm until closing time). Fridays can draw a large crowd, so arrive early to grab a seat.

Voodoo

39 Arran Quay. Much larger than its exterior might suggest, *Voodoo* is the bigger sister to the *Dice Bar* (see p.151) and packs a similarly powerful punch, often showcasing the best of the local indie-band scene.

From Capel Street to Collins Barracks   PLACES

Phoenix Park

Europe's largest urban walled park, Phoenix Park's undulating landscape sprawls across some 1750 acres. Much of the park is open space, sparsely dotted with trees, shrubs and wild flowers, though there are also areas of woodland and hawthorn, ponds and a lake. Overall, it's an ideal place to escape the city's bustle, offering plenty of pleasant spots for a picnic, as well as being a popular venue for sports, with cricket, football, hurling and even polo played regularly on its numerous pitches. Developed as a deer park for Charles II (a small herd still ranges across its fields), the park takes its name from Phoenix House, the original residence of the British viceroys, a space now occupied by the tumbledown Magazine Fort, though the area's name originates in the Irish fionn uisce ("clear water"). As well as its greenery, there are some notable monuments to explore, including the Phoenix Monument, dating from 1747, the 100-foot-high stainless steel Papal Cross, marking the place where the late Pope John Paul II celebrated Mass in 1979, and the impressive Wellington Monument. Other than open-top tour buses, no public transport runs inside the park, so be prepared to burn some shoe-leather, and bring your own refreshments as food and drink establishments are few and far between.

Dublin Zoo

☎ 01/474 8900, 🖳 www.dublinzoo.ie. Mon–Sat 9.30am–6pm, Sun 10.30am–6pm (Oct–Feb closes at dusk). Adults €13, children under 3 free, children under 16 €8.50. The second-oldest zoo in Europe once bred the lion that used to growl ferociously at the beginning of films produced by Hollywood's MGM studios. Nowadays, the zoo focuses firmly on breeding threatened species, such as Amur tigers and Siamang gibbons, for future release into the wild. Spread over sixty acres, its attractions include the African Plains, featuring giraffes, rhinos and hippos, and another devoted to South American creatures such as tamarins and toucans. Alongside aviaries and reptile houses, there are also areas for polar bears and gorillas, and the wonderfully sociable meerkats. The regular new-born arrivals draw the crowds and provide photo opportunities, and there's

▼ PAPAL CROSS

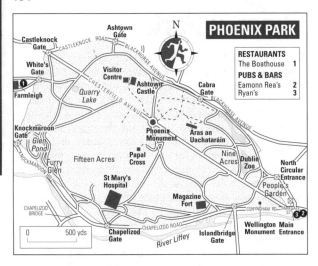

PHOENIX PARK

RESTAURANTS
The Boathouse	1

PUBS & BARS
Eamonn Rea's	2
Ryan's	3

▲ DUBLIN ZOO

a City Farm to keep younger children happy.

Áras an Uachtaráin

Sat 10.30am–4.30pm. Entry by guided tours; free; tickets from the Phoenix Park Visitor Centre (see below) on the day. The home of Britain's viceroys from the 1780s until Ireland's independence, this impressive Palladian abode, graced by a broad frontage and a four-pillared entrance, has been the official residence of the president of Ireland ever since Douglas Hyde, the first incumbent, took up office in 1938. Tours of the building only take place when the current president is not in residence and start from the Phoenix Park Visitor Centre (minibus transport is provided). A small exhibition centre is devoted to the building's history and visitors are whisked through a small section of the grandiosely decorated house, including the State Reception Rooms and the Presidential Office. Look out for some impressive stuccowork by the renowned Lafranchini brothers.

Phoenix Park Visitor Centre and Ashtown Castle

☎01/677 0095, ⊛www.heritageireland
.ie. Jan to mid-March & Oct daily
10am–5pm, mid- to end March daily
10am–5.30pm, April–Sept daily
10am–6pm, Nov & Dec Sat & Sun
10am–5pm. €2.75 (includes tour
of Ashtown Castle); Heritage Card.
Accessed via a lane just north

▲ ÁRAS AN UACHTARÁIN

10am–6pm (gates close 4.45pm). Free. Bus #37 from Hawkins St to Castleknock Gate. White's Gate on the park's northwestern fringe provides access to the splendid Georgian-Victorian Farmleigh, one of the most striking buildings in the city, famed for its gorgeous interiors. The house is set in equally impressive eighty-acre wooded grounds, which feature an attractive ornamental lake, sunken garden and a 120-foot clocktower which houses the estate's water-tank. Farmleigh was constructed in 1752 for the Trench family and later purchased by Edward Cecil Guinness, the first Earl of Iveagh, as a rustic residence offering easy access to his brewery. Extensions took place during the 1880s, and the Guinnesses remained in residence until the death of the third earl in 1992. Farmleigh was then purchased by the Irish government for use as a state guest house.

Tours commence in the dining room, whose unusual

of the Phoenix Monument, the visitor centre recounts the story of the park through the ages, focusing on its wildlife and flora. As well as displaying the chair in which the late Pope John Paul II sat to celebrate Mass in the park in 1979, you can view the rejected designs for the Wellington Monument, some of which are frankly bizarre, as well as a reconstruction of a Megalithic cist grave, thought to date from the fourth century BC, whose original was discovered in the park in 1838. An enjoyable interactive section for children encourages an understanding of forest life and there are also often other temporary exhibitions. Next door to the centre is Ashtown Castle, an early seventeenth-century tower house whose existence was only uncovered when the former residence of the Papal Nuncio, which had been constructed around it, was demolished in 1978. Guided tours reveal some of the tower's integral defensive features.

Farmleigh

☎01/815 5900, ⊛www.farmleigh.ie. House: Easter–Oct Thurs–Sun & Bank Holiday Mondays 10.30am–5pm. Tours may not be available if a visiting delegation is in residence (call in advance to check). Grounds: daily

▼ ASHTOWN CASTLE

▲ BLUE ROOM FIREPLACE, FARMLEIGH

decorations include statues of Bacchus either side of the fireplace and a clock inlaid in its centre, all set off by seventeenth-century Italian silk tapestries. The hall features Bohemian chandeliers made from Waterford crystal and a pair of debtors' chairs in which the pauper's legs would be trapped until agreeing to pay their debts. The library contains four thousand items on loan from the Iveagh Collection, including a first edition of *Ulysses* and books dating back to the twelfth century. The Blue Room, dedicated to Ireland's Nobel Prize winners, has another strange fireplace, this one situated below a window and looking out towards a fountain, in a manner reminiscent of Magritte. However, the real treat is the ballroom, decorated with ornate plasterwork in the style of Louis XVI, and featuring an Irish oak floor constructed of wood originally intended for Guinness barrels. From here, delicate linen portières fringe doors leading you to a massive, plant-stocked conservatory. Behind the house there's a tearoom in the stable block.

People's Garden

The People's Garden, by the park's main entrance on Parkgate Street, dates from 1864 and, neat and systematic, retains much of the original horticultural style of the Victorian era. Bounded by hedges, yet only a stone's throw from a major thoroughfare, this is a relatively peaceful spot in which to enjoy the sweet scent of the variety of blooms in the parterres. There's also a statue of Seán Heuston, who was executed for his part in the 1916 Easter Rising.

Wellington Monument

The Wellington Monument took some 44 years to complete before it was finally unveiled in 1861. The obelisk – the tallest of its kind in the British Isles at some two hundred feet – features bas-reliefs, using bronze from cannons captured at Waterloo, depicting scenes from the successful military campaigns of the "Iron Duke".

Magazine Fort

Alongside Military Road is the Magazine Fort, dating from 1734, and built on the site of the original Phoenix House. The fort once housed the munitions of the British garrison based in Dublin, but now lies in dereliction. It's an easy climb up the hill to take a trip around its walls and take in some fine views of the park and surrounding area.

Restaurants

The Boathouse

Farmleigh. Sat, Sun & public holidays noon–5.30pm. Set beside Farmleigh's ornamental lake, and offering alfresco waterside dining on its decking, this cheerful restaurant serves light meals with a blend of Irish and Italian influences.

Pubs and bars

Eamonn Rea's

25 Parkgate St. A comfortable and homely alternative to *Ryan's*, *Rea's* is very definitely a locals' pub, serving a more than decent pint (one of the city's cheapest) and hosting impromptu quizzes. The walls exhibit hurling memorabilia.

Ryan's

28 Parkgate St. *Ryan's* is the long-time challenger to the reputation of *Mulligan's* (see p.81) for serving the best pint of Guinness in the city, owing to its proximity to the brewery just across the river. At one time it was only a plain bar with two stout pumps and one for the lager (the latter allegedly for eccentrics and country visitors). Nowadays it's a pleasantly refurbished place – the Guinness is still grand – and dishes up fine seafood in its upstairs restaurant.

Along the Grand Canal

The Grand Canal runs through south Dublin from its confluence with the River Liffey, through the leafy, affluent suburb of Ballsbridge and the more working-class, ethnically-mixed Portobello, before heading away to the west of Ireland. Strolling the canal towpath is enjoyable in itself, especially along the verdant, surprisingly bucolic stretch between the docklands and Portobello. There are a number of attractions on the way, including three specialist museums, as well as literary connections with the poet/novelist Patrick Kavanagh and dramatist George Bernard Shaw. After years of decline, the adjacent canal docks have been earmarked for rejuvenation over the next few years and, though currently a mass of construction work, the area will feature new housing, hotels and, if plans go ahead, the newly relocated Abbey Theatre.

Waterways Visitor Centre

Grand Canal Quay ⊛www.waterwaysireland.org. June–Sept daily 9.30am–5.30pm, Oct–May Wed–Sun 12.30–5pm. €2.50. Known by Dubliners as "the box in the docks", this cubiform visitor centre is perched on stilts above the waters of the Grand Canal Dock. The nautical theme continues inside too, the interior done out with porthole-style

▼ THE GRAND CANAL

windows and wooden decking. The centre's displays explain the development of the canal system and local ecology, as well as how the waterways have inspired artists and writers. Plenty of literature is on sale for those wishing to learn more.

National Print Museum

Garrison Chapel, Beggars Bush, Haddington Rd ☎01/660 3770, ⊛ireland.iol.ie/~npmuseum/index.html. Mon–Fri 9am–5pm, Sat & Sun 2pm–5pm. €3.50. Housed in the former chapel of barracks constructed in the 1860s (and with a café next door, if you're parched), this specialist museum is devoted to all things "hot metal". Tours begin with a short video describing the history of printing before you are taken by your guide into the world of monotype and linotype and to watch the resident typesetter in action. There's an impressive range of presses to investigate, exhibits on bookbinding, and an

▲ TYPESETTER AT WORK, NATIONAL PRINT MUSEUM

Kerry monastery, record the arrival in 1079 of five Jews "from over the sea", but it was not until the late fifteenth century, following their expulsion from Spain and Portugal, that Ireland became home to a significant Jewish population. At its peak, by the end of World War II, this had reached some 5500 people, though this has now dropped to around two thousand, of whom about half live in Dublin. Tucked away on a back street just north of the Grand Canal these two former terraced houses were converted into a synagogue in the early twentieth century to serve Jews living in the area. However, by the 1970s, most of its congregation had moved out to the suburbs and the building lay dormant until 1985, when it was reopened as a museum by the then President of Israel, Chaim Herzog, who was himself born in Belfast and had studied in Dublin. The ground floor contains a number of informative and often intriguing exhibits documenting Irish Jews' social and cultural history, as well as subjects such as trade, sport and references in *Ulysses*

intriguing range of trade union banners, including one from the Bookbinders' Union itself proclaiming "Bind Right with Might". The upstairs gallery displays original newspaper pages recounting major events in world history.

Irish Jewish Museum

3–4 Walworth Rd ☏ 01/490 1857. May–Sept Tues, Thurs & Sun 11am–3.30pm, Oct–April Sun 10.30am–2.30pm. Free. The twelfth-century Annals of Inisfallen, compiled in a Co.

▼ IRISH JEWISH MUSEUM

Along the Grand Canal · PLACES

◀ ⑥ (200yds)

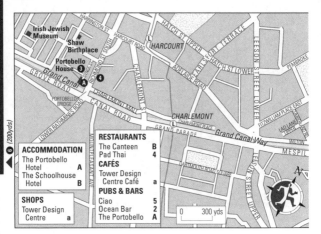

0   300 yds

(one of Joyce's protagonists, Leopold Bloom, was, of course, Jewish). The original room of worship itself is on view on the first floor, as well as displays on Judaica, including circumcision instruments, and a wedding canopy.

The Shaw Birthplace

33 Synge St ☎01/475 0854, ⊛www
.visitdublin.com. May–Sept Mon, Tues, Thurs & Fri 10am–1pm & 2–5pm, Sat, Sun & public holidays 2–5pm. €6.50.
The acclaimed playwright and all-round man of letters George Bernard Shaw was born in this unpretentious terraced house

in July 1856. His family, having fallen on hard times, stayed here for ten years before moving to Harcourt Street.

The self-guided tour of the house, which has been kitted out with appropriate period furniture, decor and plenty of Shaw memorabilia, begins in the basement kitchen where the young GBS often sought solace away from the "loveless" atmosphere of his parents' upstairs domain. On this floor too is the starkly plain maid's room and a small but neat garden replete with an austere outside privy.

A canalside stroll

One of the best canalside walks is along the path that runs from the Macartney Bridge, more commonly known as the **Baggot Street Bridge**, past Leeson Street and along to Portobello. A verdant, tree-lined stretch whose waters are populated by swans and the occasional barge, it is an area associated with the poet **Patrick Kavanagh** (1904–1967), famed for his novel *Tarry Flynn* and semi-autobiographical *The Green Fool*. Kavanagh also edited and published his own magazine, dedicated to literature and politics, and was a key figure in the city's cultural life. He lived for a while on both Pembroke Road and nearby Raglan Road, and wrote a song bearing the latter street's name, which remains one of Ireland's most popular. There are two monuments to him by the canal near the *Mespil Hotel* on Mespil Road: a **memorial seat** erected by his friends and a life-size bronze **statue** of him perched on a bench by one of his favourite spots.

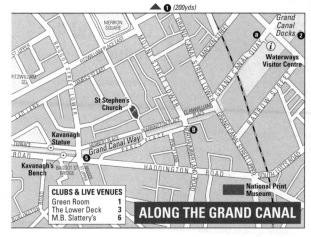

Upstairs are the family bedrooms – Shaw's is tiny – and a remarkably claustrophobic parlour, all chintz and red velvet. On the top floor is the more expansive reception room equipped with a period pianoforte. It was here that Shaw's mother held her musical soirees and the young Shaw gained his first musical insights – he was later to become a critic.

Shops

The Tower Design Centre
Grand Canal Quay. Mon–Fri 9am–5pm. The Tower's five floors house a range of studios where working craftspeople display their wares for purchase, most also accepting commissions. Several studios are devoted to jewellery while others feature hand engraving, heraldry, sculpture, leatherware, handbag design, and fine and applied arts.

Cafés

Tower Design Centre Café
Grand Canal Quay. Mon–Fri 9am–5pm. Offering coffee, sandwiches and snacks, as well as wholesome lunches at reasonable prices, this friendly place makes a good starting point for an exploration of the Grand Canal.

Restaurants

The Canteen
2–8 Northumberland Ave, Ballsbridge ☎01/614 4333. Closed Sat lunchtime and Sun evening. Justifiably popular thanks to its reasonably priced but superb gourmet lunches, such as pan-fried John Dory and tomato and gorgonzola tart, and Sunday brunch (noon–4pm), The Canteen also serves a tempting evening menu with seafood (such as Carlingford oysters) well to the fore, alongside a range of feasts to satisfy carnivores, including roast loin of smoked Kassler pork.

Pad Thai
30 Richmond St South ☎01/475 5551. This cosy place by Portobello Bridge serves a variety of snacks as well as a budget-priced set lunch. Its evening meals of delicious soups, finger food, such as the satay-like *moo ping*

▲ PAD THAI

or corn cakes, and a generous range of main courses are well worth queuing for if you've forgotten to book a table.

Pubs and bars

Ciao

Baggot St Bridge ☎01/799 6126. A spacious and convivial bar, especially busy during weekday lunchtimes, *Ciao* also provides a range of reasonably priced meals all day and offers live jazz every Friday (8.30–11pm).

Ocean Bar

Charlotte Quay Dock, Ringsend Rd. Modern, bright and stylish, the *Ocean*'s canalside location makes it a relaxed place to observe all the activity in the surrounding docklands over a rewarding pint.

The Portobello

33 Richmond St South. A roomy bar renowned for its excellent carvery lunches (12.15–3pm) – Sundays are especially popular – and range of hearty evening meals (4–8.45pm).

Clubs and live venues

Green Room

Holiday Inn, 99–107 Pearse St ☎01/670 5202, ⊛www .greenroomdublin.ie. Petite but well equipped, with a good sound-system, the *Green Room* specializes in concerts by solo artists and small groups at the traditional end of the music spectrum.

The Lower Deck

Portobello Harbour ☎01/475 1423. Dating from 1867, this large, popular bar offers well-kept ales and stouts, good service and a diverse range of nightly entertainment, including decidedly left-field indie bands.

M.B. Slattery's

217–219 Lower Rathmines Rd ☎01/497 2052. A mile south of Portobello Bridge, this friendly, long-standing landmark on Dublin's entertainment scene has a cosy front bar and a more spacious alternative to the rear. It's renowned for its music (covering everything from traditional to rock and blues), not least because entry's free.

▼ OCEAN BAR

The southern outskirts

The diffuse southern outskirts of Dublin, which extend as far as the Wicklow Mountains, hold two focuses of attention for the visitor. In the green, almost village-like suburb of Rathfarnham, you'll find a much-redeveloped sixteenth-century castle and the Irish-language school founded by revolutionary Pádraig Pearse, now a museum. Along the coast, southeast of the city, lie Sandycove's James Joyce Museum and the charming, historic neighbourhood of Dalkey. The DART train ride here is a scenic attraction in itself, displaying the great sweep of Dublin Bay before dramatically skirting Dalkey and Killiney hills and arrowing off towards Bray and Greystones (see p.179).

Pearse Museum

St Enda's Park, Grange Rd, Rathfarnham ☎01/493 4208, ⊛www .heritageireland.ie. Museum: Feb–April, Sept & Oct 10am–5pm; May–Aug 10am–5.30pm; Nov–Jan 10am–4pm; closed 1pm–2pm; free. St Enda's Park daily: Feb–March 10am–5.30pm; April, Sept & Oct 10am–7pm; May–Aug 10am–8pm; Nov–Jan 10am–4.30pm; free. Bus #16 from College Green. The informative Pearse Museum explores in detail the life and principles of Pádraig Pearse and is housed in the former St Enda's School, which he founded in 1910 with the aim of promoting Gaelic culture and Nationalist ideals. All classes were taught in Irish and students were encouraged to take part in Gaelic football and hurling. Pearse's renown, however, draws not from his educational work – the school recruited fewer pupils than expected and closed in 1916 – but from his role as one of the leaders of the Easter Rising (see p.131).

A visit best begins in the rooms to the rear where displays focus on Pearse's background, including his birth in 1879 on Great Brunswick Street (now Pearse Street). Other rooms recount the school's history and Pearse's educational philosophy, a key part of which was "special attention to character building and the development of those elements which promote true manhood, honour and good citizenship". Upstairs, the dormitory's original straw mattresses and rugged bed frames suggest that bodily comfort was not one of those elements. Pearse was also a reasonably successful playwright, but whether he was a good teacher was questioned by James Joyce, who took Pearse's Irish classes at University College but left after three months, deploring his tutor's attempts to elevate the Irish language by denigrating English.

The museum has tearooms (May–Sept weekends only) and a nature study centre where you can acquire details of the nature trail around St Enda's Park. The park also offers pleasant riverside walks and a waterfall, as well as a walled garden which hosts summer outdoor concerts (call ☎01/493 4208 for details).

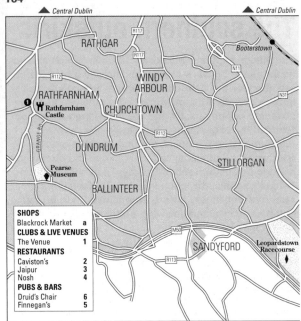

▲ Central Dublin   ▲ Central Dublin

RATHGAR

WINDY ARBOUR

RATHFARNHAM

Rathfarnham Castle

CHURCHTOWN

Booterstown

DUNDRUM

Pearse Museum

STILLORGAN

BALLINTEER

SANDYFORD

Leopardstown Racecourse

SHOPS
Blackrock Market   a
CLUBS & LIVE VENUES
The Venue   1
RESTAURANTS
Caviston's   2
Jaipur   3
Nosh   4
PUBS & BARS
Druid's Chair   6
Finnegan's   5

Rathfarnham Castle

Rathfarnham Rd, Rathfarnham
☎01/493 9462, ⊛www.heritageireland
.ie. May–Oct daily 9.30am–5pm; call
☎01/647 2466 for winter opening
hours. Guided tours €2; Heritage Card.
Bus #16 or #16A from College Green.
A squat and chunky edifice,
constructed from limestone and
brick, Rathfarnham Castle dates
from the 1580s and was built for
one Adam Loftus, a Yorkshire
clergyman who rose through
the clerical ranks to become
Archbishop of Dublin, and later
Lord Chancellor of Ireland
and the first Provost of Trinity
College. The castle was besieged
during the 1641 Rebellion and
Cromwell's troops were based
here during the English Civil
War, which began the following
year. The building subsequently
passed through numerous hands,
including those of William

Connolly of Castletown renown
(see p.183), until it was re-
acquired by descendants of
Loftus.

The castle's battlements
were removed in 1720, but
it still retains a characteristic
sixteenth-century appearance.
Its innards, however, were much
re-modelled in the 1770s, under
the direction of Henry Loftus,
Earl of Ely, who employed
notable architects and painters
to produce suitably lavish
interiors for his grand-scale
society entertaining.

The castle later fell into
serious decline and, in 1912,
was purchased by property
developers, who built houses
and a golf course in the
extensive grounds. By the
1980s the castle was semi-
derelict; hour-long guided tours
concentrate very heavily on

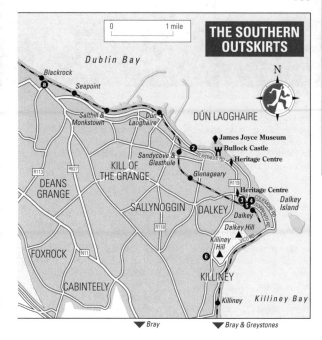

the renovation work that has subsequently taken place and draw attention to the changes in the building's structure uncovered by the process. The castle's kitchen wing has been fully restored, though work inside the main section is ongoing and now includes a room dedicated to temporary exhibitions of artwork.

Writers' Museum, Shaw Birthplace. Sandycove & Glasthule DART station, then a 10min walk, down Islington Ave then east along the seafront. This diverting memorial to Joyce is housed inside an impressive Martello tower overlooking the Irish Sea, one of fifteen such towers erected between Dublin and Bray in 1804–06 against the threat of invasion by Napoleon.

The James Joyce Museum

Sandycove Point, Sandycove ☎01/280 9265. March–Oct Mon–Sat 10am–1pm & 2–5pm, Sun 2–6pm. €6.50, or €11 combined ticket with any one of the following: Malahide Castle, Fry Model Railway, Dublin

▼ THE JAMES JOYCE MUSEUM, SANDYCOVE

▲ FORTY FOOT POOL, SANDYCOVE

Built with eight-feet-thick, circular, granite walls and an armoured door twelve feet off the ground as the only entrance, the towers never fired a shot in anger.

Joyce stayed here for just a week, in September 1904, a month before he left the country for Italy with Nora Barnacle. At the time, his host, the writer and wit Oliver St John Gogarty, was renting the tower from the War Office for £8 a year as digs during his medical studies. Joyce immortalized the tower as the setting for the opening chapter of his masterpiece, *Ulysses* – and Gogarty as "stately, plump Buck Mulligan" – and it's now the focus for readings and celebrations every year on June 16, Bloomsday (see p.208).

Opened in 1962 by Sylvia Beach, who first published *Ulysses* in Paris in 1922, the museum displays Joyce's guitar, waistcoat and walking stick, as well as one of two official death masks (the other is in Zurich, where he died in 1941). There are also copious letters, photos, and first and rare editions, notably a *Ulysses* beautifully illustrated by Matisse. On the first floor, Gogarty's living quarters in the former guardroom have been re-created as Joyce described them, and you can climb up to the gun platform on the roof for panoramic views of Dublin Bay.

Just beyond the tower on the rocky headland is Dublin's most famous bathing spot, the Forty Foot Pool (so called because of a forty-foot-deep fishing hole off the coast here). It was traditionally for male nude bathers only, but nowadays hardy, togged souls of both sexes jump-start their hearts here throughout the year.

Dalkey

Around the coast from Sandycove, Dalkey (pronounced "Dawky") is a pretty seaside suburb set against the tree-clad slopes of Dalkey Hill. In medieval times, it prospered as a fortified settlement and the main port of Dublin, until the dredging of the River Liffey in the sixteenth century took away its business. Nowadays, with the building of the railway, Dalkey's characterful old houses and villas are much sought after by well-to-do commuters, as well as celebrities seeking privacy.

Just down Railway Road from Dalkey DART station, Castle

▼ DALKEY

Street boasts two fortified warehouses from Dalkey's medieval heyday (if you happen to be making the fifteen-minute walk from Sandycove to Dalkey, you'll pass a third fortification, Bullock Castle, on Ulverton Road, built by the Cistercians in the twelfth century to protect Bullock fishing harbour). Goat Castle, across the road from Archibold's Castle, serves as an attractive and well-designed Heritage Centre (⊕01/285 8366, ⊛www.dalkeycastle.com; Jan–March Sat & Sun 11am–5pm; April–Dec Mon–Fri 9.30am–5pm, Sat & Sun 11am–5pm; €5). The detailed exhibition, with panels written by playwright and local resident Hugh Leonard, covers the town's history, especially its transport systems and literary associations, the latter including an exhibit on Joyce who set the second chapter of *Ulysses* in Dalkey. The castle interior is impressive in itself, and fine views are to be had from the battlements.

The Heritage Centre regularly organizes interesting guided tours in the town (phone for details), including a trip to Dalkey Island, three hundred yards offshore from Coliemore Harbour, where you'll find a Martello tower and the ruins of the medieval St Begnet's Oratory.

Shops

Blackrock Market

19A Main St, Blackrock. Sat 11am–5.30pm, Sun noon–5.30pm. Hugely varied and popular weekend market, just behind the high street of this southern suburb and close to the DART station. Antiques and bric-a-brac, books and CDs, crafts, jewellery, shoes and clothes are on sale.

Restaurants

Caviston's

59 Glasthule Rd, Sandycove ⊕01/280 9245, ⊛www.cavistons.com. Tues–Sat,

Dalkey and Killiney Hills

A walk up adjoining Dalkey and Killiney Hills, before descending to Killiney DART station, offers panoramic views of the city and its environs, and can all be done in an hour and a half from Dalkey DART station at a moderate pace. From Dalkey, head southeast on Sorrento Road, and then either take the easier route to the right up Knocknacree and Torca roads, or continue along cliffside Vico Road, from where steps and a path ascend steeply. On Torca Road, Shaw fans might want to track down privately owned Torca Cottage, where GBS lived for several years as a boy and where he occasionally returned to write in later years. On the way to Dalkey Hill's summit, with its crenellated former telegraph station and fine views over Dublin Bay, you'll pass Dalkey quarry, which provided the granite blocks for the massive piers of Dún Laoghaire harbour below.

From here, follow the partly wooded ridge up to Killiney Hill, where a stone obelisk, built to provide work during the severe winter of 1741, enjoys even more glorious views, north to Howth and south to Killiney Bay and the Wicklow Mountains. From the obelisk, you can quickly descend to the park gate on Killiney Hill Road and refreshment at the cosy *Druid's Chair* pub directly opposite; from there it's a fifteen-minute walk down Victoria Road and Vico Road through the leafy and exclusive borough of Killiney, to the DART station by the beach.

▲ KILLINEY BAY

3 lunch sittings: noon, 1.30pm & 3pm. Handily placed between Sandycove and Glasthule DART station and the Joyce Museum, this restaurant works to a basic but hugely successful formula – the day's freshest fish and seafood cooked simply. Booking is essential and there are a few outside tables in summer.

Jaipur

21 Castle St, Dalkey ☏01/285 0552, ⊛www.jaipur.ie. Closed lunchtime Mon–Wed. Branch of the excellent South Great George's Street Indian restaurant – see p.119.

Nosh

111 Coliemore Rd, Dalkey ☏01/284 0666, ⊛www.nosh.ie. Closed Mon. Simple, stylish contemporary bistro just off Castle Street, offering everything from pan-fried duck with lentil ratatouille to Thai prawn curry in the evening, basic dishes such as fish pie and omelette for lunch, and brunch on Saturday and Sunday.

Pubs and bars

Finnegan's

Railway Rd, Dalkey. Dalkey's watering-hole of choice, handy for the DART station and tastefully smartened up to reflect the neighbourhood's gentrification, but offering traditional hospitality and a fine pint of Guinness.

Clubs and live venues

The Venue

Rathfarnham House, 19–20 Main St, Rathfarnham, ⊛www.thevenue.ie. Major and less well-known singers and bands play gigs at this spanking new venue which also hosts club nights (Thurs–Sat till late), including a hugely popular reggae session (first Fri each month).

The northern outskirts

The northern outskirts from Glasnevin across to Howth
hold an astonishing diversity of attractions, some of
which can easily be combined on the same excursion.
You'll want fine weather for a trip to the beautiful
Botanic Gardens and the adjacent Glasnevin Cemetery,
last resting-place for the major figures in Irish history
since 1832, which is best appreciated on a guided tour.
The exquisite architecture of the Casino at Marino and
the fright-fest of the Bram Stoker Museum have quite
different appeals, while the flora and fauna of North Bull
Island's nature reserve can be appreciated by anyone.
At the end of the DART line, Howth is an attractive
seaside village, with a good concentration of places to
eat and drink and a fine cliff walk.

National Botanic Gardens

Glasnevin Hill, off Botanic Rd, Glasnevin
℡01/837 7596. Summer Mon–Sat
9am–6pm, Sun 10am–6pm, winter
daily 10am–4.30pm; free. Guided
tour Sun 2.30pm; free. Glasshouses
open daily 10am–4.15pm. Bus #13
from Merrion Square or O'Connell
St, or #19 or #19A from South Great
George's St or O'Connell St. The
Botanic Gardens' fifty acres on
the south bank of the River
Tolka are a great place to
wander on a fine day, while
their magnificent Victorian

▼ NATIONAL BOTANIC GARDENS

wrought-iron glasshouses offer
diversion and shelter whatever
the weather. Laid out between
1795 and 1825 with a grant
from the Irish Parliament, the
gardens were, in 1844, the first
in the world to raise orchids
from seed and, in August of the
following year, the first to notice
the potato blight that brought
on the Great Famine. Nowadays,
a total of around twenty
thousand species and cultivated
varieties flourish here, including
an internationally important
collection of cycads, primitive
fern-like trees. Outdoor
highlights include the rose
garden, collections of heather
and rhododendrons, the Chinese
shrubbery and the arboretum.
Among the beautifully restored
glasshouses, the Curvilinear
Range was built by Richard
Turner, a Dublin ironfounder
who also built the palm house
at Kew Gardens in London, as
well as the huge conservatories
for the Great Exhibitions in
London in 1851 and Dublin
in 1853. There's a pleasant
self-service café with picture
windows in the visitor centre,

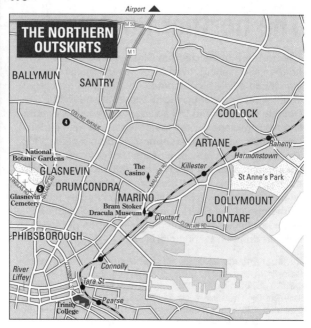

THE NORTHERN
OUTSKIRTS

Airport ▲

BALLYMUN SANTRY

COOLOCK

ARTANE Raheny
Harmonstown
Killester

National
Botanic Gardens
GLASNEVIN The
Casino
DRUMCONDRA
MARINO
Glasnevin Bram Stoker
Cemetery Dracula Museum Clontarf

St Anne's Park

DOLLYMOUNT

CLONTARF

PHIBSBOROUGH

River
Liffey Connolly

Tara St

Pearse

Trinity
College

serving cakes, sandwiches, salads
and simple hot meals.

Glasnevin Cemetery

Finglas Rd ☎ 01/830 1133, ⊛ www
.glasnevin-cemetery.ie. Mon–Sat
8am–4.30pm or later, Sun 9am–
4.30pm or later; free. Fascinating
guided tours Wed & Fri 2.30pm;
90min; free. Bus #40, #40A/B/C/D
from Parnell St. Fifteen minutes'
walk from the Botanic Gardens
(down Botanic Road, then
right into Prospect Way and
Finglas Road) lies the entrance
to Glasnevin Cemetery (aka
Prospect Cemetery), which
was founded as a burial
place for Catholics by the
nationalist political leader
Daniel O'Connell in 1832. It's
now the national cemetery,
open to all denominations and
groaning with Celtic crosses,
harps and other patriotic

emblems. O'Connell himself
is commemorated near the
entrance by a 160-foot-high
round tower, which managed to

▼ GLASNEVIN CEMETERY

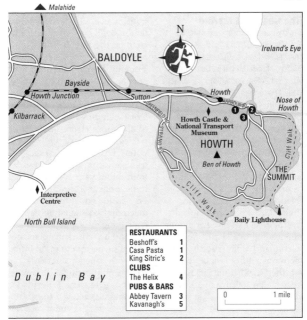

RESTAURANTS	
Beshoff's	1
Casa Pasta	1
King Sitric's	2
CLUBS	
The Helix	4
PUBS & BARS	
Abbey Tavern	3
Kavanagh's	5

survive a Loyalist bomb in the 1970s. His corpse was interred in the tower's crypt in 1869, having been brought home from Genoa where he died (in fact, not all of his body is here: his heart was buried in Rome).

To the left of the round tower, O'Connell's political descendant, Charles Stewart Parnell, who asked to be buried in a mass grave among the people of Ireland, is commemorated by a huge granite boulder from his estate at Avondale, County Wicklow. Other notable figures among the 1.2 million dead at Glasnevin – most of them gathered around O'Connell's tower – include Countess Markiewicz (see p.91), Éamon de Valera, prime minister, president and architect of modern Ireland, and his old rival Michael Collins, the most charismatic leader of the successful independence struggle. From the arts, there's Gerard Manley Hopkins (unmarked, in the Jesuit plot), W.B. Yeats's muse, Maud Gonne MacBride, Brendan Behan (see p.15) and Alfred Chester Beatty (see p.112). To the right of the tower is the Republican plot, with a memorial to hunger strikers, from Thomas Ashe who died in 1917 to Bobby Sands in 1981, while in front of the tower lie the recent graves of 18-year-old Kevin Barry and eight other Volunteers hanged by the British during the War of Independence; originally buried in Mountjoy Prison, their bodies were moved here with the full honours of a state funeral in October 2001.

The Casino at Marino

Cherrymount Crescent, off Malahide Rd, Marino ☎01/833 1618, ⊛www .heritageireland.ie. Guided tours Jan–March, May & Oct daily 10am–5pm; April Sat & Sun noon–5pm; June–Sept daily 10am–6pm; Nov & Dec Sat & Sun noon–4pm. €2.75; Heritage Card. Bus #20B from St Stephen's Green, #27 from Talbot St, #27B from Eden Quay or #42 from Lower Abbey St; or DART to Clontarf, then a 15min walk. Sited in the now unpromising suburb of Marino, the Casino is probably the finest piece of Neoclassical architecture in Ireland. It was commissioned by the first Earl of Charlemont, the leading intellectual figure of Georgian Dublin, shortly after he returned from eight years on the Grand Tour. Seeking to recreate an Italianate park with a *casino* ("little house" in Italian) as its focus, emphasizing the fine views of Dublin Bay that his estate then enjoyed, Charlemont turned to Sir William Chambers, the architect of Somerset House in London. Started in 1757, construction lasted nearly twenty years and cost £20,000 (equivalent to about €5 million today), almost bankrupting the estate.

The exterior is covered in exquisite carving in Portland stone, which reflects, notably in the ox skulls symbolizing animal sacrifice, the Enlightenment's preoccupation with pagan antiquity. To maintain the pristine Neoclassical appearance, Chambers disguised chimney pots as urns and used hollow Doric columns as drainpipes (with bronze chains inside to reduce the noise of the falling water). His most remarkable trick, however, was one of scale: from outside, the Casino appears to be a single-storey villa, but once inside you'll find three ingeniously designed floors containing a total of sixteen rooms. The remarkable standards of craftsmanship continue inside too, with ornate plasterwork and beautiful wooden floors inlaid in geometric patterns. Nothing was allowed to mar guests' views: the entrance doors convert into a window, and a series of tunnels was built under the surrounding land, including one that ran to the main house (now demolished) so that the servants wouldn't blot the landscape.

Bram Stoker Dracula Museum

Bar Code, West Wood Club, Clontarf Rd ☎01/805 7824. Fri–Sun noon–10pm; €7, children €4. DART to Clontarf. Buried deep within a leisure centre, this well-designed attraction combines museum and fairground show, much to the delight of kids who love frights. It's run by a great Dracula enthusiast whose mission is to establish Stoker, born across the road on The Crescent in 1847 and educated at Trinity College, among the pantheon of Irish writers. Things begin fairly conventionally with some engaging display boards on Stoker's life and influences,

▼ THE CASINO AT MARINO

but take an eerie turn with a disorientation tunnel; from here on, you walk through a series of ghoulish scenes – Dracula's lair, Renfield's lunatic asylum – punctuated by regular shocks and surprises.

North Bull Island

Interpretive centre at the end of the causeway road, by the beach in the centre of the island ☎01/833 8341. Mon–Thurs 10.15am–1pm & 1.30–4.30pm, Fri 10am–1.30pm, Sat & Sun 10am–1pm & 1.30–5.30pm (till 4.30pm in winter); free. DART to Raheny, then a 30min walk to the interpretive centre, or bus #130 from Lower Abbey St along Clontarf Rd, then walk along North Bull Wall. Flanked by Dollymount Strand, a three-mile beach on its seaward side, North Bull Island is an impressive resource for nature-lovers – now designated a UNESCO Biosphere Reserve – just five miles from the city centre. Originally no more than a sandbank visible at low tide, the island grew in the tidal shadow of the North Bull Wall, which was built, along with the South Bull Wall, in 1821 on the advice of Captain William Bligh (of HMS *Bounty* fame) to prevent the mouth of the Liffey from silting up. Besides golfers and day-tripping Dubliners, the island provides accommodation for up to 40,000 migrating birds from more than fifty species in winter, including a sixth of the world's population of Brent geese – it's one of the most northerly sites in Europe where the foreshore doesn't freeze. In summer, you'll see cormorants, oystercatchers and curlews wading on the mudflats. As well as a rich and varied flora – notably thrift, a mass of pink flowers in June, and several types of orchid – the grasslands

▲ HOWTH HARBOUR

PLACES The northern outskirts

behind sustain shrews, badgers and one of the few remaining large indigenous mammals, the much-harassed Irish hare.

Howth

DART to Howth station. Clinging to the slopes of a rocky peninsula and overlooking an animated fishing harbour, the village of Howth is a fine place to escape the rigours of the city centre. The windy walk along the harbour's east pier will blow away any Guinness-induced cobwebs and give you the chance to stare out Ireland's Eye, an island sea-bird sanctuary that shelters a ruined sixth-century monastery and a Martello tower; during the summer, boats from the pier (☎01/831 4200 or 087/267 8211) run across to the island when they have enough takers. To the west of the harbour, about ten minutes' walk beyond the DART station, Howth Castle, built in 1564 and now the oldest inhabited house in Ireland, is closed to the public, but a barn in the grounds has been turned into the National Transport Museum (June–Aug Mon–Fri 10am–5pm, Sat & Sun 2–5pm, Sept–May Sat & Sun 2–5pm;

Howth Cliff Walk

The best way to appreciate Howth, if the weather's fine, is to do the **Cliff Walk** around the peninsula, taking in great views south to the Wicklow Mountains and north to the Boyne Valley. The footpath runs for some five miles clockwise from the village round to the west-facing side of the peninsula, followed by a two-mile walk by the sea along Strand Road and Greenfield Road to Sutton DART station; allow at least three hours in total.

You first head out east along Balscadden Road to the **Nose of Howth**, before the path turns south, crossing the slopes above the cliffs, which are covered in colourful gorse and bell heather in season; for refreshment on this stretch, the area known as **The Summit**, just inland of the path, has a pub and a café. The southeast point is marked by the Baily Lighthouse, which until March 1997 was the last manned lighthouse on Ireland's coastline. The path along the south-facing coast of the peninsula is the most spectacular part of the walk, providing close-up views of cliffs, secluded beaches and rocky islands.

€3), containing rustic tractors, a horse-drawn fire engine and an old Hill of Howth tram.

Restaurants

Beshoff's
10 Harbour Rd, Howth. Well-run fish and chip shop, all gleaming chrome and tiles, serving great fishcakes, chunky chips, deep-fried fresh prawns and nice extras like garlic mayonnaise.

Casa Pasta
12 Harbour Rd, Howth ☎01/839 3823. Popular Italian restaurant with a buzzing, family-friendly atmosphere and views of the harbour. The moderately priced menu of pastas, salads and pizzas doesn't stray far from the usual suspects, but it's enlivened by daily specials and a few Thai main courses.

King Sitric's Fish Restaurant
East Pier, Howth ☎01/832 5235, ⊛www.kingsitric.ie. Closed Sat lunchtime & Sun. Excellent, plush restaurant with panoramic sea views, offering fish landed at the nearby pier, lobster and crab from adjacent Balscadden Bay,

and plenty of other delicious seafood and game. Though it's expensive, the set menus at lunchtimes and on Monday to Thursday evenings are good value. Smart bedrooms are available (doubles from €138) if you really want to push the boat out.

Pubs

The Abbey Tavern
Abbey St, Howth ☎01/839 0307, ⊛www.abbeytavern.ie. Welcoming traditional pub, smartly furnished with dark wood, flagstones and open fires, and

▼ THE ABBEY TAVERN, HOWTH

popular for its four-course meals with Irish dancing and ballads on summer evenings in the back room (€50). The bar serves decent lunches – sandwiches, seafood platters, hot specials – and a good pint of Guinness.

Kavanagh's

Prospect Square, Glasnevin. One of the city's finest old pubs, aka *The Gravediggers*, a dimly lit classic of bare wooden floors, benches and trestles. Sandwiches are served Monday to Friday lunchtimes. Located just outside the old entrance to Prospect Cemetery, where it has consoled mourners (and changed little) since 1833, it's best reached from the present-day entrance by retracing your steps along Finglas Road and taking the first small lane on the left along the cemetery walls.

Clubs and live venues

The Helix

Dublin City University, Collins Ave, Glasnevin ☎ 01/700 7000, ⊛ www .thehelix.ie. *The Helix* is a modern, 1250-seater venue, providing a very broad range of entertainment, including rock bands, classical music and ballet, musicals, ice shows and special events, plus a variety of performances in its smaller theatre.

PLACES The northern outskirts

Day trips

Dublin is an excellent base from which to explore some of the wonderful countryside within a thirty-mile radius of the city. You can enjoy Neolithic discoveries at the awesome Brú na Bóinne sites, early Christian monuments and remains at Glendalough, set deep in the Wicklow Mountains, as well as castles and impressive Georgian mansions in gorgeous parkland. Alternatively, if you fancy the seaside experience, just head to Bray, which offers both the "cheap-and-cheerful" and more refined delights. Efficient transport networks make it easy and not too expensive to reach these outlying sights, or if you're short of time or feeling spoilt for choice, then taking a tour might be worth considering (see box, p.178).

Malahide Castle

Malahide, Co. Dublin ☎01/846 2184, ⓦwww.malahidecastle.com. April–Sept Mon–Sat 10am–12.45pm & 2–5pm, Sun closes 6pm; Oct–March Mon–Sat same hours, Sun 11am–12.45pm & 2–5pm. €6.50; combined ticket with Fry Model Railway, Dublin Writers' Museum, Shaw Birthplace or Joyce Tower €11. DART or suburban train from Connolly Station to Malahide. It's a fifteen-minute walk from Malahide station through the pretty parkland known as Malahide Demesne to a cluster of tourist attractions, chief among them Malahide Castle. A twelfth-century tower-house with many additions, mainly from the seventeenth to nineteenth centuries, the castle was the seat of the Anglo-Norman Talbot family for eight hundred years, until the death of the last lord, Milo, in 1973 (it's now owned by Fingal County Council). Highlights of the tour include the drawing rooms of the west wing, with their beautiful rococo cornicing, and the sixteenth-century carved panelling of the Oak Room, which incorporates copies of Raphael's Vatican

frescoes of Adam and Eve, and Joseph and his brothers, as well as rich, swirling floral patterns. The fifteenth-century Great Hall, complete with minstrels' gallery and hammer-beam ceiling, contains a painting of the Battle of the Boyne by van Wyck, flanked by portraits of the Earl of Tyrconnell, "Fighting Dick" Talbot, who led the Jacobites, and other family members who fought with him – it's said that fourteen Talbots breakfasted at the castle before riding out to their deaths in the battle. In the adjoining library, furnished with a beautiful marquetry table and eighteenth-century Flemish floral wall-hangings, some of James Boswell's papers were discovered, including an early draft of *The Life of Samuel Johnson*.

Fry Model Railway

Malahide Castle ☎01/846 3779. April–Sept Mon–Thurs & Sat 10am–1pm & 2–5pm, Sun 2–6pm. €6.50; combined ticket with Malahide Castle, Dublin Writers' Museum, Shaw Birthplace or Joyce Tower €11. In the castle's former corn store, the Fry

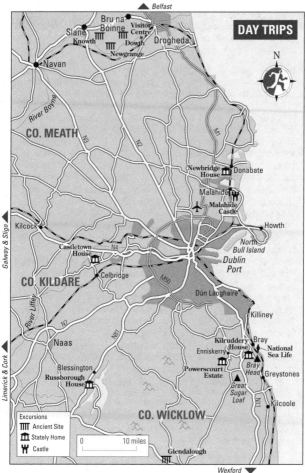

Model Railway is one of the world's largest working miniature railways, covering 2500 square feet. The handmade models include historical and modern Irish trains, as well as trams, buses, barges and the DART.

Talbot Botanic Gardens

Malahide Castle ☎01/846 2456. May–Sept daily 2–5pm; guided tours Wed 2pm. €3. Laid out by the last Lord Talbot, Milo, after World War II, this attractive, twenty-acre botanical garden contains a walled garden, glasshouses and around five thousand species from Australia, New Zealand and Chile.

Tara's Palace and the Museum of Childhood

Malahide Castle ☎01/846 3779. April–Sept Mon–Fri 10.45am–4.45pm, Sat & Sun 11.30am–5.30pm; Oct Sun 11.30am–5.30pm. €2. Pride of

Day trips PLACES

Organized tours

Several companies operate tours to Dublin's outlying sights and all admission charges are usually included in the price.

Bus Éireann (℡01/836 6111, ⊛www.buseireann.ie) runs tours to Glendalough and Powerscourt (mid-March to Oct daily; Nov to mid-March Wed, Fri & Sat; 10.30am; €27; 7hr 15min) and Newgrange (mid-March to Oct daily except Fri; Nov to mid-March Thurs–Sat; €27; 7hr 45min), leaving from Busáras, Store Street.

Day-Tours (℡087/258 6298, ⊛www.day-tours.net) covers both the north coast of Dublin Bay, including Malahide and Howth (Mon & Thurs 9am; €20; 3hr 30min) and its southern counterpart, including Sandycove and Dalkey (Mon & Thurs 1.30pm; €20; 3hr 30min). Its all-day Wicklow tour (Tues, Fri & Sat 9am; €30; 8hr) includes the mountains and Glendalough. All tours depart from opposite the Kilkenny Design Centre on Nassau Street.

Dublin Bus (℡01/873 4222, ⊛www.dublinbus.ie) operates daily tours from its office at 59 O'Connell St Upper, including "South Coast and Gardens" (11am; €20; 4hr 30min), which runs along the coast to Bray and then to Powerscourt; "North Coast and Castle" (10am & 2pm; €20; 3hr), which explores Malahide, Howth and Dollymount Strand.

Irish Tours (℡01/872 9010, ⊛www.irishcitytours.com) runs daily tours from outside The Gresham Hotel, O'Connell Street Upper, including its "Coast and Garden Tour" down to Bray and on to Powerscourt (10.15am; €20; 4hr); "Dublin Bay and Castle" to Malahide and Howth (2.30pm; €20; 3hr); and the "Wicklow Tour" to Glendalough and the mountains (10am;

€30; 7hr). It also operates an excursion to Newgrange (April–Oct Mon, Tues, Fri & Sat 10am; €30; 6hr) from the Suffolk Street tourist office; and a tour of the Wicklow Mountains, including Glendalough and Russborough House (April–Oct Sun 10.30am; €38; 7hr 30min), from outside its offices at 33 Bachelors Walk.

Mary Gibbons Tours (℡01/283 9973, ⊛www.newgrangetours.com) takes in Newgrange and the Boyne Valley (Mon–Fri 9.40am; €35; 6hr), leaving from outside the North Star Hotel, Amiens Street, and calling at the Suffolk Street tourist office at 10.15am.

Over the Top Tours (℡01/838 6128, ⊛www.overthetoptours.com) uses a minibus to visit Glendalough and the Wicklow Mountains (€24; 8hr) leaving from outside The Gresham Hotel, O'Connell Street Upper at 9.20am, calling at the Suffolk Street tourist office at 9.45am.

Railtours (℡01/856 0045, ⊛www.railtours.ie) operates combined rail and coach tours, including the "Dublin Bay Explorer" (Mon–Sat 1.30pm; €29; 4hr), which heads off to Greystones and then to Powerscourt; and the "Wicklow Mountaineer" (Mon–Sat 11.45am; €39; 6hr 45min), which visits Glendalough. Tours depart from Connolly Station.

The Wild Wicklow Tour (℡01/475 3313, ⊛www.discoverdublin.ie) explores Glendalough and heads off the beaten track into the mountains (€28; 7hr), departing from outside The Shelbourne Hotel, St Stephen's Green at 8.50am daily.

place in the Craft Courtyard behind the model railway goes to the Museum of Childhood. Downstairs is a display of toys from 1720 to 1960, including a rare travelling dolls' house, and houses from the collections of Oscar Wilde's mother, Speranza, and Vivien Greene, wife of author Graham. The first floor shelters Tara's Palace, a meticulous re-creation of an

▲ NEWBRIDGE HOUSE

eighteenth-century mansion, including a chapel and billiards room, at one-twelfth scale, based on Leinster House, Castletown House and Carton House. Proceeds from the museum's takings go to Irish children's charities.

Newbridge House

Donabate, Co. Dublin ☏01/843 6534. April–Sept Tues–Sat 10am–1pm & 2–5pm, Sun 2–6pm; Oct–March Sat & Sun 2–5pm. House €6.50, farm €3.50. Suburban train to Donabate from Connolly Station or Malahide. Built by Richard Castle in 1740 for Charles Cobbe, later archbishop of Dublin, Newbridge House is a trim, two-storey manor with a fine Georgian interior, featuring some lovely rococo stucco ceilings. From Donabate station, it's a pleasant fifteen-minute walk to the house across the parkland of Newbridge Demesne. The house's finest room is the magnificent Red Drawing Room, which has been left almost exactly as it was after its 1820s redecoration, while the Cobbe family's Museum of Curiosities nearby displays all manner of weird artefacts, mostly Oriental but including some ostrich eggs laid in Dundalk. In sharp contrast to these extravagances, you can see the laundry and kitchen below stairs, and in the restored courtyard, a labourer's cottage furnished in nineteenth-century style. Kids will especially enjoy the attached traditional farm, which stretches over nearly thirty acres. Work is afoot in the grounds to restore the nineteenth-century walled kitchen garden, which will include a rose walk, ornamental glasshouses and a herb garden.

Bray

Just across the border in County Wicklow, the formerly genteel Victorian resort of Bray now draws a great influx of day-tripping Dubliners down the DART line on summer weekends, when the seafront amusement arcades and fast-food outlets go into overdrive. The attractive sand and shingle beach, however, dramatically set against the knobbly promontory of Bray Head, is long enough to soak up the crowds, and the enterprising town lays on a diverse roster of festivals to broaden its appeal, including the Bray Jazz Festival in May and the Oscar Wilde Autumn School in October (see p.208). Details of all these events are available from the tourist office, in the nineteenth-century former courthouse on Main Street, a ten-minute walk inland from the DART station (June–Aug Mon–Fri 9am–1pm & 2–5pm, Sat 10am–3pm; Sept–May Mon–Fri 9.30am–1pm & 2–4.30pm, Sat 10am–3pm; ☎01/286 6796, ⊛www.bray.ie). The attached heritage centre (same hours; €3) is devoted to local history, focussing on the achievements of Sir William Dargan, who built the Dublin–Kingstown (now Dún Laoghaire) railway, the world's first suburban line, in 1831–34, and helped to establish Dublin's National Gallery.

National Sea-Life

Strand Rd, Bray ☎01/286 6939, ⊛www.sealife.ie. Early March to mid-Oct Mon–Fri 10am–6pm, Sat & Sun 10am–6.30pm; mid-Oct to early March Mon–Fri 11am–5pm, Sat & Sun 10am–5.30pm. €8.50, children €5.50. Bray's main attraction, especially popular with children, is National Sea-Life, on the seafront, an aquarium run by fishy enthusiasts, who lay on plenty of activities for kids, as well as informative display boards that'll keep adults interested. The full range of sea and freshwater habitats is covered – including "probably the largest shoal of piranhas in Ireland" – with a strong emphasis on the need for

▼ NATIONAL SEA-LIFE

conservation. Inevitably, the more exotic, far-flung creatures provide the big thrills, notably the blacktips in the tropical shark tank, and the scary giant Japanese spider crab, a species which can grow up to twelve feet from claw to claw.

Killruddery House and Gardens

Off Southern Cross Rd, Bray ☎01/286 3405, ⊛www.killruddery.com. Gardens: April Sat & Sun 1–5pm; May–Sept daily 1–5pm; €5. House: May, June & Sept daily 1–5pm; €8 (gardens included). Finnegan's bus from Bray DART station, or a 20min walk from the southern end of the seafront (via Putland Rd, Newcourt Rd, Vevay Rd and Southern Cross Rd). Used as a film location on many occasions, including for *My Left Foot* and *Dancing at Lughnasa*, the Killruddery estate is most notable for its gardens, which were laid out in the seventeenth century in early French formal style and added to in the nineteenth. As such, they're the oldest gardens in Ireland, featuring an original "sylvan theatre" framed by a high bay hedge and terraced banks, where plays are still staged in the summer, and extensive walks flanked by hornbeam, beech and lime hedges. The two-hundred-yard-long twin ponds, once stocked with fish for the table, were designed as "water mirrors" in front of the main house. The latter, in Tudor Revival style, is still home to the Brabazon family (the earls of Meath), and boasts some fine plasterwork ceilings. When the house is open, you can get into the Orangery, which was built in the 1850s after the fashion of London's Crystal Palace and restored in 2000 – so styling itself "Ireland's Millennium

A walk over Bray Head to Greystones

There's an excellent two- to three-hour walk from Bray seafront south across Bray Head to Greystones, a small commuter town at the end of the DART line. You can follow the comparatively flat cliff path that runs above the rail tracks for most of the way, giving close-up views of rocky coves and slate pinnacles, lashed by magnificent waves on windy days. Alternatively, take on the steep climb over the top of Bray Head for great views of Killiney Bay and the cone-shaped hills inland known as Little Sugar Loaf and Great Sugar Loaf, with a distant backdrop of the Wicklow Mountains the route ascends rapidly from the end of Bray seafront through pine woods and over gorse slopes to a large cross, 656ft above sea level; from here a track winds across the ridge below the 860ft summit of Bray Head, before you turn sharp left down to join the cliff path which will bring you into Greystones.

Dome". Kilruddery features prominently in the Wicklow Gardens Festival from May to July every year (see p.208).

Powerscourt Estate

Enniskerry, Co. Wicklow ☏ 01/204 6000, ⊛ www.powerscourt.ie. Gardens daily: March–Oct 9.30am–5.30pm; Nov–Feb 9.30am to dusk; €7. Exhibition daily: March–Oct 9.30am–5.30pm; Nov–Feb times may vary slightly; €2.50. Waterfall daily: summer 9.30am–7pm; winter 10.30am–dusk; €4.50. Bus #44 from Westland Row and St Stephen's Green East or #185 from Bray DART. Given good weather you could easily spend a whole day enjoying Powerscourt, a massive 34,000-acre estate just half a mile south of Enniskerry. Powerscourt's centrepiece is the magnificent Georgian mansion, designed by Richard Castle for Richard Wingfield, the first Viscount Powerscourt, on the site of a medieval castle constructed by the Anglo-Norman le Poer family (whose name, when Anglicized, became Power – hence the estate's title).

Completed in 1741 and topped by two copper domes, the house remains impressive from a distance, but, sadly, much of its interior was destroyed by a fire in 1974. Parts have since been renovated and include the exhibition centre by the main entrance, featuring displays on the house's former glories and a video on its history, as well as several shops, including a branch of the Avoca department store (see p.74) with its own café (daily 9.30am–5.30pm).

From the café terrace you can enjoy sumptuous views of the gardens – the estate's main attraction – some 47 acres in size and set against the backdrop of the Wicklow Mountains. Highlights include the walled garden, entered by a gilded gate from Bavaria's Bamberg

▼ POWERSCOURT WATERFALL

Cathedral, and the terraced Italian Gardens overlooking Triton Lake, from the centre of which a statue of the sea-god shoots a jet of water high into the air. Among other sights are the curious, and aptly named, Pepper Pot Tower, as well as a splendidly fragrant Japanese Garden. The final attraction is Ireland's highest waterfall – three miles from the main gate, but well signposted – which leaps and bounds down a four-hundred-feet rock face to replenish the waters of the River Dargle in the valley below.

Glendalough

Co. Wicklow ☎0404/45325, ⊛www .heritageireland.ie. Glendalough Visitor Centre: mid-March to mid-Oct 9.30am–6pm; rest of year 9.30am–5pm. €2.75; Heritage Card. St Kevin's bus service (☎01/281 8119, ⊛www.glendaloughbus.com) runs from opposite the Mansion House on Dawson Street, Dublin via Bray to Glendalough (Mon–Sat 11.30am & 6pm, Sun 11.30am & 7pm; €10 single, €16 return). Set deep in a glacier valley on the eastern fringe of the Wicklow Mountains, Glendalough, with its two lakes, provides

▼ ROUND TOWER, GLENDALOUGH

a delightfully atmospheric location for the striking remains of one of Ireland's best-preserved monastic sites. The monastery was founded by St Kevin in the sixth century and played a vital role in the development of learning in pre-medieval Europe. You can find out more about its history via the visitor centre's informative displays and videos and by taking the excellent guided tour.

The site comprises no fewer than five churches and an impressive, though now roofless, ninth-century cathedral, containing slabs marking many graves, as well as a round tower, nearly 100ft high, one of the country's most noteworthy. Just by the cathedral stands St Kevin's Cross, a monolith featuring one of the most characteristic designs from the post-Celtic period, a wheel overlaid by a cross. Above the doorway of the nearby twelfth-century Priest House are carvings of figures believed to depict the Saint and two later abbots.

Heading west from here along the "Green Road", past the Lower Lake, you'll come to the ruins of the tiny Romanesque Reefert Church and the path leading to St Kevin's Cell, similar in style to a typically Celtic "beehive" hut, and St Kevin's Bed, a small cave into which he reputedly moved to avoid the allures of an admirer called Caitlín; he supposedly ended up chucking the poor woman into the lake in a last-ditch attempt to fight off her advances.

Wicklow Mountains Visitor Centre

Glendalough, Co. Wicklow ☎0404/45425, ⊛www.heritageireland .ie. April & Sept Sat & Sun 10am–6pm;

May–Aug daily 10am–6pm. Free. At the eastern end of the Upper Lake at Glendalough is the Wicklow Mountains Visitor Centre, which provides information on the mountains and bogland conservation, as well as details of suitable exploratory walks in the area.

Russborough House

Russborough, Blessington, Co. Wicklow ☎045/865239. April & Oct Sun & public holidays 10am–5pm; May–Sept daily 10am–5pm. Guided tours €6. Bus #65 from Eden Quay or College Green. Situated three miles south of Blessington, Russborough House is a gorgeously lavish Palladian country house, designed by Richard Castle for Joseph Leeson, the son of a wealthy Dublin brewer. Castle died before the end of the project, and the fulfilment of his grand design was overseen by Francis Bindon. Completed in 1751, the granite stone building's 700-foot-wide frontage, with its colonnaded wings, is the longest of its kind in Ireland. The interior is sumptuously decorated and furnished and its expansive hall features a massive chimney-piece manufactured from black Kilkenny marble. The ground-floor rooms are accessible on guided tours, taking in the stylish saloon, whose ceiling bears the grandiose rococo plasterwork of the Lafranchini brothers and whose walls are covered with Genoese velvet. Here, and in the equally luxurious dining and tapestry rooms, are displayed paintings from the collection of Alfred Beit, a German

▲ RUSSBOROUGH HOUSE

entrepreneur who derived his vast fortune from the De Beers Diamond Mining Company. His nephew of the same name purchased Russborough in 1952 and donated much of his inherited art collection to the Irish state – several paintings are on display in the National Gallery (see p.85). Only a selection of the remaining masterpieces, including works by artists such as Goya, Rubens, Hals and Gainsborough, is on display at any one time. The Beit collection has proved attractive to thieves and the house was burgled on four occasions between 1974 and 2002, though almost all of the stolen paintings have subsequently been recovered.

Castletown House

Celbridge, Co. Kildare ☎01/628 8252, ⊛www.heritageireland.ie. Easter to Oct Mon–Fri 10am–6pm (Oct closes 5pm), Sat, Sun & public holidays 1pm–6pm; Nov Sun 1pm–5pm. Guided tours €3.50; Heritage card. Bus #67 or #67A

▲ CASTLETOWN HOUSE

from Wellington Quay to Celbridge. The largest Palladian country house in Ireland, Castletown is accessed by gates at the northern end of Celbridge's high street and then by a long, straight-as-a-die tree-lined avenue. Like many a grandiose Irish construction, Castletown has a brewing connection, being built for William Connolly, son of a Donegal publican who made his fortune from land deals and became Speaker of the Irish House of Commons in 1715. The house took an extraordinarily long time to complete – from 1722 till 1770 – and employed the designs of a range of architects. Visits are only possible on hour-long guided tours, which highlight an impressive array of ornamentation, including, not least, stucco work by the Lafranchini brothers in the main hall and alongside the impressive cantilevered staircase, as well as rooms featuring walls covered in damask, silk and prints of old masters. The upstairs Long Gallery contains the busts of famous philosophers and poets, Pompeiian murals and a false door, included for symmetrical effect, while its windows offer views of the Connolly Folly, some two miles north – an arcane edifice consisting of an

obelisk perched shakily on top of a cascade of arches.

Brú na Bóinne
Donore, Co. Meath
☎ 041/988 0300,
🌐 www.heritage ireland.ie. The valley of the River Boyne, some thirty miles north of Dublin, is scattered with numerous Neolithic remains, the most important of which are the passage graves at Newgrange, Knowth and Dowth, although the last-named is still being excavated. Newgrange and Knowth are accessed from the impressive Brú na Bóinne Visitor Centre at Donore, which provides detailed information on the significance of the sites and their probable means of construction (as well as housing a tourist information desk and café).

Brú na Bóinne is one of Ireland's foremost attractions and, as the numbers visiting each site daily are strictly limited (and there's no advance booking), it's advisable to arrive

▼ STAIRCASE, CASTLETOWN HOUSE

early in the day or be prepared for a long wait before the minibus whisks you away for the guided tours of the sites themselves.

Newgrange is unquestionably the most striking passage-grave, a mound, 250-foot in diameter, constructed some 5000 years ago, surrounded by the later addition of a circle of colossal standing stones. The stone used to construct the tomb's interior came from as far afield as Counties Down and Wicklow, an unfathomable feat of transportation. The tomb's pivotal feature is a roof-box above the entrance whose slit is perfectly positioned to receive the light of the rising sun on the day of the winter solstice (December 21); the light first peeps into the tomb before spreading its rays along the length of the passage and into the burial chamber itself – the tour provides an electrically-powered simulation.

Excavations at Knowth have produced a wealth of Neolithic and later art, including many ornamented stones. The main passage-grave is almost double the size of Newgrange and the tunnel leading to its central chamber features much decoration – there's a second, smaller, tomb here, too, as well as much evidence of later settlement in the surrounding area.

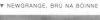
▼ NEWGRANGE, BRÚ NA BÓINNE

PLACES Day trips

Visiting Brú na Bóinne

Opening times

The Brú na Bóinne Visitor Centre and Newgrange are open daily: March, April & Oct 9.30am–5.30pm; May & mid- to end Sept 9am–6.30pm; June to mid-Sept 9am–7pm; Nov–Feb 9.30am–5pm; last tours 90min before closing. Knowth has the same times, but is open May–Oct only.

Admission prices

Admission to the visitor centre is €2.75; combined ticket with Newgrange €5.50; combined ticket with Knowth €4.25; all three €9.75. The Heritage Card is valid for all of these.

Access

Take Bus Éireann service #100 from Busáras (or suburban train from Pearse, Tara Street or Connolly stations) to Drogheda and then #163 to Donore. Alternatively, a Newgrange shuttlebus (☎01/860 0405; €10 single, €15 return) leaves Suffolk Street tourist office daily at 8.45am & 11am, stopping outside the *Royal Dublin Hotel*, O'Connell Street Upper at 9am & 11.15pm; 45min; tickets can be purchased on board or in advance at tourist offices.

Restaurants

The Hungry Monk

Church Rd, Greystones ☎01/287 5759. Restaurant Wed–Sat evenings, Sun 12.30–8pm; wine bar Tues–Sun evenings. A fine, traditional restaurant, specializing in game in winter and seafood in summer, with an excellent, wide-ranging wine list; especially popular for Sunday dinner (or "linner" as they call it), served all day. There is a cheaper, simpler menu available in the wine bar downstairs.

Hush

12A New St, Malahide ☎01/806 1928. East of Malahide station off the Dublin Road, *Hush* is a bright, informal place, serving everything from lobster fettuccini to great burgers, at reasonable prices.

Jaipur

5 St James's Terrace, Malahide ☎01/845 5455, ⊛www.jaipur.ie. Closed lunchtimes Mon–Thurs. Just off The Mall, a branch of the excellent South Great George's Street Indian restaurant – see p.119.

Tree of Idleness

The Strand, Bray ☎01/286 3498. Closed lunchtimes and all day Mon. Bray's outstanding restaurant option, a Greek-Cypriot establishment on the seafront, specializes in smoked lamb, suckling pig and seafood, complemented by an extensive wine list, excellent service and a groaning dessert trolley.

Pubs and bars

Castletown Inn

Upper Main St, Celbridge. A handy watering-hole a hundred yards from the main entrance to Castletown House that also serves exceptionally good bar meals in gargantuan portions.

Lynham's

Laragh, Co. Wicklow. A mile or so east of Glendalough, *Lynham's* is a welcoming pub where you can get excellent food in its lively bar and spruce restaurant or just sip a pint at one of its outdoor riverside tables.

The Porterhouse

The Strand, Bray ☎01/286 0668, ⊛www.porterhousebrewco.com. A branch of the excellent Temple Bar microbrewery-pub, serving its own great stouts, lagers and ales, as well as good, basic fare such as Irish stew, salads and burgers. There's a beer garden overlooking the esplanade, and live music and DJs Friday to Sunday nights till late.

Accommodation

Hotels and guesthouses

Though Dublin has a plethora of accommodation possibilities, the city's hotels and B&Bs rank amongst Europe's most expensive; finding a bed can be especially problematic during July and August, major festivals and public holidays such as around St Patrick's Day, and at the time of major gigs or sporting events. Book directly via telephone or online. Alternatively, any Bord Fáilte (Irish tourist board) or Northern Irish Tourist Board office will be able to book you a room for a fee of €4 or £2.

Suburban B&Bs will generally charge around €60–80 for a double room, while their more upmarket central equivalents may charge anything from €100 to €300. As for hotels, the price ranges from the bargain to the extravagant, though good deals can be discovered by booking in advance via Gulliver (☎066 979 2030, ◉www.gulliver.ie) or Dublin Tourism (◉www .visitdublin.com), especially midweek in the city centre and, conversely, at weekends for places that specialize in business travellers.

Trinity College, Grafton Street and around

The Westbury Harry St, off Grafton St ☎01/679 1122, ◉www.jurysdoyle.com. The glossy lobby of this luxurious five-star hotel is an indicator of the treats that lie in store. Its bedrooms are not so much furnished as designed to pamper and the range of facilities on offer includes a fitness centre, a svelte bar specializing in champagne cocktails, and underground parking. €510 rack rate, but high-season bargains without breakfast can be as low as €179.

The Westin Dublin Westmoreland St ☎01/645 1000, ◉www.westin.com /dublin. Hiding behind the facade of the old Allied Irish Bank building just north of Trinity College, *The Westin* is a marvellously luxurious establishment. Its 163 bedrooms are designed with character and elegantly equipped, while the bar is housed in the former bank's vaults, and the lounge has a stunning glass roof. €375 (breakfast not included).

Kildare Street and Merrion Square

Buswells Hotel 23–27 Molesworth St ☎01/614 6500, ◉www.quinnhotels .com. Popular with politicians through its proximity to Leinster House, *Buswells* offers 68 pleasantly designed en-suite rooms in a converted Georgian townhouse. Ornate plasterwork and fireplaces testify to those origins and the hotel also has a splendid carvery/restaurant, its own bar and secure overnight parking. €225.

Fitzwilliam 41 Fitzwilliam Street Upper ☎01/662 5155, ◉www.fitzwilliamguest house.ie. Probably the friendliest central Southside guesthouse, this converted Georgian residence provides thirteen tastefully decorated en-suite rooms, including doubles, triples and a family room. Non-smoking throughout, this is a very popular

A guide to prices

For hotels, guesthouses and B&Bs, the prices quoted in this chapter are for the cheapest double room in the summer high season, and include breakfast unless otherwise specified. For hostels, we've given the price of the cheapest dorm bed in high season, as well as the cost of a private (double or twin) room, where available. A light breakfast is usually included, but we've specified exceptions to that rule.

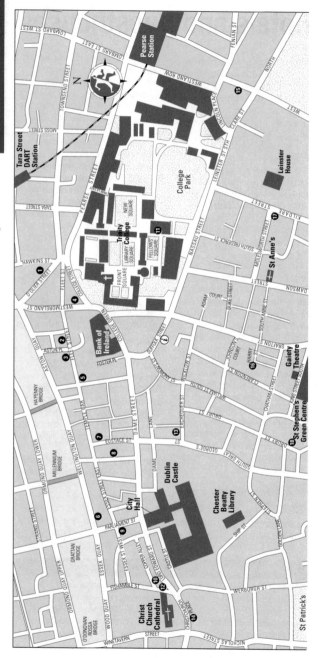

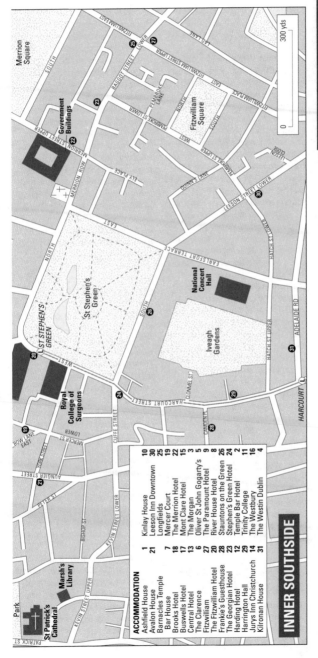

ACCOMMODATION

Ashfield House	1
Avalon House	21
Barnacles Temple Bar House	7
Brooks Hotel	18
Buswells Hotel	17
Central Hotel	13
The Clarence	6
Fitzwilliam	20
The Fitzwilliam Hotel	27
Frankie's Guesthouse	28
The Georgian Hotel	23
Harding Hotel	12
Harrington Hall	29
Jurys Inn Christchurch	14
Kilronan House	16
Kinlay House	10
Leeson Inn Downtown	30
Longfields	25
Mercer Court	19
The Merrion Hotel	22
Mont Clare Hotel	15
The Morgan	3
Oliver St John Gogarty's	5
The Paramount Hotel	9
River House Hotel	8
Stauntons on the Green	26
Stephen's Green Hotel	24
Temple Bar Hotel	2
Trinity College	11
The Westbury	4
The Westin Dublin	31

INNER SOUTHSIDE

Hotels and guesthouses

choice, so weekend bookings must be for two nights or more and a discount of €10 per night is offered to those staying at least three nights. €119.

The Georgian Hotel 18–22 Baggott St Lower ☎01/634 5000, ✆www.georgian hotel.ie. A wonderful haven of calm on a busy thoroughfare, this renovated Georgian property's bedrooms feature stylish decor and soothing colours. Breakfast (an additional €15 per person) is served in the attached *Maguires Bar*. Off-peak disounts often available. €165.

Longfields Hotel 9–10 Fitzwilliam St Lower ☎01/676 1367, ✆www.longfields .ie. *Longfields* fully proves the point that size isn't everything. Its 26 en-suite rooms are furnished and decorated to a high standard and include elegant drapes, prints and some four-poster beds. Run by a helpful team, the facilities include a cosy lounge as well as an excellent restaurant, *Number 10.* €250.

The Merrion Hotel Merrion St Upper ☎01/603 0600, ✆www.merrionhotel .com. The Duke of Wellington's dismissal of his Irish connections, "being born in a stable doesn't make one a horse", rings even hollower now that his birthplace at no. 24 is part of this opulent hotel. Four eighteenth-century townhouses have been redecorated in Georgian style and hung with a superb collection of Irish art, overlooking a private landscaped garden. Facilities include the luxurious Tethra Spa and *Restaurant Patrick Guilbaud* (see p.99). Main House €450, Garden Wing €370.

Mont Clare Hotel Merrion St Lower ☎01/607 3800, ✆www.ocallaghanhotels .com. Just off Merrion Square (and with its own secure car park) the *Mont Clare* offers over seventy recently refurbished air-conditioned rooms, providing a degree of comfort for which you might pay double elsewhere, as well as an attractive location. Facilities include a bar and restaurant. €155.

St Stephen's Green to the Grand Canal

The Fitzwilliam Hotel St Stephen's Green ☎01/478 7000, ✆www .fitzwilliamhotel.com. With a grand and expansive foyer and luxurious rooms

designed by Sir Terence Conran, the *Fitzwilliam* offers deluxe accommodation in a marvellous central location. The double-room rate ranges considerably depending on size and facilities, and there's also a beauty salon, roof garden, bars, secure parking and restaurant. €195.

Frankie's Guesthouse 8 Camden Place ☎01/478 3087, ✆www.frankiesguest house.com. By some distance the best gay- and lesbian-friendly guesthouse in Dublin, *Frankie's* occupies a fine mews location and proffers a dozen rooms, including standard singles and doubles as well as en-suite doubles and twins – though note that there's minimum stay of two/three nights for respectively doubles/twins and singles at weekends. There's a glorious roof garden and a sumptuous breakfast included. €85.

Harrington Hall 70 Harcourt St ☎01/475 3497, ✆www.harringtonhall.com. Occupying elegant Georgian premises and offering equally stylish interiors, this guesthouse just south of St Stephen's Green has 28 thoughtfully furnished and generously sized en-suite rooms, complete with secondary glazing and ceiling fans. Fifty percent discounts available in low season. €268.

Kilronan House 70 Adelaide Rd ☎01/475 5266, ✆www.dublinn.com. It's hard to top the welcome at this fine Georgian townhouse which features elegant decoration, including Waterford crystal chandeliers, and orthopedic mattresses in all its rooms. Often offers substantial off-peak discounts. €152.

Leeson Inn Downtown 24 Leeson St Lower ☎01/662 2002, ✆www.leesoninn downtown.com. Some three hundred yards from the southeast corner of St Stephen's Green, the *Leeson's* tastefully furnished 24 en-suite rooms give respite from the city's hurly-burly and at a reasonable price too. €139.

Stauntons on the Green 83 St Stephen's Green ☎01/478 2300, ✆www.stauntons onthegreen.ie. Set in an unbeatable location on the south side of the Green with its own private gardens, this is a luxurious guesthouse whose 38 en-suite rooms offer both comfort and style befitting this Georgian building. €152.

Stephen's Green Hotel St Stephen's Green ☏01/607 3600, ⊛www .ocallaghanhotels.com Swish, classy, yet thoroughly modernist, this utterly enjoyable hotel occupies a spot overlooking the south-western corner of the Green. As well as its lively bar and economically priced bistro, fitness centre, libraries and wireless Internet access, the hotel provides 64 spacious air-conditioned double rooms equipped with fridges and power showers and a number of suites, including the sixth-floor Presidential (€550 a night), complete with two bathrooms and an enormous balcony. €260.

Temple Bar

The Clarence 6–8 Wellington Quay ☏01/407 0800, ⊛www.theclarence.ie. Formerly a bolt-hole for priests and lawyers up from the country, *The Clarence* retains the distinctive light oak panelling of its former incarnation, but has been transformed into a hip, informal, luxury hotel. Owned by U2, it contains the *Tea Room* restaurant in the former ballroom (see p.104) and the stylish *Octagon Bar* (see p.105), as well as a two-storey penthouse suite used by sundry rock stars. All fifty rooms come with a state-of-the-art multimedia system. €330.

The Morgan 10 Fleet St ☏01/679 3939, ⊛www.themorgan.com. Sheer bliss in terms of the quality of its accommodation and crisply designed throughout, this establishment fully merits the term bijou. Rooms vary in size and facilities and the hotel is currently enjoying a revamp which will see its room-count rise to 106. €126.

The Paramount Hotel Parliament St ☏01/417 9900, ⊛www.paramounthotel .ie. Situated at the eastern end of Temple Bar (and entered via Essex Gate), *The Paramount* combines thoroughly modern facilities with deluxe accommodation, its 66 rooms decorated using tones and furniture reminiscent of the 1930s. Its *Turks Head* bar is a stylish hang-out and serves bistro-style meals throughout the day. €220.

River House Hotel 23–24 Eustace St ☏01/670 7655, ⊛www.riverhousehotel .com. Tucked away on one of Temple Bar's quieter streets, the red-fronted *River House* is one of the few family-run establishments in the centre, with 29 thoughtfully decorated double rooms. Excellent breakfasts, especially the freshly-baked scones, add to the attraction. €120.

Temple Bar Hotel 13–17 Fleet St ☏01/677 3333, ⊛www.templebarhotel .com. Tastefully designed throughout, from its bright and airy lobby to its attractive, modern en-suite bedrooms, the *Temple Bar* has a high reputation for service, though some of its front-facing rooms can suffer from late-night street noise. The hotel's *Buskers* bar is a popular spot and there's reduced-rate secure car parking nearby. €200.

The old city and South Great George's Street

Brooks Hotel Drury St ☏01/670 4000, ⊛www.brookshotel.ie. Compact, four-star boutique hotel, on a quiet road that's handy for Temple Bar and Grafton Street, with stylish bedrooms and public rooms, a small gym and sauna, and very friendly service. €210.

Central Hotel 1–5 Exchequer St ☏01/679 7302, ⊛www.centralhotel.ie. Centrally located, as its name suggests, this hotel is one of the city's oldest, having been in business since 1887. Rooms are stylishly furnished, appointed and reasonably well soundproofed, though some can feel a little cramped, and the hotel's *Library Bar* has recently been refurbished. All rooms are en suite. €175.

Harding Hotel Copper Alley, Fishamble St ☏01/679 6500, ⊛www.hardinghotel .ie. Massively popular due to its budget-conscious high-season room rate of €106 and roomy twins, doubles, triples and family accommodation, the *Harding* also includes the atmospheric *Darkey Kelly's* bar (taking its name from an eighteenth-century Copper Alley brothel-keeper), supplying good food and a regular programme of live entertainment. €106.

Jurys Inn Christchurch Christchurch Place ☏01/454 0000, ⊛www.jurysinn .com. Bang opposite the Cathedral (though don't compare the relative architectural merits) *Jurys* is a well-liked spot for families thanks to its low-cost room rate per night (breakfast is not included). Rooms are both restful and functional and the hotel offers a restaurant, café and bar. €108.

O'Connell Street and around

Academy Hotel Findlater Place, Cathal Brugha St ☎01/878 0666, ⊛www .academy-hotel.ie. Tucked away behind O'Connell Street, this well-appointed hotel offers tastefully furnished air-conditioned en suites as well as a fine range of breakfasts and a friendly bar, plus free wireless Internet access. Off-season bargains can begin as low as €98. €178.

The Gresham Hotel 23 O'Connell St Upper ☎01/874 6881, ⊛www.gresham -hotels.com. *The Gresham* isn't just a splendidly equipped 4-star hotel, but one of Dublin's landmarks, a place where you don't have to be a guest to enjoy afternoon tea in the opulent surroundings of its lobby or sample the meals in its restaurant. Rooms are stylish and spacious while the individually designed penthouse suites offer differing views of the city. €241.

Hotel Isaacs Store St ☎01/813 4700, ⊛www.isaacs.ie. Though its setting opposite Busáras isn't exactly auspicious, *Isaacs'* tastefully designed interior, friendly staff and 99 well-accoutred bedrooms more than compensate. The hotel has its own attached Italian restaurant, *Il Vignardo*, as well as a suitably cosmopolitan café-bar, *Le Monde*. €140.

Jurys Inn Custom House Custom House Quay ☎01/607 5000, ⊛www.jurysinns .com. The riverside location really is hard to beat and the views of Dublin's developing docklands are staggering from rooms on the upper storeys. Facilities include a bar, café and restaurant. €108.

The Morrison Ormond Quay Lower ☎01/887 2400, ⊛www.morrisonhotel.ie. Black remains the new black as far as this swish temple of minimalism is concerned. While that colour dominates the lobby and ultra-cool bar (see p.137), the luxurious rooms also feature chocolate and cream decor using natural materials (fashion designer John Rocha was employed as consultant). The exclusive penthouse offering lush decor and all manner of creature comforts has spectacular riverside views. €230.

Othello House 74 Gardiner St Lower ☎01/855 4271, ⊛www.othelloguest house.com. A good option on a busy street, this comfortable B&B provides 22 en-suite rooms, all equipped with TV, telephone and

INNER NORTHSIDE

0   200 yds

N

ACCOMMODATION

Abbey Court	17
Abraham House	6
Academy Hotel	5
Ashling Hotel	18
Chief O'Neill's	16
Clifden Guesthouse	2
Comfort Inn	4
Dublin International Youth Hostel	3
Globetrotters	11
Gresham Hotel	7
Hotel Isaacs	12
Isaacs Hostel	10
Jacobs Inn	9
Jurys Inn Custom House	14
Litton Lane Hostel	15
Marian Guest House	1
The Morrison	19
Othello House	8
The Townhouse	13

Collins Barracks

NORTH CIRCULAR ROAD

PHIBSBOROUGH ROAD

PEVENSIE STREET

DOMINICK STREET

CHANCERY STREET

KING STREET NORTH

St Michan's Church

FOUR COURTS

Four Courts

BENBURB ST

WOLFE TONE QUAY

MUSEUM

ELLIS QUAY

SMITHFIELD

ARRAN QUAY

MARY'S

Heuston Station

VICTORIA QUAY

HEUSTON

tea/coffee-making facilities, as well as an excellent Irish breakfast. Parking is available. €110.

The Townhouse 47–48 Gardiner St Lower ☏01/878 8808, ⊛www.townhouseof dublin.ie. This superbly converted Georgian house remains an oasis of calm in one of the city's busiest streets. Stylish twins, doubles, triples and a family room are thoughtfully decorated and include sizeable en-suite facilities. A buffet breakfast is served in an elegant dining room with a balcony and there are secure off-street parking spaces. €115.

North from Parnell Square

Clifden Guesthouse 32 Gardiner Place ☏01/874 6364, ⊛www.clifdenhouse .com. One of the Northside's most reliable options, this comfortable Georgian house is well maintained by very friendly hosts. Fifteen pleasant en-suite rooms include doubles as well as a triple and a family room. Off-street parking is available. €110.

Comfort Inn Great Denmark St ☏1850/266 3678, ⊛www.comfortinn dublin.com. A welcome recent addition to the inner Northside, the *Comfort's* Georgian exterior encompasses a stylish modern hotel. Rooms are attractively furnished, bright and airy and the hotel's bar, *The Belvedere*, is becoming a popular meeting-place. Broadband access is available in all rooms and the hotel is wheelchair accessible. Big discounts available in off season. €229.

Marian Guest House 21 Gardiner St Upper ☏01/874 4129, ⊛www.marian guesthouse.ie. Immensely popular due to its budget prices and warm welcome, the *Marian* offers five clean and comfortable en-suite double rooms as well as one standard. Off-street parking is available and buses #16 and #41 stop just around the corner on Dorset Street Upper. €70.

From Capel Street to Collins Barracks

Chief O'Neill's Smithfield Village ☏01/817 3838, ⊛www.chiefoneills .com. Named after the Cork-born traditional music collector and erstwhile police chief of Chicago, this splendidly stylish modern hotel presents chic bedrooms, each incorporating unique music-inspired prints on the walls

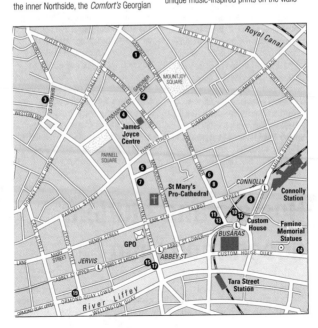

and accoutrements such as CD players. Served in the basement, the breakfast buffet offers possibly the city's widest choice and there's a swish ground-floor bar too, sometimes providing live music. €179.

Phoenix Park

Ashling Hotel Parkgate St ☎01/677 2324, ⊛www.ashlinghotel.ie. Handily placed near Heuston Station, this modern hotel offers almost 150 bedrooms providing tastefully designed comfort and plenty of space, as well as a pleasant bar and excellent breakfast. €220.

Along the Grand Canal

Belgrave House 6–10 Belgrave Square, Rathmines ☎01/496 3760, ⊛www .belgraveguesthouse.com. Set in a quiet square, near the Ranelagh stop on the LUAS Green Line, *Belgrave House* provides tasteful modern rooms in a Victorian setting. The breakfast range is extensive and the "full Irish" will keep you going till teatime. €180.

The Berkeley Court Lansdowne Rd, Ballsbridge ☎01/665 3200, ⊛www .jurysdoyle.com. Lansdowne Rd DART station or buses #5, #7 and #45. Its drab exterior offers barely a hint of the luxuries lying within this 5-star hotel, though one glance of the lavish, open-plan foyer will convince you otherwise. The hotel's 186 bedrooms offer luxurious comfort and it prides itself on its family-friendliness, offering both a children's menu in its restaurant and a babysitting service. €338.

Butlers Town House 44 Lansdowne Rd, Ballsbridge ☎01/667 3690, ⊛www .butlers-hotel.com. Lansdowne Rd

DART station or buses #5, #7 and #45. Discretion is the byword at this splendid establishment, from its stately exterior to the opulent comfort of its twenty en-suite, air-conditioned bedrooms, each designed to reflect a more unhurried era. The breakfast is a delight and there's also secure parking available. €180.

Montrose House 16 Pembroke Park, Ballsbridge ☎01/668 4286. The rooms in this elegantly furnished townhouse are extremely sizeable. Two of the three are en suite with TV and there are plenty of books available if you're short of reading matter. Breakfast is taken communally around the same table. On-street parking requires a disc available from nearby machines. €100.

The Portobello Hotel 33 Richmond St South ☎01/475 2715, ⊛www.portobello hotel.ie. Actually accessed by the canal-side Charlemont Mall (see map p.160) and with reception on the first floor, this welcoming 24-room establishment has incredibly spacious and reasonably priced en-suite doubles. Most have views of the canal and to the Dublin mountains beyond and all also have a bath as well as a shower. The hotel has recently been refurbished. €140.

The Schoolhouse Hotel 2–8 Northumberland Rd, Ballsbridge ☎1850 344 000, ⊛www.schoolhousehotel.com. A gem by the canal (see map p.160), *The Schoolhouse* provides 31 superbly furnished and spacious rooms in premises that first opened as a National School in 1861. Each room is individually named, including one appropriately after Pádraig Pearse (see p.163), and facilities include a bar and the *Canteen* restaurant (see p.161). Substantial discounts available most weekends. €199.

Hostels and student accommodation

Dublin has numerous hostels and the majority of these offer both beds in dormitory accommoda-

tion (around €15–25, depending on the season) and private rooms, usually sleeping between two and four persons (€25–45 per person). Private rooms are en suite and the standard is often as good as a B&B. Most hostels in Dublin belong to the IHH (Independent Holiday Hostels of Ireland ⓦwww.hostels-ireland.com) though a few are members of the IHO (Independent Hostel Owners ⓦwww.hostellingireland.com). Additionally, several of the city's educational establishments open up their student accommodation to visitors during the summer vacation. Prices are generally higher than hostels (€45–70 per person per night), but still cheaper than many hotels offering similar city-centre locations.

Trinity College, Grafton Street and around

Ashfield House 19–20 D'Olier St ☏01/679 7734, ⓦwww.ashfieldhouse .ie. One of the centre's most popular choices provides over 100 beds in a variety of bright and spacious rooms, all with en-suite facilities. Dorms come in a variety of sizes, most four- and six-bed and there are comfortable doubles), as well as a kitchen and Internet access. Dorms from €15, doubles €80.

Trinity College College Green ☏01/608 1177. ⓦwww.tcd.ie.conferences /visitor2.htm. The College opens its 800 residential rooms to visitors from mid-June to the end of September. Although not the cheapest budget option, it has an unbeatable, historic location. There's a range of single, twin and four-bed standard- or en-suite rooms with shared kitchen, plus a campus restaurant, bar and sporting facilities. €42–69 per person per night.

St Stephen's Green to the Grand Canal

Mercer Court Campus Accommodation Mercer Street Lower ☏01/474 4120, ⓦwww.mercercourt.ie. Open from late June to late September during the Royal College of Surgeons' holidays, Mercer Court has 100 en-suite bedrooms, all with TV

and continental breakfast is included in the price. €85.

Temple Bar

Barnacles Temple Bar House 19 Temple Lane ☏01/671 6277, ⓦwww.barnacles .ie. This modern hostel's lobby is strangely reminiscent of a sub-post office, but don't be dissuaded because its en-suite rooms and facilities cover all essentials. Dorms from €16, doubles €54.

Oliver St John Gogarty's 18–21 Anglesea St ☏01/671 1822, ⓦwww.gogartys .ie. Not to be recommended at weekends thanks to its popularity with British hen and stag parties, this well-equipped hostel has more than a 100 beds in a range of accommodation, including standard and en-suite twins, up to eight- and ten-bed dorms as well as stylish one- to three-bed apartments. Kitchen and laundry facilities are available. Dorms €18, doubles €60, apartments €120–200.

The old city and South Great George's Street

Avalon House 55 Aungier St ☏01/475 0001, ⓦwww.avalon-house.ie. Five minutes' walk south of South Great George's Street, *Avalon House* occupies a former medical school and has a variety of accommodation available, including various sized dorms, as well as twin-bedded rooms. It's a large hostel (281 beds) and has a café, kitchen, Internet access, TV and games rooms. Dorms €18, doubles €62.

Kinlay House 2–12 Lord Edward St ☏01/679 6644, ⓦwww.kinlayhouse .ie. A very lively and busy hostel near Christ Church Cathedral, *Kinlay House* offers good-value private rooms as well as both small six-bed and much bigger 24-bed dorms. There's a large kitchen as well as a café, and residents qualify for reductions at *Darkey Kelly's* restaurant. Internet access is available. Dorms €17, doubles €64.

The Liberties and Kilmainham

Brewery Hostel 23 Thomas St ☏01/453 8600, ⓦwww.irish-hostel.com. This IHO hostel's inauspicious location (see map p.124) is certainly mitigated by the friendliness of its welcome and all-round cosiness. More like a country hostel than its Dublin cousins, the hostel offers 70 beds, including four private rooms. Facilities include a large lounge, a well-equipped kitchen and well-maintained showers, plus a courtyard for alfresco conviviality. Dorms €18, doubles €75.

O'Connell Street and around

Abbey Court 29 Bachelors Walk ☎01/878 0800, ⊛www.abbey-court .com. Right next to O'Connell Bridge, this upmarket, well-designed hostel provides en-suite twins/doubles and dorms ranging from four to twelve beds. Very security conscious, access is via keycards and there are lockers in every room. Add to that a café, kitchen, laundry, two TV lounges, a conservatory and a barbecue area, plus Internet access. Dorms €21, doubles €88.

Abraham House 82–83 Gardiner St Lower ☎01/855 0600, ⊛www.abraham -house.ie One of the larger Northside hostels, *Abraham House* has both a friendly staff and atmosphere. En-suite rooms range in size from doubles and triples to four-, six-, eight-, ten- and sixteen-bed dorms. There's a good kitchen, lockers, Internet access and a small car park. The stop for bus #41 to and from the airport is adjacent. Dorms €18, doubles €92.

Globetrotters 46 Gardiner St Lower ☎01/873 5893, ⊛www.globetrotters dublin.com. Under the same excellent management as *The Townhouse* (see p.195) this 94-bed hostel offers 6- to 12-bed dorms, equipped with some of the most comfortable bunks in Dublin. All are en suite and there's a good kitchen too plus free Internet access. Dorms €19.

Isaacs Hostel 2–5 Frenchman's Lane ☎01/855 6125, ⊛www.isaacs.ie. Dublin's oldest independent hostel is still one of its best and consists mostly of eight- and ten-bed dorms and some cosy twin-bedded private rooms, though none are en suite. Efficiently run and very welcoming, facilities include a high-quality kitchen, a café, a small garden hosting barbecues in summer, Internet access and live acoustic music on Fridays. Dorms €18, twins €72.

Jacobs Inn 21–28 Talbot Place ☎01/855 5660, ⊛www.isaacs.ie. Entered via a

bright and breezy communal area, this is Dublin's largest independent hostel which, despite its size, remains one of the most convivial. En-suite private rooms are well-furnished and the larger twelve-bed dorms are comfortable too. Internet facilities are available and the hostel is wheelchair accessible. Dorms €16, doubles €62.

Litton Lane Hostel 2–4 Litton Lane ☎01/872 8389, ⊛www.irish-hostel.com. Housed in a former recording studio in a quiet side street off Bachelors Walk, this popular and efficient hostel offers eight- and ten-bed dorms as well as comfortable private rooms. There's a sizeable kitchen too and a pool table. There are also some self-contained apartments sleeping from two to four. Dorms €22, doubles €75, apartments €90–120.

North from Parnell Square

Dublin International Youth Hostel Mountjoy St ☎01/830 1766, ⊛www.irelandyha .org. A gargantuan 293-bed establishment in a somewhat grim Northside area, just west of the Black Church and Dorset Street Upper, this An Óige flagship is more homely inside than its forbidding exterior might suggest. Much of the accommodation is in largish dorms though there are some private and four-bedded rooms. Non-An Óige or International Youth Hostelling Association members are charged a supplement of €2. There's a reasonably priced restaurant and Internet access too. Dorms €20, doubles €52.

Along the Grand Canal

Bective Hostel 2 Eglinton Terrace, Donnybrook ☎01/260 5994, ⊛www .bectivehostel.com. Occupying a beautifully converted Victorian house off Morehampton Road, a couple of miles southwest of the centre (buses #10, #46A and #46B stop nearby), this recent arrival on the hostel scene is Dublin's smallest (just 36 beds) and certainly the only one to feature a jacuzzi. Rooms range include doubles, a triple and to four-, six- and twelve-bed dorms. All are en suite, equipped with a TV and well furnished. There's a sizeable common room, plus a laundry, kitchen BBQ area and Internet access. Dorms €20, doubles €75.

Essentials

Arrival

No matter how you arrive Dublin's efficient transport network means you'll soon be in the city centre, though bear in mind that journeys by road from the airport and ferry terminals may take much longer during rush-hour periods.

By air

Dublin Airport (☎01/874 1111, ⓦwww .aer-rianta.com) is some seven miles north of the centre. The arrivals hall contains a tourist office (daily 8am–10pm), a travel information desk, a *bureau de change*, several ATMs and a number of car-rental outlets.

Buses to the centre depart from outside the arrivals exit. The most direct are the **Airlink** bus #747 (every 10–15min Mon–Sat 5.45am–11.30pm, every 15–20min Sun 7.15am–11.30pm; €5 single, €9 return) which runs via O'Connell Street to Busáras, the central bus station; and #748 (every 30min Mon–Sat 6am–8.05pm, Sun 7am–8.40pm; same prices), which takes a similar route but continues to Heuston railway station. Alternatively, the **Aircoach** service (daily every 15min 4.30am–midnight, hourly midnight–4.30am; €7 single, €12 return; ⓦwww.aircoach.ie) runs into the centre via College Green and onwards to hotels in Donnybrook and Ballsbridge. If you are staying near a DART station (see p.203), the **Aerdart** bus #A1 (every 15min Mon–Fri 5.45am–11.45pm, Sat & Sun 6.30am–11.45pm; €5.50 single, price includes rail travel) runs from the airport to connect with the rail service at Howth Junction.

The slower but cheaper option (€1.75) is to take one of the regular **Dublin Bus** services such as the #16A to O'Connell Street and College Green (every 20–30min Mon–Fri 7.45am–10.40pm, Sat 7am–10.20pm, Sun 9.20am–9.15pm) or #41, #41B and #41C to Eden Quay by O'Connell Bridge (every 10–20min Mon–Sat 6.20am–11.30pm, every 15–30min Sun 7.10am–11.30pm).

Additionally, the #746 (every 30min–1hr 15min Mon–Fri 9.15am–9.45pm, hourly Sat 9.45am–9.45pm & Sun 10am–7pm) runs to the centre and thence to Dún Laoghaire.

Alternatively a **taxi** to the centre should cost around €30.

By bus

Busáras, Dublin's central bus station, is on Store Street behind the Custom House, some ten minutes' walk east of O'Connell Street. It serves Bus Éireann express coaches from all parts of Ireland (North and South) as well as the Airlink service and coaches from Britain. City buses run into the centre along Talbot Street, a block to the north, while there are LUAS Red Line (see p.203) stops just to the north outside Connolly station or to the west on Abbey Street Lower. Alternatively, a taxi can usually be hailed on Beresford Place just south of Busáras.

Private coaches terminate at a variety of locations – check with the service operator for precise details.

By ferry

All services – except Stena Line's HSS (see below) – arrive at **Dublin Port**, two miles east of the centre. An unnumbered Dublin Bus service (€2.50) meets arrivals and runs directly to Busáras. The return service leaves Busáras at 7.30am, 11am, 4.30pm and 7.30pm. Stena Line HSS ferries arrive at **Dún Laoghaire**, nine miles southeast of the city centre. The DART station is directly opposite the terminal and trains (€1.90) run every 20 minutes to the centre (including the central Pearse, Tara Street and Connolly stations). Alternatively, bus #46A (daily every 10–30min; €1.75) runs from outside the Crofton Road entrance to the station via Donnybrook to St Stephen's Green and O'Connell Street. The ferry terminal has a tourist office (Mon–Sat 10am–1pm, 2–6pm).

By train

Trains from Belfast, Sligo, Wexford and Rosslare terminate at **Connolly Station** on Amiens Street, fifteen minutes' walk east of O'Connell Street via Talbot Street and connected to the centre by regular buses and LUAS trams. The station is also on the DART line. **Heuston Station**, on the south bank of the Liffey, two miles west of the centre, serves trains from Ballina, Cork, Galway, Kilkenny, Killarney, Limerick, Tralee, Waterford and Westport. Heuston is connected to the centre by buses #91 and #92 while #90 runs between the station and Connolly. Two other Southside stations, Tara Street and Pearse serve DART and suburban railways. Information on train services and timetables is available from ☎ 01/836 6222, ✆ www.irishrail.ie.

By car

Almost all major trunk roads entering Dublin are linked by the M50 motorway which runs in a semi-circle around the city's outskirts. The M1/N1 (from Belfast and Drogheda), N2 (Derry and Monaghan) and N3 (Cavan) eventually converge on Dorset Street, just north of Parnell Square and O'Connell Street. The N4 (from Sligo, linking with the N6 from Athlone) runs past Heuston Station and thence along the Northside Quays of the Liffey. The N7 (from the southwest, linking with the N9 from Waterford) runs along Crumlin Road, entering the centre via Patrick Street and Christchurch. Lastly, the N11 (from the southeast, linking with the N21 from Dún Laoghaire) runs through Ballsbridge and on to Merrion Square.

City transport and tours

Getting around the city couldn't be easier, thanks to an extensive system of buses, trams and railway services, as well as many taxis.

Buses

Dublin Bus (✆ www.dublinbus.ie) operates a network of routes covering just about everywhere in the city and extending far beyond its boundaries into the county, as well as counties Kildare, Meath and Wicklow. Most of its bus stops display route maps and ticket prices. A free guide to the services, timetables and an excellent, free visitors' map are available from the company's offices at 59 O'Connell St Upper (Mon 8.30am–5.30pm, Tues–Fri 9am–5.30pm, Sat 9am–2pm) while travel information is also available from ☎ 01/873 4222. If your mobile is connected to an Irish network you can also send **text message** enquiries to ☎53503 – type "BUS" followed by the route number (such as "BUS46A") to receive details of the next three buses in each direction. You can also specify different times using the 24-hour clock (such as "BUS19 2100" or even "BUS15 0830 TOMORROW").

All bus fares are exact-change only and ticket prices range from €0.90 for a short ride to €1.85 for the longest journeys (child fares €0.60–0.80). Most services operate around 6.30am–11.30pm on weekdays, starting later and finishing earlier on Sundays. Special **Nitelink** buses run in the small hours (Mon–Wed 12.30am–2am; Thurs 12.30–3.30am, hourly; Fri & Sat 12.30–4.30am, every 20min). These buses run from College Street, D'Olier Street and Westmoreland Street, all routes carry the suffix "N" (e.g. 46N) and tickets cost a flat-fare rate of €4 for the shorter routes and €6 for longer journeys to places such as Ashbourne and Maynooth.

LUAS

Introduced in 2004, LUAS (the Irish for "speed") currently operates two overground **tramway** routes (more are in the pipeline) which are much quicker

Travel passes

A bewildering range of **travel passes** is available from the Dublin Bus office (see p.201), newsagents and other shops displaying the Dublin Bus sign, and from DART and suburban railway stations. Bus-only **Rambler** passes are accepted on all routes except Aerdart, Airlink and Nitelink and cover one day (€5), three (€10), five (€15) and seven (€18) days. Alternatively, the Rambler Handy Pack (€16) consists of five one-day passes and is useful if you don't intend to travel every day. Additionally, the family one-day Rambler (€7.50) covers travel by two adults and up to four children.

One-day passes for the LUAS service (see opposite) cost €4.50 and a seven-day pass is €16 when purchased from station vending machines, but they're cheaper (€4 and €14) when bought from shops bearing the LUAS sign (usually found near the station).

The price of most DART railway (see below) passes depends on the starting and finishing points of your journey. A three-day pass ranges from €5.50–14.20 and a seven-day pass from €9.20–23.80. A combined bus/DART/suburban rail one-day pass costs €7.70, rising to €15 for three days and €26 for seven. A one-day family pass covering the short-hop zone (basically, Malahide to Bray) is €11.60.

than buses and avoid traffic congestion. The Red Line runs from Connolly Station along Abbey Street to Collins Barracks before crossing the river at Heuston Station then heads southwest to the suburb of Tallaght; while the Green Line commences at St Stephen's Green, then heads down Harcourt Street before cruising along to the southeastern suburbs of Dundrum and Sandyford. Trams run every 5–15 minutes (Mon–Fri 5.30am–12.30am, Sat 6.30am–12.30am, Sun 7am–11.30pm) and singles cost €1.30–2 and returns €2.50–3.80 (children €0.80 and €1.60 respectively). Tickets are bought from vending machines at the tramway stops.

DART and suburban trains

The trains of the Dublin Area Rapid Transit system or **DART** (Mon–Sat 6.20am–midnight, Sun 9.20am–11.40pm) link Howth and Malahide to the north of the city with Bray and Greystones to the south via places such as Lansdowne Road, Dún Laoghaire and Dalkey. It's certainly the quickest option for visiting some of the outlying attractions (see Day trips, p.176). Single fares range from €1.10–3.50 with returns at €1.95–6.40 (children's fares €0.70–1.50 and

€1.20–2.75), though buying a travel pass (see above) is a cheaper option. The **suburban train services** operated by Iarnród Éireann utilize the same tracks as the DART, but stop at fewer stations (Connolly, Tara Street and Pearse in the centre, Dún Laoghaire and Bray to the south and Howth Junction to the north). The Northern Commuter line from Pearse Station via Tara Street and Connolly is the quickest means of making day trips to Malahide and Drogheda for Brú na Boinne.

Taxis

Dublin's **taxis** vary in shape and size from London-style black cabs and saloon cars to people carriers, though all are readily identifiable by an illuminated box on the roof displaying the driver's taxi licence number. Taxis can be hailed on the street, but it is often easier to head to one of the various ranks, such as at the northwest corner of St Stephen's Green, next to the Bank of Ireland on College Green, outside The Westin Hotel on Westmoreland Street or in front of The Gresham Hotel on O'Connell Street.

Finding a taxi after 11pm on a busy night can be arduous, especially at weekends in the city centre, so it's advisable to book one earlier. Conversely, if you're heading back to the centre from the suburbs, it can often be easy to hail a cab returning the same way. City Cabs (☎01/872 7272 or 01/490 0099), Satellite Taxis (Northside ☎ 01/836 5555, Southside ☎01/454 3333) and Eurocabs (☎01/623 4100) are all generally reliable options. Eurocabs can also supply a wheelchair-accessible taxi if booked one hour or more in advance.

As for fares, a short hop will usually cost around €6–8 while a trip from the centre to one of the closer suburbs, such as Clontarf or Ballsbridge will cost around €10–12. Metered taxis tend to be cheaper than the flat-fare variety and can use the city's bus lanes.

Cars and parking

Dublin's "rush-hour" covers the entire weekday periods from 7–10am and 4–7pm and some areas, such as The Quays and Dame Street, are best avoided at all times. As for car parks, a good Southside option is the Royal College of Surgeons multi-storey off the west side of St Stephen's Green. On-street spaces are hard to find, but Merrion Square and Fitzwilliam Square are usually safe bets.

Unless you're planning to use the city as a tour base there's no need to **rent a car** in Dublin. The cost of a week's rental ranges from around €200–300 depending upon vehicle size and insurance costs. Major reductions can be found by advance Internet booking.

Open-top bus tours

One of the simplest ways of seeing the sights if time is short is to take a ride on one of the several hop-on-and-off **open-top bus tours**. Commentary is provided either by the driver (some of whom also readily break into appropriate songs), an on-board guide or a prerecorded tape. All tickets offer a range of discounts to the city's attractions.

All the tours follow roughly the same route covering Parnell Square, Trinity College, St Stephen's Green, Dublin Castle, the cathedrals, the Guinness Storehouse, the Irish Museum of Modern Art (or Kilmainham Gaol), Phoenix Park and Collins Barracks. The full circular tour lasts around 1hr 15min.

Dublin Bus (☎01/873 4222, ⊛www .dublinbus.ie) offers the daily Dublin City Tour, commencing from outside its office at 59 O'Connell St Upper (daily every 10min 9.30am–3pm, every 15min 3–5pm and also June–Aug every 30min 5–6.30pm). Tickets cost €12.50 and can be purchased from the office or driver and from certain hotels. The company also operates a Ghost Bus Tour (Mon–Fri 8pm, Sat 7pm & 9.30pm; €22; not suitable for under 14s) visiting the city's spookier spots.

Irish Tours (☎01/872 9010, ⊛www .irishcitytours.com) operates a City Sightseeing Tour (daily every 10–15min; mid-March to mid-July 9am–5pm, mid-July to Sept 9.30am–5.30pm, Oct 9.30am–4pm, Nov to mid-March 9.30am–3.30pm; €15). Tickets can be purchased at the company's office, 33 Bachelors Walk, from the driver, tourist information offices and some hotels. Tours commence from outside 14 O'Connell St Upper.

Car rental companies

Argus Airport ☎01/814 4013 and Dublin Tourism Centre, Suffolk St ☎01/605 7701, ⊛www.argusrentals.com.
Atlas Airport ☎01/864 4859, ⊛www .atlascarhire.com.
County Airport ☎01/854 5689 and Dublin Tourism Centre, 14 O'Connell St Upper ☎01/874 6084, ⊛www .countycar.ie.

Dan Dooley Airport ☎01/844 5156 and 42 Westland Row ☎01/677 2723, ⊛www.dan-dooley.ie.
Hertz Airport ☎01/844 5466 and 151 South Circular Rd ☎01/709 3060, ⊛www.hertz.co.uk.
Irish Car Rentals Airport ☎01/844 4199, ⊛www.irishcar rentals.com.

Land and water tour

The award-winning **Viking Splash** tour (64–65 Patrick St ☎01/707 6000 ⊛ www.vikingsplashtours.com) uses reconditioned World War II amphibious vehicles known as Ducks and guides in Norse costume to provide a lively tour of the centre, culminating in a voyage from the Grand Canal Basin (mid-Feb to mid-March Wed–Sun 10am–4pm; mid-March to Oct daily 9.30am–5pm; Nov Tues–Sun 10am–4pm; 1hr 15min). Tours operate from Bull Alley Street (next to St Patrick's Cathedral) and tickets (June Sat & Sun and July & Aug daily €17.50; rest of year €15.50) can be bought at the company office or the Suffolk Street tourist office.

Walking tours

Historical Insights (☎ 01/878 0227, ⊛ www.historicalinsights.ie) operates a two-hour tour run by Trinity history graduates covering Dublin's development and major events. Tours (April–Oct daily 11am, May–Sept 11am & 3pm; Nov–March Fri–Sun noon; €10) start from Trinity College's front gate.

The **1916 Rebellion** tour (☎086/858 3847, ⊛ www.1916rising.com) covers the events leading up to the Easter Rising, the rebellion itself and its aftermath. Tickets cost €10 and tours commence inside the *International Bar*, Wicklow Street (Nov to mid–March Sat 11.30am, Sun 1pm; mid-March to Oct Tues & Wed 11.30am, Thurs–Sat 11.30am & 2.30pm, Sun 1pm; 2hr).

The **Zozimus Ghostly Experience** (☎01/661 8648, ⊛ www.zozimus.com) is a ghoulish tour of the medieval city led by actors in which the blind storyteller Zozimus and his fellow cast recreate notorious events. Advance booking is essential and tours commence outside the gates of Dublin Castle nightly June–Aug 9pm, Sept–May 7pm; 1hr 30min; €10).

For something less fiendish there's the **Jameson Dublin Literary Pub Crawl** (☎01/670 5602, ⊛www.dublinpubcrawl.com) which commences upstairs at *The Duke* on Duke Street and involves actors performing extracts from major works in a number of pubs with literary connections (April–Nov daily 7.30pm, also Sun noon; Dec–March Thurs–Sun; 2hr 15min; €10).

Lastly, the **Traditional Irish Music Pub Crawl** (☎01/478 0193, ⊛www.discoverdublin.ie/musicalpubcrawl.html) sees two musicians guide you on a tour of half a dozen pubs, performing songs and music while recounting Ireland's musical history. Tours (daily April–Oct 7.30pm, Nov–March Thurs–Sat only; 2hr 30min) begin upstairs at *Oliver St John Gogarty's*, Fleet Street.

Information

Tourist offices

The main Dublin Tourism Centre (Mon–Sat 9am–5.30pm, July & Aug until 7pm, Sun and Public Holidays 10.30am–3pm; ⊛www.visitdublin.com) occupies the former St Andrew's Church on Suffolk Street, a short distance west of the Grafton Street junction with Nassau Street. A numbered-ticket queuing system operates for information and accommodation reservations (see p.189 for more on the latter) and there are also desks for currency exchange, car rental and the purchase of tickets for events. Outside is a touch-screen information console that accepts credit card accommodation bookings. Dublin Tourism's other offices are at the airport (see p.201), Dún Laoghaire ferry terminal (see p.201), 14 O'Connell St (Mon–Sat 9am–5pm) and Baggott Street Bridge (Mon–Fri 9.30am–noon & 12.30–5pm).

Tourist passes

Available at any tourist information office or online at ⊛ www.dublinpass.com, the **Dublin Pass** provides free entry to more than thirty attractions as well as a range of other special offers and a one-way journey to the airport on the Aircoach service (see p.201). A one-day pass costs €29 with two-, three- and six-day passes at €49, €59 and €89 respectively. It can also be worth acquiring a **Heritage Card** (€20) for free entry to attractions run by the Heritage Service (☎01/647 2453, ⊛ www.heritageireland.ie), such as the Casino at Marino, Kilmainham Gaol, Dublin Castle, Rathfarnham Castle, Phoenix Park Visitor Centre and, further afield, Glendalough Visitor Centre, Castletown House and Brú na Boinne. Cards are available from Heritage Service sites or tourist offices.

Newspapers and listings magazines

The heavyweight daily *Irish Times* (€1.50) and the *Evening Herald* (€1) are both useful sources of information, including cinema and theatre listings, and the former also produces a weekly listings supplement, *The Ticket*, on Fridays. Free listings magazines include the weekly *In Dublin*, the fortnightly *Event Guide* and the monthly *Totally Dublin*, and copies of all of them can be picked up in bars, cafés, record and CD shops and shopping malls. *Mongrel* (monthly; free) also has articles on the local arts scene. Music listings can also be found in the fortnightly rock and style magazine *Hot Press* (€3.50) while traditional music is covered by the monthly *Irish Music* (€2.95). The O'Connell Street Lower branch of Eason's (see p.135) stocks just about every magazine published in Ireland, along with all Irish and British newspapers.

Dublin on the Internet

Dublin Tourism's ⊛ www.visitdublin.com site is a useful entry point, particularly for details of attractions, events and booking accommodation.

⊛ **www.browseireland.com** A massive all-Ireland portal with plenty of useful Dublin links.

⊛ **www.ddda.ie** Events and activities both on the water and in the surrounding Docklands.

⊛ **www.dublincity.ie** Dublin Corporation's site includes information on various facilities provided – handy if you fancy a swim.

⊛ **www.dublinfinder.net** Another huge portal with links for everything from shopping to entertainment.

⊛ **www.dublinpubscene.com** Pub review site with details of live-music and comedy nights.

⊛ **www.entertainment.ie** Bucketloads of information about the latest shows, screenings and events.

⊛ **www.temple-bar.ie** Everything that's happening around this vibrant area.

Entertainment

Cinema

Mainstream cinemas include UGC, 17 Parnell St ☎01/872 8444, ⊛ www.ugc .ie; Savoy, O'Connell Street ☎01/874 6000; and Screen, Townsend Street, ☎ 01/672 5500. Fans of world and independent cinema should head for the Irish Film Institute (see p.101).

Classical music

The National Concert Hall (Earlsfort Terrace, ☎01/417 0000, ⊛ www.nch.ie) is

Dublin's largest classical music venue, featuring weekly concerts by the resident RTÉ National Symphony Orchestra as well as visiting orchestras and soloists and a varied programme of jazz and traditional music.

Other places regularly staging classical music events include the Bank of Ireland Arts Centre, Foster Place ☎01/671 2261, ⊛ www.bankofireland .ie; National Gallery, Merrion Square West ☎01/661 5133, ⊛ www.nationalgallery .ie; St Mary's Pro-Cathedral (see p.133); SS Michael and John, Essex Street West ☎ 01/858 6644; St Patrick's Cathedral, St Patrick's Close ☎01/453 9472, ⊛ www.stpatrickscathedral.ie; and Trinity College Chapel, Trinity College Street ⊛ www.tcd.ie.

Theatre

The most renowned theatres are the Abbey (see p.132) and the Gate (see p.139). Other worth seeking out include Andrew's Lane Theatre, 12 St Andrew's Lane ☎ 01/679 5720, ⊛ www.andrewslane .com; Gaiety Theatre, King Street South ☎01/677 1717 ⊛ www.gaietytheatre .net; The Helix (see p.175); Liberty Hall, Eden Quay ☎ 01/872 1122; Olympia Theatre (see p.106); Pavilion Theatre, Marine Road, Dún Laoghaire ☎01/231 2929, ⊛ www.paviliontheatre.ie; Peacock Theatre (see p.133); and SFX City Theatre, 23 Upper Sherrard St ☎01/855 4090, ⊛ www.sfx.ie.

Also of note is the Lambert Puppet Theatre, 5 Clifton Lane, Monkstown ☎01/280 0964 ⊛ www.lambertpuppet theatre.com which stages daily shows during May and June (call for times) and all-year performances (Sat & Sun 3.30pm), as well as an international puppet festival in mid-September.

Sporting venues

Croke Park St Joseph's Avenue ☎01/836 3222, ⊛ www.gaa.ie. The home of the Gaelic Athletic Association hosts both hurling and Gaelic football matches and other major events (see p.143 for more details).

Lansdowne Road ☎01/647 3800, ⊛ www.irfu.ie/top/lansdowne.asp. The ageing stadium continues to stage rugby internationals and other major matches, as well as football internationals and occasional rock gigs. However, events will transfer to Croke Park (see p.143) when redevelopment starts in 2007.

Shelbourne Park Greyhound Stadium South Lotts Rd, Ringsend ☎01/668 3502, ⊛ www.shelbournepark.com. Greyhound racing every Wed, Thurs & Sat 8pm (€8). Alternatively, there's also Harold's Cross Stadium, off Harold's Cross Road (☎01/497 1081), Mon, Tues & Fri (same times and price).

Horse racing

There are several racetracks within easy reach of Dublin and Bus Éireann (☎01/836 6111, ⊛ www.buseireann.ie) lays on special services on race days, leaving from Busáras (see p.201).

The Curragh 31 miles southwest of the capital, near Kildare town ☎045/441205, ⊛ www.curragh.ie. Home to the flat-racing classics: the Irish 2000 Guineas and 1000 Guineas in May, the Irish Derby in June, the Irish Oaks in July and the Irish St Leger in September. Trains from Heuston Station stop at The Curragh on the big race days.

Fairyhouse Ratoath, 15 miles northwest of Dublin ☎01/825 6167, ⊛ www.fairyhouse racecourse.ie. Venue for the Irish Grand National on Easter Monday.

Leopardstown in the southern suburb of Foxrock ☎01/289 0500, ⊛ www.leopards town.com. Races are held at weekends throughout the year and on Wed and Sat evenings in summer, but the main events are the four-day Christmas Festival starting on St Stephen's Day (Dec 26), and the Hennessy Cognac Gold Cup in February. LUAS to Sandyford station then a 15min walk.

Punchestown 25 miles southwest of Dublin near Naas ☎045/897704, ⊛ www.punchestown.com. Home to the four-day Irish National Hunt Festival in April.

Festivals and events

February

Dublin Chinatown Festival ☎01/448 7777, ⊛www.chinatown.ie. Set over the Chinese New Year in early February, this festival features numerous events around the city, including plenty of music and dance, as well as activities at the two Dublin branches of the National Museum.

Jameson Dublin International Film Festival ☎01/661 6216, ⊛www.dubliniff .com. Held at cinemas and other venues across the city centre in mid-February. While screening the latest in new Irish cinema, the festival also has a decidedly international flavour and its hundred or so films include special themes and retrospectives.

RTÉ Living Music Festival ☎01/208 2617, ⊛www.rte.ie/music. Three days of contemporary classical music concerts and events, featuring leading Irish and international figures held in mid-February at The Helix (see p.175).

March/April

Easter Rising Commemorations take place on Easter Sunday, featuring speeches and a march from the General Post Office to Glasnevin Cemetery.

St Patrick's Festival ☎01/676 3205, ⊛www.stpatricksfestival.ie. Running for six days on and around St Patrick's Day (March 17), this city-wide festival includes a parade, Europe's biggest fireworks display, a music village, funfair, exhibitions and a *ceili mor* (a day of traditional dancing).

Poetry Now Festival ☎01/205 4873, ⊛www.dircoo.ie/arts. A major four-day event, held over the first weekend in April at The Pavilion Theatre, Dún Laoghaire, the festival features readings by major Irish and international poets, master classes, exhibitions and children's events.

Feis Ceoil ☎01/676 7365, ⊛www .siemens.ie/feis. Spread over two weeks at the beginning of April, this is Europe's longest running classical music festival and celebrates its 110th anniversary in 2006. Competitions feature some 8000 contestants and take place at a variety of locations, culminating in a grand prizewinners' concert at the Royal Dublin Society's Showgrounds, Merrion Road, Ballsbridge.

Convergence Sustainable Living Festival ☎01/674 6396, ⊛www.sustainable.ie. Run by the Sustainable Ireland Cooperative, and focusing on ecological and environmental matters, the festival takes place in Temple Bar over five days in late April. Featuring a diverse range of events, including plenty for children.

May

Heineken Green Energy ☎0818/719 300, ⊛www.ticketmaster.ie. Major music acts play outdoors at Dublin Castle over the first weekend in May; previous performers have included The White Stripes, Lou Reed, Faithless and Manic Street Preachers.

Bray Jazz Festival ☎01/272 4030, ⊛www.brayjazz.com. Three days of gigs, featuring international singers and musicians at more than a dozen venues over the first weekend in May.

Wicklow Gardens Festival ☎0404/20070, ⊛www.wicklow.ie/tourism. A variety of privately owned gardens close to Dublin throw open their gates to the public between May and August.

June

Diversions Temple Bar ☎01/677 2255, ⊛www.templebar.ie. This series of free outdoor events runs from June to September in and around Meeting House Square and includes film screenings, music performances, family fun days and other entertainment.

Bloomsday ☎01/878 8547, ⊛www .jamesjoyce.ie. The James Joyce Centre organizes a week of events in mid-June, culminating in Bloomsday itself (June 16), the day on which Joyce's *Ulysses* is set.

Docklands Maritime Festival ⊛www .ddda.ie. Tall ships open their decks to visitors in mid-June at North Wall Quay, plus there's a market, art exhibition and a variety of events for children.

Dublin Writers Festival ☎01/671 3639, ⊛www.dublinwritersfestival.com. Major Irish and international writers and poets take part in four days of readings, discussions and other events around the city centre in mid-June.

July

Outlook ⊛www.gcn.ie/dlgff/home.asp. Dublin's Lesbian and Gay Film Festival takes place at the Irish Film Institute (see p.101) at the end of July and features a strong programme of new feature and documentary works.

August

Dublin Horse Show ☎01/668 0866, ⊛www.dublinhorseshow.com. Five days of equestrian events in August at the RDS arena in Ballsbridge, featuring major international showjumpers, including the Nations Cup.

September/October

All-Ireland Senior Hurling and Gaelic Football finals Two of Ireland's major sporting events are staged at Croke Park (see p.143) in September: the hurling final on the second Sunday and the football final on the fourth.
Dublin Fringe Festival ☎1850/374 643, ⊛www.fringefest.com. Ireland's biggest performing arts festival takes place over three weeks from mid-September to October and features all manner of music, dance, street theatre, comedy and children's events.

Dublin Theatre Festival ☎01/677 8439, ⊛www.dublintheatrefestival.com. A major celebration of theatre, held during the first two weeks in October, this includes performances of new and classic drama at various city centre venues.
Oscar Wilde Autumn School ☎01/286 5245. Six days devoted to the dramatist, novelist and man of letters, set around Wilde's birthday (Oct 16), featuring various shows, lectures, readings, walks and musical events, including some activities geared towards children. The venue for indoor events is usually the *Esplanade Hotel* on the seafront.
Dublin City Marathon ☎01/623 2250, ⊛www.dublincitymarathon.ie. Featuring 10,000 entrants, the race takes place on the last Monday in October and involves a roughly circular course starting from Kildare Street and terminating at Merrion Square West.

Directory

ATMs Virtually all banks have ATMs which accept cards bearing the Cirrus, Maestro, Switch or Visa symbol and dispense funds from your account in euros.
BANKS AND EXCHANGE Most banks open Mon–Fri 10am–4pm, Thurs until 5pm. The majority of bank branches will change Travellers' Cheques and there are also foreign exchange desks at the airport. Centrally located *bureaux de change* include Thomas Cook, 118 Grafton St (Mon–Sat 9am–5.30pm, Thurs until 8pm), the GPO, O'Connell Street Lower (Mon–Sat 8am–8pm) and the Dublin Tourism Centre, Suffolk Street (Mon–Sat 9am–5pm).
DISABLED TRAVELLERS Both the government agency Comhairle, 7th Floor, Hume House, Dublin 4 ☎01/605 9000, ⊛www.comhairle.ie, and Dublin Tourism (see p.205) offer advice and information to people with disabilities visiting Ireland. The latter's annual accommodation guide (available from all offices) indicates which of the city's establishments are wheelchair-accessible. The Irish Wheelchair Association, Aras Chúchulain, Blackheath Drive, Clontarf, Dublin 3 ☎01/818 6403, ⊛www.iwa.ie also provides advice on accessible accommodation and other amenities in Ireland and

its website lists contact details of companies offering wheelchairs for hire. In terms of transport, Dublin Bus (see p.202 and ⊛www.dublinbus.ie/about_us/accessibility.asp) operates low-floor fully accessible buses on almost fifty routes and some of its tours. Similarly, with advance notice, Iarnród Éireann (☎01/836 6222, ⊛www.irishrail.ie/about_us/disabled_access.asp) will make sure that staff meet and assist you on your DART or railway journey. Information on taxis can be found on p.203.
ELECTRICITY The standard electricity supply is 220 volts and three-pin plugs are the norm. All appliances purchased in Britain should function normally, but those from North America will need a transformer and a plug adapter (available from most electrical suppliers and airport shops). Those from Australia and New Zealand will only require an adapter.
EMBASSIES Australia, Fitzwilliam House, Wilton Terrace ☎01/664 5300; Canada, 65 St Stephen's Green ☎01/417 4100; UK, 31 Merrion Rd ☎205 3700; USA, 42 Elgin Rd ☎01/668 8777.
EMERGENCIES Dial ☎112 or 999 for emergency medical assistance, fire services or police.

GAY AND LESBIAN TRAVELLERS *GCN* (Gay Community News; @ www.gcn.ie) is a free monthly magazine which includes events listings – copies can usually be found at gay venues or Books Upstairs, 36 College Green (see p.74). Outhouse, 105 Capel St ☎01/873 4932, @ www.outhouse. ie is a gay and lesbian resource centre with a café (Mon–Fri 1.30–5.30pm, Sat 1–5pm, also Tues 6.30–9.30pm, Thurs 7–10pm – women only, and Fri 7–10pm – men only) and a small library, and is used for meetings by various groups. Gay Switchboard (Mon–Fri 7.30–9.30pm, Sat 3.30–6pm; ☎01/872 1055) provides advice and information. Useful websites include @ www .queerid.com for events and news, @ dublin .gaymonkey.com for community news and events, and @ www.out.ie for online chat.

HOSPITALS Hospitals with accident and emergency departments include: Beaumont Hospital, Beaumont Rd ☎01/809 3000; Mater Misericordiae, Eccles St ☎01/885 8888; and, St James's, James St ☎01/410 3000. For dental emergencies there is the Dublin Dental School and Hospital, Lincoln Place ☎01/812 7200 @ www.tcd.ie /dental_school.

INTERNET CAFÉS Central options include Central Cyber Café, 6 Grafton St; Global Internet Café, 8 O'Connell St Lower; Internet Exchange, 3 Cecilia St, Temple Bar; Oz Cyber Café, 39 Abbey Street Upper; and, Planet Cyber Café, 13 St Andrew's St. Access costs from as little as €2–3 per hour.

LEFT-LUGGAGE Left-luggage lockers are available in Busáras (in the station basement) and on the concourse of Connolly and Heuston train stations.

LOST PROPERTY Dublin Bus ☎01/703 1321; Bus Éireann ☎01/703 2489; Connolly Station ☎01/703 2355; Heuston Station ☎01/703 2102; Airport ☎01/814 4483.

OPENING HOURS City centre shops tend to open from 9.30am or 10am until 6pm Mon–Sat with many staying open until 8pm on Thurs. Some also open from noon–6pm on Sun. Standard pub opening times are Mon–Thurs 10.30am–11.30pm, Fri & Sat 10.30am–12.30am and Sun noon–11pm. Café hours tend to be Mon–Sat 8am–6pm with most in the city centre opening on Sun from around 9am or 10am–6pm. Restaurants generally serve lunch from noon–3pm and dinner from 6pm onwards. Exceptions to these hours have been detailed in the listings section of each chapter.

PHARMACIES Central pharmacies include Dame Street Pharmacy, 16 Dame St ☎01/670 4523 and O'Connell's at both 55 O'Connell St Lower ☎01/873 0427 and 17 Westmoreland St ☎01/677 8440, all open daily until 10pm.

POLICE The main police station (Garda Siochana) is on Harcourt Terrace ☎01/666 9500). A free Tourist Victim Support service is also offered here (Mon–Sat 10am–6pm, Sun noon–6pm; ☎ 01/478 5296, @ www .touristvictimsupport.ie).

POST OFFICES The largest is the General Post Office on O'Connell Street Lower (Mon–Sat 8am–8pm, ☎01/705 8833). There are also central branches at St Andrew's St (by the Suffolk St Tourism Centre), Ormond Quay Upper and Clare St. For mail enquiries call ☎1850/575 589. Many newsagents sell postage stamps.

PUBLIC HOLIDAYS New Year's Day; St Patrick's Day (March 17); Good Friday, Easter Monday; first Monday in May, June and August; last Monday in October; Christmas Day; St Stephen's Day (December 26). Virtually all attractions are closed on Good Friday and from Christmas Eve to St Stephen's Day.

SMOKING You can't smoke in any enclosed workplace in the Republic of Ireland, including all bars and pubs, clubs, cafés and restaurants. However, many establishments provide outdoor, sometimes heated, space for smokers.

SWIMMING POOL Markievicz Leisure Centre, Townsend St ☎01/672 9121, @ www .dublincity.ie.

TAX-FREE SHOPPING Visitors from outside the EU can claim a VAT refund on all goods bought in Ireland, as long as these are taken out of the country within three months of purchase. Not all retailers participate in the VAT refund scheme, but those who do will display a sticker (for more information see @ www.globalrefund.ie).

TELEPHONES Public phones are widely available and making a local call costs a minimum €0.50. Most phones will also accept pre-paid cards purchasable from post offices and newsagents. Mobile phones from the UK usually switch to an Irish network automatically on arrival (though you should check call costs with your network provider); US cell phones need to be GSM compatible. US Operator assistance, including reverse-charge calls, is available by dialling ☎10 for Ireland and the UK and ☎114 for the rest of the world.

TIME Ireland is on Greenwich Mean Time like Britain and operates a similar daylight saving scheme, putting clocks forward by one hour in March and back again at the end of October.

TIPPING It's usual to reward good restaurant service with a tip of 10–15 percent, a sum also expected by most taxi drivers too. A growing number of restaurants and hotels automatically add a discretionary service charge to your bill.

TOILETS Note that the Irish words *fir* (men) and *mná* (women) may appear on some establishment's toilet doors.

Stay in touch

Rough Guides FREE full–colour newsletter News, travel issues, music reviews, readers' letter and the lastest dispatches from authors on the road

If you would like to receive Rough News, please send us your name and address:

Rough Guides

80 Strand London
WC2R 0RL

4th Floor, 345
Hudson St, New York
NY10014, USA

newslettersubs@roughguides.co.uk

Small print & **Index**

A Rough Guide to Rough Guides

Dublin DIRECTIONS is published by Rough Guides. The first *Rough Guide to Greece*, published in 1982, was a student scheme that became a publishing phenomenon. The immediate success of the book – with numerous reprints and a Thomas Cook prize short-listing – spawned a series that rapidly covered dozens of destinations. Rough Guides had a ready market among low-budget backpackers, but soon also acquired a much broader and older readership that relished Rough Guides' wit and inquisitiveness as much as their enthusiastic, critical approach. Everyone wants value for money, but not at any price. Rough Guides soon began supplementing the "rougher" information about hostels and low-budget listings with the kind of detail on restaurants and quality hotels that independent-minded visitors on any budget might expect, whether on business in New York or trekking in Thailand. These days the guides offer recommendations from shoestring to luxury and cover a large number of destinations around the globe, including almost every country in the Americas and Europe, more than half of Africa and most of Asia and Australasia. Rough Guides now publish:

• Travel guides to more than 200 worldwide destinations
• Dictionary phrasebooks to 22 major languages
• Maps printed on rip-proof and waterproof Polyart™ paper
• Music guides running the gamut from Opera to Elvis
• Reference books on topics as diverse as the weather and Shakespeare
• World music CDs in association with World Music Network

Visit **www.roughguides.com** to see our latest publications.

Publishing information

This 1st edition published February 2006 by
Rough Guides Ltd, 80 Strand, London WC2R 0RL.
345 Hudson St, 4th Floor, New York, NY 10014, USA.
14 Local Shopping Centre, Panchsheel Park, New
Delhi 110017, India.

Distributed by the Penguin Group
Penguin Books Ltd, 80 Strand, London WC2R 0RL
Penguin Group (USA), 375 Hudson Street, NY
10014, USA
Penguin Group (Australia), 250 Camberwell Road,
Camberwell, Victoria 3124, Australia
Penguin Group (Canada), 10 Alcorn Avenue,
Toronto, Ontario M4V 1E4, Canada
Penguin Group (New Zealand), Cnr Rosedale and
Airborne Roads, Albany, Auckland, New Zealand
Typeset in Bembo and Helvetica to an original
design by Henry Iles.

Printed and bound in China
© Paul Gray, Geoff Wallis February 2006

224pp includes index

A catalogue record for this book is available from
the British Library

ISBN-10: 1-84353-543-2

The publishers and authors have done their best
to ensure the accuracy and currency of all the
information in **DUBLIN DIRECTIONS**; however, they
can accept no responsibility for any loss, injury, or
inconvenience sustained by any traveller as a result
of information or advice contained in the guide.

1   3   5   7   9   8   6   4   2

Help us update

We've gone to a lot of effort to ensure that the first edition of **DUBLIN DIRECTIONS** is accurate and up to date. However, things change – places get "discovered", opening hours are notoriously fickle, restaurants and rooms raise prices or lower standards. If you feel we've got it wrong or left something out, we'd like to know, and if you can remember the address, the price, the phone number, so much the better.

We'll credit all contributions, and send a copy of the next edition (or any other DIRECTIONS guide or Rough Guide if you prefer) for the best letters. Everyone who writes to us and isn't already a subscriber will receive a copy of our full-colour thrice-yearly newsletter. Please mark letters: "**DUBLIN DIRECTIONS Update**" and send to: Rough Guides, 80 Strand, London WC2R 0RL, or Rough Guides, 4th Floor, 345 Hudson St, New York, NY 10014. Or send an email to **mail@roughguides.com**

Have your questions answered and tell others about your trip at **www.roughguides.atinfopop .com**

SMALL PRINT

Rough Guide credits

Text editors: Edward Aves, Andy Turner, Ruth Blackmore
Layout: Amit Verma
Photography: Mark Thomas
Cartography: Animesh Pathak

Picture editor: JJ Luck
Proofreader: Madhulita Mohapatra
Production: Julia Bovis
Design: Henry Iles
Cover design: Chloë Roberts

The authors

Paul Gray has been a regular visitor to Dublin since 1990 and lived in the city for three years until 2004. He is co-author of the *Rough Guide to Ireland* and the *Rough Guide to Thailand*, and has edited and contributed to many other guidebooks, including updating his native Northeast for the *Rough Guide to England*.

Nottingham-born **Geoff Wallis** has been visiting Ireland for the last quarter of a century and is co-author of the *Rough Guide to Ireland* and the *Rough Guide to Irish Music*. Apart from travel writing, he is a respected music journalist who contributes articles and reviews to *fRoots*, *Songlines* and *Musical Traditions* magazines while continuing to follow the declining fortunes of his native city's football team.

Acknowledgements

The authors would like to thank: John Lahiffe and all at Tourism Ireland; Dublin Tourism; the staff of all the tourist attractions that assisted our research; and our editor, Ed Aves.
Paul would also like to thank: Jan; Brooks Hotel, the Clarence, the Leeson Inn and the Merrion Hotel;

Ciarán and Eimear; Nick and Niamh; the Gurkleys; Julia and Delphine.
Geoff would also like to thank: Marian Ryan; Theresa Quinn; Joan McDermott; Nicholas Carolan; Tom Sherlock; Finbar Boyle; George Hook; Áine Kelly; P.J. Malone; Grainne Lafferty.

Readers' letters

Thanks to all those readers of the third edition of the *Rough Guide to Dublin* who took the trouble to write in with their amendments and additions. Apologies for any misspellings or omissions.

Jessica Backlund, John Barth, Chris Burin, Pete Campbell, Stéphane Catelain, Brian Cotterill, Brian Donnellan, Marie Victoria Ellwood, Lionel Frewin, Sarah Growcott, Bryce Jones, Geraint Jones &

Helen Dixon, Mr I Lisk, Brendan McEvoy, Chris and Noreen Malone, Bri Miles, Ruth Pertab, John Roberts, Simon Shaw.

Photo credits

All photos © Rough Guides except the following:

Front cover: Ha'penny Bridge © Alamy.
p.5 Ha'penny Bridge, River Liffey © Jon Arnold Images/Alamy.
p.5 *Book of Kells*, Gospel of St Matthew (vellum) © The Board of Trinity College, Dublin.
p.8 *The Four Seasons* by Felim Egan. Commissioned by OPW (Office of Public Works) for the new atrium at the National Gallery of Ireland.
p.8 Temple Bar © PCL/Alamy.
p.8 *Portrait of Alice Liddell, after Lewis Carroll* by Vik Muniz © Collection Irish Museum of Modern Art.
p.12 *Akbar discourses with two Jesuit Priests* by Narsingh, India © Chester Beatty Library.

p.13 *Woman writing a letter, with her Maid* by Johannes Vermeer. Courtesy of the National Gallery of Ireland. Photographer: Roy Hewson.
p.13 Gold Collar, Gleninsheen, Co. Clare © Image courtesy of the National Museum of Ireland.
p.15 McDaid's © DK Images.
p.16 Two men celebrating Bloomsday © Richard T. Nowitz/Corbis.
p.17 James Joyce Tower, Sandycove © JJ Museum.
p.19 Oysters © Rougemont Maurice/Corbis Sygma.
p.21 U2 – Bono and The Edge © Stephane Cardinale/People Avenue/Corbis.
p.22 Newman House. Courtesy of Newman House.

p.30 Frost at St Kevin's kitchen and graveyard, Glendalough © Richard Cummins/Corbis.

p.32 Doheny and Nesbitt © Massimo Listri/Corbis.

p.35 Robert Emmet (1778–1803) death mask © Image courtesy of the National Museum of Ireland.

p.37 Merrion Hotel spa – swimming pool. Courtesy of the Merrion Hotel.

p.37 Interior, Restaurant Patrick Guilbaud. Courtesy of Restaurant Patrick Guilbaud.

p.37 Penthouse Suite at The Clarence. Courtesy of The Clarence.

p.38 Swimming off Forty Foot © Michael St Maur Sheil/Corbis.

p.39 Picnic in Merrion Square gardens © Geray Sweeney/Corbis.

p.40 Dublin marathon © Brendan Moran/ SPORTSFILE.

p.40 Hurling championship, Croke Park © Ray McManus/SPORTSFILE.

p.41 Irish Greyhound Derby, Shelbourne Park © Ray McManus/SPORTSFILE.

p.41 Leopardstown racecourse © Matt Browne/ SPORTSFILE.

p.41 Rugby, Lansdowne Road © Brendan Moran/ SPORTSFILE.

p.45 *House of Prince* by Tal R © Douglas Hyde Gallery.

p.45 *Eye of the Storm* by Michael Craig-Martin © Collection Irish Museum of Modern Art.

p.45 *Untitled (Kneeling Figure – Back View)* by Francis Bacon © The Estate of Francis Bacon, courtesy of the Hugh Lane Gallery.

p.47 Hodges Figgis facade. Courtesy of Hodges Figgis.

p.47 Brown Thomas department store. Courtesy of Brown Thomas.

p.48 Taking aim at the wrongdoers in the pillory, Dublinia. Courtesy of Dublinia.

p.49 Billy goats. Courtesy of the Lambert Puppet Theatre.

p.49 Sunflower, The Ark. Courtesy of The Ark.

p.53 DART ride to Bray/Greystones © Vitalii/Alamy.

p.53 Powerscourt © Si Howard/Alamy.

p.53 View of the city from Smithfield Observation Chimney © David Sanger photography/Alamy.

p.55 Drawing rooms at the Merrion Hotel. Courtesy of the Merrion Hotel.

p.56 Interior, the Helix Theatre. Courtesy of the Helix Theatre.

p.57 Exterior, the Gate Theatre. Courtesy of the Gate Theatre.

p.57 Nora and children, the Abbey Theatre. Courtesy of the Abbey Theatre.

p.57 Fringe Festival poster. Courtesy of the Fringe Festival.

p.57 The Project Arts Centre. Courtesy of the Project Arts Centre.

p.59 Curlew © David Tipling/Alamy.

p.59 Dalkey and Killiney Hills © DK Images.

p.60 St Patrick's parade © Bruno Barbier/Robert Harding.

p.60 Diversions festival, Temple Bar. Courtesy of Temple Bar Properties Ltd.

p.61 RDS Horse Show. Courtesy of the RDS Horse Show.

p.61 Henri Texier, Bray Jazz Festival © Robert Goode.

p.61 Docklands Maritime Festival. Courtesy of the Docklands Maritime Festival.

p.62 Smithfield horse market © Network Photographers/Alamy.

p.63 Busker, Grafton Street © Peter Titmuss/Alamy.

p.64 Avenue of horse chestnut and lime trees in Phoenix Park © R.A. Murphy/Alamy.

p.88 Whale skeleton, The Natural History Museum © National Museum of Ireland.

p.112 Mummified cat and rat, ambulatory, Christ Church Cathedral © DK Images.

p.113 Strongbow's tomb, Christ Church Cathedral © DK Images.

p.114 "A busy medieval street", Dublinia © Ken Walsh.

p.118 Covered market © DK Images.

p.143 The GAA Museum. Courtesy of the GAA Museum.

p.150 Japanese head armour. Courtesy of the National Museum of Ireland.

p.156 Blue Room fireplace, Farmleigh. Courtesy of Farmleigh, Phoenix Park.

p.165 James Joyce Tower © JJ Museum.

p.166 Forty Foot Pool © Michael St Maur Sheil/ Corbis.

p.166 Goat Castle, Dalkey © DK Images.

p.168 Killiney bay © Chris Warren/Alamy.

p.179 Newbridge House © Dave G. House/Corbis.

p.180 National Sea-Life Centre, Bray © Kevin Eaves.

p.181 Powerscourt waterfall © Richard Cummins/Corbis.

p.182 Round tower, Glendalough © DK Images.

p.183 Russborough House © DK Images.

p.184 Facade of Castletown House © Richard Cummins/Corbis.

p.184 Staircase, Castletown House © DK Images.

p.185 Standing stone and the main mound at Newgrange © Travelog Picture Library/Alamy.

Index

Maps are marked in **colour**

INDEX